MY 28 '02 -S

FEB 0 5 20 S

11/19/07

BV 3777 .S4 M33 1980
Macfarlan, D. (Duncan), 1771-1857.
 The revivals of the eighteenth century,
particularly at Cambuslang : with three
sermons by the Rev. George Whitefield,

CAMBUSLANG—SCENE OF THE OUT-DOOR RELIGIOUS SERVICES.
Vide Preface, p. vi.

THE REVIVALS

OF

THE EIGHTEENTH CENTURY,

PARTICULARLY AT

CAMBUSLANG.

WITH THREE SERMONS

BY THE REV. GEORGE WHITEFIELD,

TAKEN IN SHORT HAND.

COMPILED FROM ORIGINAL MANUSCRIPTS AND CONTEMPORARY PUBLICATIONS.

By D. MACFARLAN, D.D.,
RENFREW.

RICHARD OWEN ROBERTS, PUBLISHERS
WHEATON, ILLINOIS
1980

PUBLISHED IN 1847
BY JOHNSTON & HUNTER OF EDINBURGH

REPRINTED IN 1980
BY RICHARD OWEN ROBERTS, PUBLISHERS
WHEATON, ILLINOIS 60187

Printed in the United States of America

PREFACE.

THE manuscripts from which this volume was prepared were chiefly left by the Rev. William M'Culloch of Cambuslang, and are now the property of the Free Church Library, of Mrs. Coutts, Mr. M'Culloch's grand-daughter, and another lady. The contemporary publications made available are partly the property of the Free Church library, partly of James Hog, Esq. of Newliston, and partly of the undersigned.

The preparation of the work was undertaken at the request of the Assembly's Publication Committee, but something of the kind had long been contemplated by the writer, as a means of awakening a thoughtless and sleeping generation.

It must be known to all conversant with the history of the period referred to, that a painful controversy took place between some of the early Seceders and friends of the revivals connected with the Establishment. It was thought injudicious to mix up matters of a controversial nature with the historical details of a work believed to be of God, but it was not meant to conceal or suppress these. A Review of the whole was prepared and sent to the printer, which could not be admitted without greatly exceeding the fixed limits of the volume; and the same reason prevented the insertion of a greater number of Mr. Whitefield's sermons. In absence of the review above referred to, it may be stated, that there were circumstances on both sides leading to temptation; that these were allowed, especially on the one side, a very undue influence; that much may be learned from what then took place to guard parties similarly circumstanced against falling into similar errors; but that there is nothing going either to weaken the evidence of the work being of God, or to discourage in seeking anew times of refreshing.

The Frontispiece was taken on the spot; but from the extent of the scene and the narrow limits of the sketch, farther description may be useful to enable the reader to understand the references which occur in the volume. It was taken from the top of the bank on the south side of the church-yard, and therefore the church, which has been rebuilt, does not appear. Immediately in front, but at the extremity of the low ground nearly southward, will be seen the meeting of two small streams, which flow together past the church under the name of the Kirk-burn. From the meeting of these streams, northward along the east side, there is a comparatively level green, having near its centre two aged hawthorn trees, growing so much together as scarcely to fail in attracting notice. On this green, and probably on the south side of these trees, stood the communion tables at the great meetings in July and August, 1742, and the principal tent on these occasions is said to have stood on the stripe of ground separating the two streams. Preaching from this, the minister would be looking to the north-east, having the brae from the south-east all the way round to the north before him, as well as the level tract of ground immediately in front of the tent—a space altogether capable of containing many thousands, and remarkably well adapted for sitting and hearing. West of the burn and nearly opposite the church, the hill slopes so away as to admit of a separate meeting very much out of hearing from the tent already described, and here a second tent was pitched on these sacramental occasions, and a second congregation formed. The church-yard rests on a sandstone cliff, with the burn passing deep below on the west; and there was a third tent with a separate congregation. The old manse stood a little way to the south-east of the church-yard, and not far from the top of the brae on the east. And all round, but especially southwards in the direction of the farm seen in the distance, are the braes so often referred to as places of retirement for devotional purposes. The hollow space given in the sketch and the brae round the east side, were occupied not merely on communion occasions, but generally, when weather permitted, throughout the Revival period, the church being both small and out of repair.

It is necessary only to add, that the state of religion preparatory to the Revivals of the last century, and the longing desires of many who, in discouraging circumstances, feared God, were not unlike what may be observed at present. May God grant us the farther likeness of experiencing, as they did, the power of the Highest!

D. MACFARLAN.

Free Church Manse,
Renfrew.

CONTENTS.

		PAGE
CHAPTER I.—Introductory sketch of the times, and of the Revivals generally		9
CHAPTER II.—The same continued		19
CHAPTER III.—Some account of Mr. M'Culloch of Cambuslang, chiefly as furnished by his son, the Rev. Dr. Robert M'Culloch, minister of Dairsie, and published with a volume of sermons in 1793		34
CHAPTER IV.—Means and circumstances apparently employed in bringing about the Revival at Cambuslang		38
CHAPTER V.—The first three months of the Revival at Cambuslang		45
CHAPTER VI.—The First Communion		61
CHAPTER VII.—The Second Communion		70
CHAPTER VIII.—The condition of Cambuslang after the Revival of 1742 had subsided		88
CHAPTER IX.—Some account of two manuscript volumes left by Mr. M'Culloch, and of the Cases which they contain		105
CHAPTER X.—A selection of Cases prepared from the first volume, and approved of by the original examiners		113
William Baillie		ib.
Janet Jackson		117
Elizabeth Jackson		123
Catherine Jackson		127
George Tassie		135
Alexander Roger		140
Elizabeth Dykes		142
James Kirkland		148
R. Shearer		151
R. Barclay		157
Archibald Bell		162
James Tenant		167

CONTENTS.

	PAGE
CHAPTER XI.—A selection of Cases prepared from the second manuscript volume	173
Bailie Weir	ib.
Mrs. Weir	175
John Parker	177
Daniel M'Larty	186
Bessie Lyon	188
Sarah Gilchrist	191
Catherine Anderson	198
Jean Walker	202
Andrew Faulds	203
Margaret Borland	205
Archibald Smith	207
CHAPTER XII.—The extension of the work to other parts of Scotland	213
The Presbytery of Hamilton	218
The Presbytery of Irvine	219
The Presbytery of Paisley	221
Glasgow	ib.
The Barony Parish	224
The City of Glasgow	226
The Parish of Calder	230
The Parish of Baldernock	231
The Parish of Kirkintilloch	233
The Parish of Campsie	234
The Parish of Kilsyth	237
Parishes lying East and North of Kilsyth	239
The Parish of Gargunnock	240
The Presbytery of Auchterarder—Parish of Muthill	242
Other Parishes in Presbytery of Auchterarder—Parish of Monivaird	247
Crief	248
The Town of Dundee	ib.
The Synod of Ross	250
The Parish of Rosskeen	ib.
The Parish of Nigg	251
The Parish of Rosemarkie	253
Other Parishes in the same District	254
The Parish of Golspie, in Sutherland	ib.
Other Parishes in the District	256
The City of Edinburgh	ib.

SERMONS BY THE REV. GEORGE WHITEFIELD.

SERMON I.—The duty of a gospel minister	3
SERMON II.—The method of grace	18
SERMON III.—The kingdom of God	34

THE REVIVAL OF THE EIGHTEENTH CENTURY,

ESPECIALLY AT CAMBUSLANG.

CHAPTER I.

INTRODUCTORY SKETCH OF THE TIMES IN WHICH THE REVIVAL OCCURRED.

An interesting subject, connected with the history of practical godliness, is the recurrence of reviving power after long seasons of deadness. Occasions of this kind are most noticeable when confined to particular churches or countries; but they are more wonderful when they occur in churches and countries widely apart. It seems, on such occasions, as if the voice of the Bridegroom were heard, saying to the church at large, "Rise up, my love, my fair one, and come away; for, lo, the winter is past, the rain is over and gone: the flowers appear on the earth; the time of the singing of birds is come, and the voice of the turtle is heard in our land; the fig tree putteth forth her green figs, and the vines with the tender grape give a good smell. Arise, my love, my fair one, and come away." (Cant. ii. 10–13.)

About the end of the seventeenth and beginning of the eighteenth century most of the churches, whether in the United Kingdom or the American colonies, were in a comparatively low state. Arianism and Deism prevailed in England. In Scotland, the old style of preaching was being fast laid aside, and cold formal addresses, verging towards a kind of Socinianism, were becoming fashionable. Old Mr.

Hutchison, minister of Kilellan, in Renfrewshire, who saw but the beginning of this progress, used to say to Wodrow the historian: "When I compare the times before the restoration with those since the revolution, I must own that the young ministers preach accurately and methodically; but there was far more of the power and efficacy of the Spirit and of the grace of God went along with sermons in those days than now. For my own part (all the glory be to God), I seldom set my foot in a pulpit in those days, but I had notice of some blessed effects of the word." The Arianism of England was carried to the north of Ireland, and finding a state of feeling suited to its reception, it took root and grew up, so as to characterize a distinct section of the presbyterian church, and now distinguished by the name of the Remonstrant Synod. The south and west of Ireland were subjected to a blight not less withering, though of a different kind, and which continued much longer—continued, to a great extent, throughout the whole of the last century.

The following extract is from a letter now before us, written in 1838 by a highly honoured servant of God in the Irish establishment, and who, perhaps more than any one else, is able to speak of what God has since done in these parts: "The state of the south and west of Ireland is very peculiar. The counties have twice changed their landholders. In the time of Cromwell and of king William there were forfeitures, and these continued till the reign of George I. The principal lands were given to military officers and soldiers connected with the two armies; but some of the estates were purchased by English adventurers —all, however, protestants. In some places the original land tenants were driven out, in others they were allowed to remain, but nearly all the original *proprietors* went to the continent, most of them to France. The gentry were now all soldiers, and utterly regardless about religion, education, morality, or anything tending to the instruction or improvement of the people. They gave themselves to sporting and carousing, leading a kind of half-savage life. Many noblemen and gentlemen rose above this; but, as their manners got more refined, they generally went to England, leaving the country at the disposal of mere fox-hunters—few of them remaining longer than during the sittings of the Irish parliament. As agriculture extended, benefices became more valuable, unions were multiplied, and large districts of country were in consequence severally placed under one clergyman. The clergy were usually all sons of the gentry, and accustomed to their sporting, drinking, and riotous habits. They had no preparation for ministerial duties but a college degree; and no education, either literary or moral, which had not been obtained among wild young men at college. According to the interest which they happened to have, they passed at once from college to ministerial charges, and again mixed in all the dissipation of the districts where these lay. Ignorant of the truth, they and their congregations were satisfied with some short moral discourse. The people were very generally as ignorant of the Scriptures and Scripture truth as the inhabitants of Hindostan. The priests were meanwhile at work among the people, and they had many helping them. The sick and dying were watched; their fears were wrought upon. They were told of the power which the priests had—of the influence possessed by the Virgin, and much about the OLD CHURCH; and as soon as any seemed to give way, on whatever point, the priest was sent for—he plied them anew, and seldom failed in succeeding with the poor ignorant people. They were now ready to receive absolution; but he had farther conditions to propose. The whole family must submit to be rebaptized, or at least promise to attend mass; and this, also, was not infrequently gained—the protestant clergyman being all the while at a distance, neither knowing nor caring much about what was going on. *In this way more than two-thirds of the lower and middle classes of protestants went over to the church of Rome.* Throughout whole districts our churches were almost emptied, and many in country places were allowed to fall into ruins."

In New England, the visitation of barrenness was much more of the kind common to most of the other countries, and its continuation was, like theirs, temporary. Dr. Increase Mather, writing towards the end of the seventeenth century, says: "Prayer is necessary on this account, that conversions have become rare in this age of the world. They that have their thoughts exercised in discerning things of this nature, have sad apprehensions that the work of conversion has come to a stand. *During the last age scarcely a sermon was preached without some being apparently converted, and sometimes hundreds were converted by one sermon.* Who of us now can say that we have seen anything such as this? Clear, sound conversions are not frequent in our congregations; the great bulk of the present generation are apparently poor, perishing, and, if the Lord prevent not, undone; many are profane, drunkards, lascivious, scoffers at the power of godliness, and disobedient; others are civil outwardly, conformed to good order, because so educated, but without knowing aught of a real change of heart." The same esteemed writer says, in 1721: "I am now in my eighty-third year, and having had an opportunity of conversing with the first planters of this country, and having been for *sixty-five years* a preacher of the gospel, I feel as did the ancient men, who had seen the former temple, and who wept aloud as they saw the latter. The children of New England are, or once were, for the most part, the children of godly parents. What did our forefathers come into this wilderness for? Not to gain estates as men do **now**, but for religion, and that they might have their children in a hopeful way of being truly religious. There was a famous man who preached before one of the greatest assemblies that ever was addressed—it was about seventy years ago—and he said to them, 'I lived in a country seven years, and all that time I never heard a profane oath or saw a man drunk.' And where was that country? It was New England! Ah, degenerate New England! what art thou come to at this day? How are those sins become common that were once not even heard of!"

It was amidst circumstances such as these that the revivals of the eighteenth century took their rise. There is perhaps no time during which the natural tide is not either ebbing or flowing, and yet there is a period during which it would be difficult to say, *from observation*, whether the one has ceased or the other begun. In this case, our difficulty is dependent on our judging from appearances, instead of observing the relation of the heavenly bodies. The same thing occurs in those changes which affect the state of religion. Judging from appearances, it is often difficult to say whether a progress for the better has begun, or whether matters are not still growing worse; but we know that in the purposes of God there is nothing doubtful; and even the observer may sometimes detect, in the under-current, a change in the flow of the stream, although not yet perceptible to all. Early in the eighteenth century there were, in many places all over the countries referred to, a feeling of the evil, inquiries as to the remedial means which should be employed, and an enlarged measure of the spirit and exercise of prayer; not a few of the pious were stirred up to unusual wrestlings with God. Societies were formed in various places, but especially in London, for discouraging vice and instructing the ignorant; missionary societies were formed, and missions sent forth to the heathen—the Danish missionaries set sail for the East Indies in 1705; and as regarded societies, something like what occurred towards the end of the last century, though far less in amount, made its appearance; in 1701, the society for the propagation of the gospel in foreign parts was established, under the auspices of king William, and towards the end of the same year, a society was formed for promoting Christian knowledge at home; in Scotland, also, a society for propagating Christian knowledge in the highlands and islands, and in foreign parts, began to be formed in 1704, and in 1709 received, according to the fashion of the times, a charter from the crown. In the course of a few years, these and many similar undertakings began to lay hold of the religious mind; and this was, no doubt, indicative of divine power, though as yet apparent only, or chiefly, *in what concerned others*. But it was not long after this, when the power of the Spirit became manifest, and it appeared, not merely *in the doings* of men, but *on men themselves*, even the disobedient.

To begin where we stopped—in reviewing the preceding period, and passing over less remarkable manifestations of divine power, so early as 1734, a very wonderful revival took place in Northampton, New England, under the ministry of the celebrated Jonathan Edwards, a man of deep thought and guarded language, and not at all likely to be either himself carried away with strong feelings, or to be the instrument of mere excitement among others. His own narrative of what took place is so generally known as to render any notice of it here unnecessary. But we ought not to take leave of the labours of Edwards without reminding the reader of that blessed work, some ten years later, among the poor Indians, under the ministrations of the holy and self-denied Brainerd—a work brought before the public through Edwards, and connected also with the society in Scotland. But on casting our eye across the white harvest fields, which were from 1734 downwards heard rustling and falling beneath the gospel sickle, all over New England, and other parts of the colonies, south and north, we are at a loss where to begin or how to shape our way. The vast number of publications issued about the middle of the last century on American revivals, greatly injure the effect which fewer would have produced.* On the history of revivals, whether here or in other parts of the world, we know of no single work, on the whole, better than Dr. Gillies' Historical

---

* We have examined upwards of a score of these, including some full of the most virulent abuse. One, entitled "A faithful Narrative of the Remarkable Revival of Religion in East Hampton, Long Island, by the Rev. Samuel Buell," is, among others, truly interesting and satisfactory.

Collections. But the letters and journals of Whitefield shed a strong, though rapidly passing light, over the whole of that interesting scene. And as some very naturally call in question strong statements made under strong feelings, they will find a calm and judicious review of the whole in the Constitutional History of the Presbyterian Church, by Professor Hodge of Princeton college—a living author, equally distinguished for talents and orthodoxy. As this work is, we fear, but little known in this country, we shall extract from it the more largely. After describing the general deadness which prevailed on both sides of the Atlantic at an earlier period, he adds: "The earliest manifestation of the presence of the Holy Spirit, in our portion of the church (meaning the presbyterian), was at Freehold, New Jersey, under the ministry of the Rev. John Tennent, who was called to that congregation in 1730, and died in 1732." "The settling of that place," says his brother, the Rev. William Tennent, "with a gospel ministry, was owing, under God, to the agency of some Scotch people that came to it; among whom there was none so painstaking in this blessed work as one Walton (Walter?) Ker, who, in 1685, for his faithful and conscientious adherence to God and his truth, as professed by the church of Scotland, was there apprehended and sent to this country, under a sentence of perpetual banishment. By which it appears that the devil and his instruments lost their aim, in sending him from home, where it is unlikely he could ever have been so serviceable to Christ's kingdom as he has been here. He is yet alive (in 1744), and, blessed be God, flourishing in his old age, being in his eighty-eighth year."

This incident is full of interest. In 1685 there was much blood shed in Scotland, many wanton cruelties were practised, and many hundreds were banished to the colonies; and among these *New Jersey* is particularly mentioned. The name of "*Walter* Ker" also occurs as "banished to the plantations, September 3, 1685." (Wodrow.) What wisdom but that of God could so overrule, that the puritans driven from England, and the presbyterians from Scotland, should be as the sowing of that glorious harvest which was to be so largely reaped towards the middle of the following century; and that this should be a chief means of reviving the cause of God, both in England and Scotland? Yet so it was, as might be shown from other and detailed evidence. " O the depth of the riches, both of the wisdom and knowledge of God! how unsearchable are his judgments, and his ways past finding out!" (Rom. xi. 33.)

After detailing, to some extent, this work of God, not only among the presbyterians, but also the congregationalists and others, the author goes on to remark respecting its character, as genuine or otherwise: " We can compare the doctrines then taught, the exercises experienced, and the effects produced, with the word of God, and thus learn how far the work was in accordance with that infallible standard. The first of these points is a matter of primary importance. How will the revival under consideration abide this test? Is there any doubt as to the doctrines taught by Whitefield, the Tennents, Blair, Dickinson, and the other prominent preachers of that day? They were the doctrines of the reformation, and of the standards of the presbyterian church. The doctrines preached," says Turnbull, " by those famous men, who were owned as the principal instruments of this remarkable revival of God's work, were the doctrines of original sin, of regeneration by the supernatural influences of the Divine Spirit, and of its absolute necessity; of effectual calling, of justification by faith, wholly on account of the imputed righteousness of Christ; of repentance towards God, and faith towards our Lord Jesus Christ; of the perseverance of the saints, of the indwelling of the Holy Spirit in them, and of its divine consolation and joy." The second criterion is the nature of the experience professed by its subjects. When we come to ask, What was the experience of the subjects of this revival? we find, amidst much that is doubtful or objectionable, the essential characteristics of genuine conversion. In a great multitude of cases, the same feelings were professed which we find in the saints whose spiritual life is detailed in the Bible, and which the children of God, in all ages, have avowed; the same sense of sin, the same apprehension of the mercy of God, the same faith in Christ, the same joy and peace in believing, the same desire for communion with God, and the same endeavours after new obedience. Such, however, is the ambiguity of human language, such the deceitfulness of the human heart, and such the devices of Satan, that no mere detail of feeling, and especially no description which one man may give of the feelings of others, can afford conclusive evidence of the nature of those feelings in the sight of God. We must, therefore, look farther than mere professions or detail of experiences for evidences of the real character of this work. We must look to its effects. What, then, were the fruits of this revival? Mr. William Tennent says, that the subjects of this work, who had come under his observation, were brought to approve of the doctrines of the gospel, to delight in the law of God, to endeavour to do his will, to love those who have the divine image: that the formal had become spiritual; the proud, humble; the wanton and vile, sober and temperate; the worldly, heavenly-minded; the extortioner, just; and the self-seeker, desirous to promote the glory of God. The convention of ministers, that met at Boston in 1743, state, that those who were regarded as converts confirmed the genuineness of the change which they professed to have experienced, by the external fruits of holiness in their lives, so that they appeared to those who had the nearest access to them, as so many epistles of Jesus Christ, written not with ink, but by the Spirit of the living God.

And after rehearsing the opinion of president Edwards, which we need not copy, he adds: "Turnbull, a later witness, says, 'The effects on great numbers were abiding and most happy. They were the most uniformly exemplary Christians with whom I was ever acquainted. I was born, and had my education in that part of the town of Albany, in which the work was most prevalent and powerful. Many, who at that time imagined that they were born of God, made a profession of their faith in Christ, and were admitted to full communion, and appeared to walk with God. They were constant and serious in their attendance on public worship, prayerful, righteous, and charitable, strict in the government of their families; and not one of them, so far as he knew, was ever guilty of scandal. Eight or ten years after the religious excitement, there was not a drunkard in the whole parish. It was,' he adds, ' the most glorious and extensive revival of religion and reformation of manners which this country has ever known. It is estimated, *that in two or three years, thirty or forty thousand souls were born into the family of heaven in New England,* besides great numbers in New York, New Jersey, and the more southern provinces.'"

CHAPTER II.

INTRODUCTORY SKETCH OF THE TIMES CONTINUED.

ON now turning to England, we are at once met with the full blush of a returning summer. On looking back, we see, so early as 1729, a few students in the university of Oxford meeting for prayer, giving themselves wholly to God, and going forth among the poor and the ignorant to instruct and comfort them. And in the course of ten years, those who had thus been a small and despised meeting of students, went forth as apostles, over England and Wales, and into the American colonies, and were accompanied, especially at home, with men of extraordinary gifts and devotedness. There was now active and open war between the men so raised up and their followers on the one hand, and the world on the other. The history of this period, and especially of the methodists, whether of the school of the Wesleys, or of Whitefield, is large and diversified, and is to a greater or less extent within the reach of most. It would lead us altogether beyond our limits were we to enter upon it. But as the labours of Whitefield are to some extent interwoven with the Scottish revivals, it is necessary to say something of his proceedings before his coming to Scotland.

He was one of the little society in Oxford, and began to attract attention as soon as he received orders, though he was still a very young man—little more than twenty-one years of age. In 1737, the year after he obtained ordination, he went to Georgia, where he projected an orphan institution. Towards the end of 1738, he returned to make collections. This gave him occasion to go forth over England, very much as an evangelist. Early in 1739 he was at Bristol, and preparing to return to America, when it was said to him, " Why go abroad? have we not Indians enough at home? If you have a mind to convert Indians, there are colliers enough in Kingswood." He had before this thought of the duty of going forth to the highways and the hedges, that he might compel sinners to come in, but had not yet ventured on what was then altogether unusual. But it seemed to him now that he had a call in providence. The colliers, he was told, were exceedingly rude, so much so that few cared about visiting them, and they had no place of worship. After much prayer and many inward struggles, he went one day to Hannam Mount, and standing on a hill, he began to preach to about a hundred colliers. This soon took air, and meeting after meeting his audience increased, till he found himself addressing nearly *twenty thousand* persons. His own account of the effects produced is very striking. " The first discovery," says he, " of their being affected, was in the white gutters made by their tears, which plentifully fell down their black cheeks, as they came out of their coal-pits. Hundreds and hundreds of them were soon brought under deep convictions, which happily ended in sound and thorough conversion. As the scene was quite new, and I had just begun to be an extempore preacher, I had often many inward conflicts. Sometimes, when twenty thousand people were before me, I had not, as I thought, a word to say; but I was never deserted, and I was often so assisted as to understand what that meaneth, ' Out of his belly shall flow rivers of living water.' The open firmament above; the prospect of the adjacent fields; the sight of thousands and thousands, some in coaches, some on horseback, and some in the trees, and some of all affected, so as to be drenched with tears, amidst the solemn stillness of the approaching night, were almost too much for me; I was occasionally all but overcome."

From this time forward, his course was as that of an

apostle. But as it is not necessary for the present to follow him much farther, we shall here allow him to introduce us to a separate corner of the Lord's vineyard less known than England, and which, from its smallness, can be more easily judged of. Wales was at that time more than now separated from England in language, and generally in whatever characterizes a people. The history of God's work in that country is intensely interesting, and may be, to some extent, learned from a well written life of the great Rowland, and another of Charles of Bala, both of which are in general circulation. But, having access to contemporary information, we shall furnish a few extracts of what is perhaps less generally read.

An awakening had by this time existed in Wales for several years. It is said to have commenced through the labours of Griffith Jones, a truly eminent man, particularly in doing good and devising means of usefulness; and it was being carried forward, especially by Howell Harris, a very extraordinary character, to whom Whitefield will by-and-by introduce us. Whitefield had himself taken leave of his friends in Bristol, and the following entry was made in his journal on his landing in Wales:—

"*Cardiff, March* 8, 1739.—Arose before twelve at night, sung psalms, and prayed; and the wind being fair, we had a speedy passage over to the Welsh shore. Our business being in haste, God having of his own providence sent one to guide us, we rode all night, stopped at Newport to refresh ourselves, where we met with two friends, and reached Cardiff about eleven in the morning.

"The town, I soon found, was apprehensive of my coming; and therefore, whilst I was giving a word of exhortation to some poor people at the inn, who hung upon me to hear the word, Mr. Seward went to ask for the pulpit. But being denied, we pitched on the town-hall, which Mr. Seward procured; and at four in the afternoon, I preached from the judge's seat to about four hundred hearers. Most of them were very attentive, but some mocked. However, I offered Jesus Christ freely to them, and would have rejoiced if they had accepted him; but their foolish hearts were hardened. Lord, make them monuments of thy free grace!

"After I came down from my seat, I was much refreshed with the sight of my dear brother, Howell Harris, whom I knew not in person, but long loved in the bowels of Jesus Christ, and on whose behalf I have often felt my soul drawn out in prayer.

"He is now about twenty-five years of age. Twice has he applied for holy orders, being every way qualified, and yet refused, under the pretence of his not being of age, although he was then twenty-two years and six months. About a month ago he offered himself again, and was put off. On this he was, and is still, resolved to go on, and he has already shown indefatigable zeal in his Master's work. During these three years, he has discoursed, as he told me, almost twice every day, for three or four hours together; not authoritatively as a minister, but as a private person, exhorting his Christian brethren. He has been, I believe, in seven counties, and has made it his business to go to wakes, and to turn people from their lying vanities. Many ale-house people, fiddlers, harpers, &c., cry out against him for spoiling their trade. He has been the subject of many rumours, has been threatened with public prosecution, and has had constables sent to apprehend him; yet God has blessed him with inflexible courage, and he still goes on conquering and to conquer. He is of a most catholic spirit, loves all who love Christ, and is therefore styled by bigots a dissenter. He is despised by all who are lovers of pleasure more than lovers of God; but God has greatly blessed his endeavours. Many call, and even venerate him as their spiritual father, and would, I believe, lay down their lives for his sake. He discourses generally in a field, but at other times in some house, from a wall, or a table, or anything else. He has established nearly thirty societies in South Wales, and still the field of his labours is becoming wider. He is full of faith and of the Holy Ghost.

"When I first saw him, my heart was knit closely to him. I wanted to catch some of his fire, and I gave him the right hand of fellowship with all my heart. After I had saluted him, and given a warm exhortation to a great number of people, who followed me to the inn, we spent the remainder of the evening in taking sweet counsel together, and telling one another what God had done for our souls. My heart was still drawn out towards him more and more. There seemed to be a strong and divine sympathy between us, and I resolved to promote his interest with all my might. Accordingly, we took an account of the several societies, and agreed on such measures as seemed most conducive to promote the common interests of our Lord. Blessed be God, there seems to be a noble spirit going out into Wales, and I expect that ere long the fruits will be more visible. After much comfortable and encouraging conversation, we knelt down and prayed with great enlargement of heart. This done, we had a little supper, sung a hymn, and went to bed, praising God for having brought us face to face. Satan, I doubt not, envied our happiness; and we hope, by the help of God, that we shall make his kingdom shake. God loves to do great things by such instruments, that the power may be seen to be of God, and not of man."

Being thus introduced to Howell Harris, we shall next furnish an extract from a letter written by Rowland to Harris, and which is descriptive of both, and of the work of God in their common and much loved country, Wales:—

"*October* 20, 1742. My dear Brother,—I bless you for your letters; they were like showers of rain to a dry land. Indeed, the Lord gave you the tongue of the learned. But O what am I? A painted hypocrite, a miserable sinner! I know all the to's and fro's, ups and downs that are in religion; but the blessed liberty that remains for the children of God is still hidden from me. God grant that you may prevail. I wish I could skip and leap over all the mountains of pleasure and laziness, hard-heartedness, unbelief, and rest on the breast of the beloved and never-enough praised Jesus. O blessed time, when all prisoners of hope shall be released, and enter into the rest of their dear Immanuel! I doubt not that your soul joins me in saying, Amen, amen.

"I have been of late in Montgomeryshire, and had great power to convince and build up. Persecution increases. Some of the brethren have been excommunicated. I hope you will consult with the brethren in London, and send us word what we ought to do. At Brecknock, I preached in several churches and houses with uncommon power. I have heard since, that I am brought into court for preaching in an ale-house while there. Your sentiments about this, too, would be very serviceable. Last week I was in Carmarthenshire and Glamorgan, and brave opportunities indeed they were. Whole congregations were under concern and crying out, so that my voice could not be heard. Some persons of quality entertained me with more than ordinary respect. O what am I, that my ears and eyes should hear and see such things? Help me to bless the God of heaven. I hope his kingdom begins to come. Be packing, Satan; flee, flee with trembling, lest the God of Israel overtake thee. Lord, chastise him. Lord, down with him. Let his kingdom be shattered, and let him be himself trampled under the feet of thy children! How long shall he domineer over thy little ones? My dear brother, up, up with your arms; yield not an inch. That God whom we serve can, yea and will, deliver us. Through his might, we shall win the field. Don't you hear all the brethren in Wales crying out loudly, Help, help, help, help, brother Harris—the bold champion, where art thou? What! in London! though it is now the day of battle! What! has not London champions enough to fight her battles? Where are the great W——, C——, &c.* Must poor Wales send help to England? O poor Wales! thine own ingratitude has caused all this. Good Lord, pity poor Wales! Send our dear brother back among

* Probably Whitefield and Cennick.

us with thy power, and in the fulness of thy blessing; and let the devil tremble before him. Amen, amen.

"My poor flock increases daily. They would be heartily glad to see and hear you. Brother W——s* was here last Sunday, and a sweet day it was. I love him more and more, because of his simple, honest, plain way of dealing with the people. His parishioners are highly incensed against him. *I trust we shall have him out before long.*† Methinks I hear you inquiring after Carnarvonshire. B——n T——s‡ is there. They come by thousands to hear. Brother H——ll D——s (Howell Davies) promised to go there; what detains him I know not. I cannot possibly go this winter, for want of one to supply my room at my churches.§ The next week I promised to be at Pembroke and the lower part of Carmarthen, shortly after at Colvill, &c. Dear brother, never fail to intercede for me, who am your loving friend, well-wisher, and unworthy brother, DANIEL ROWLAND."

This letter from Rowland was written in October, 1742. The following extract is from a letter written by the Rev. Edmond Jones, a dissenting minister in Wales, and is dated the 8th of December, 1743, fully a year later: "As for the three ordained church of England ministers mentioned by Mr. Howell Harris, namely, Mr. William Williams, Mr. Howell Davies, and Mr. Daniel Rowland, I know them very well, although they live at a great distance from this place. They are all three men of unblemished character, very zealous, laborious, and popular. Mr. Williams labours chiefly in Brecknockshire and Carmarthenshire; Mr. Howell Davies lives in Pembrokeshire, and labours there and in Carmarthenshire and Cardiganshire,

---

* Probably William Williams.

† Rowland, as well as Williams, had been a parish minister, but was outed because of his *zeal* in his Master's work, episcopally called his *irregularities*, and so he and others united in setting up the Calvinistic methodist communion.

‡ Mr. John Thomas was at this time minister there.

§ He had four to supply.

and likewise in some parts of Glamorganshire, with great zeal and effect; and Mr. Rowland in Cardiganshire, chiefly where his churches are—but he preaches in many other parts of both North and South Wales. His people are the most zealous in the kingdom, or perhaps in the world. They sing psalms and hymns night and day, when going and returning from their places of worship, and also when at their work. It is with them as it was in St. Jerome's time in the primitive church. Some time ago, at Landewe Brevi-Church, he had above two thousand communicants; and Mr. Philip Pugh, a dissenting minister not far distant, had about five hundred. And besides, there are other meetings and congregations in the same country; so that the lower part of Cardiganshire is almost all over religious. I have been informed, that in one of Mr. Rowland's parishes there are but two men who are not well affected to religion; and even these come to hear, and are not grossly immoral. I desire both you and Mr. M'Culloch (he is writing to Mr. Robe) to be pleased to print some of your best notes of sermons, especially if you have anything remarkable on subjects rarely handled. We, who in this kingdom are for the doctrines of free grace, do greatly affect the sermons and writings of Scots ministers, and desire to have more of them. I do assure you that the works of those famous gospel preachers, the Erskines, are greatly valued, and have been of much use. The sermons entitled Law Death and Gospel Life, are in course of being translated into Welsh, in order to be printed. Also Mr. Willison's Balm of Gilead is come into some hands in this country, and is greatly and deservedly valued. It would be long before we would be wearied of such books, especially as they strengthen our hands against the adversaries of the doctrines of free grace."

The following extract, or rather abstract, is from a letter dated 14th February 1745: "Last night I came home, after a month's journey, which our dear Lord carried me through in the most tender manner. More of the divine presence and power I never knew; and such congregations

I never before saw. The meetings are generally out of doors, no house being sufficient to contain them. The work is even greater than it was some years ago. The word is quicker and more powerful—the mystical glory of Christ more set forth. The hearts of many are as if on fire, and they seem to set on fire others also. They live as if in the suburbs of heaven, and use much of its language. Others have still to struggle with the bondage of a legal spirit, though hopefully. Some are brought under conviction gradually, and others all at once. Some of the wealthier classes are growing less prejudiced—are coming even to hear; and of them, too, some have been awakened. In several parts of Carmarthen, Pembroke, and Cardigan shires, it is difficult to say where the gospel runs most, and where divine power is most seen. Mr. Rowland is one of the most surprising men that ever I heard. Such wisdom to divide the word rightly, such light in reaching the spirituality of the word, and such power in applying it, I never witnessed. He has four congregations; but the people come from six, seven, or eight counties round. It is impossible to express what life and power, what warmth and holy fire, what praises from some, what mournings and groanings from others, what tears of love and joy, and what looks of happiness, are manifested. These indications can be properly understood only by such as have experienced what they express. Mr. Rowland is assisted by Mr. Williams of Carmarthenshire, who is younger in years and in grace, but is much honoured by his Lord. He is a flaming instrument, and is day and night on the stretch in his Master's service. In Pembroke, Cardigan, and part of Carmarthenshire, the laborious Mr. Davies sounds the glad tidings of the gospel with great success. He is also young, but greatly owned, especially to the English-speaking population of Pembrokeshire, who were, till he went among them, utter strangers to the very forms of godliness. Under his ministry, the Lord does very manifestly display his great power in wounding and healing. These men preach day and night, in houses, in barns, and in the fields; the whole country being open to them."—It will perhaps occur to some, that these extraordinary effects were the result of the extraordinary gifts of the men described. And so in some sense they were. But these very gifts were of God. Rowland's mind was once unawakened, and his ministrations were barren. The awakening was of God, and so were the gifts. And it is very observable that such men grew in wisdom as well as eloquence.

On taking leave of Wales, it may be right to notice the extension of this work to the army even in foreign parts. Some will recollect a very interesting account in the Life of Walker of Truro, concerning a work of God not many years after this, among soldiers who were for some time at Truro, before going abroad. But it is more remarkable when found in the army while abroad, and wanting in the opportunities which they had at home. There was a British army at this time in Flanders; and letters were written by some of the soldiers and others on the spot, and published in the journals of the day. Most of those we have seen are by Englishmen, but the following extracts are from letters written by Scotchmen—the one " by a private Christian," probably an officer at Bruges, dated 20th March 1745; and the other dated 25th May 1745, from a common soldier; and both are addressed to ministers in this country: " Indeed, there is a great awakening in our army. There is one John Haime, a dragoon in major-general Cope's regiment; likewise one Clemens in the First Regiment of Guards; and one Evans in the Train of Artillery, who met together for searching the Scripture, for prayer and other duties, as also for rebuking others in following sinful ways, and for setting before them their dreadful state, from Scripture and reason. In our last campaign, there was open field preaching, and there is now, *in most of all our regiments, a remarkable awakening*. In this company there are three, who were notoriously wicked, and now desire only to know Christ, and him crucified. There is also a society of praying people in this and several other regiments. This society was erected before the awakening. There are two of colonel Johnston's regiment who preach. The dragoon belonging to Cope's regiment and these two preach every night, in a house they have taken. The general gave them liberty to go to the church, and preach every day. Major-general Ponsonby, who commands here, seems to be more religious; for he both encourages these men, and causes the ministers to go to church every morning and read prayers to the men that mount guard. In Ghent there is another assembly of the awakened soldiers."—The following extract is from the soldier's letter: "Rev. Sir,—I received the book which ye sent me. I am obliged to you for your love and kindness to me, and to all my father's family, and especially as I am but a prodigal, and that I refused all your good advices, and those of my friends. I desire to be very thankful to God that he hath, by your hand, sent me such a book. I hope it will be useful to me, and also to some others of this army, who are ten thousand times more deserving, and who on all occasions seek to do me good. There are a few who, in this wilderness, where we are deprived of those refreshing ordinances which you have among you, that assemble together; which we believe to be our duty. There are nearly forty of us, who meet as often as we can. But we have not in this campaign the same opportunities we had in the last; and in winter quarters, we commonly meet on Sabbath and Wednesday, and oftener when we can. We begin with prayer, we then sing, then read a chapter, we have then prayer again, and questions on practical heads of divinity, such as are in the writings of Mr. Isaac Ambrose. There is one young lad in the company who sent to London for his whole works. He got it over in winter; but we could not get it to camp with us. After the question has gone round, duty is gone about, and we conclude with praise. There are amongst us men of different regiments, who take upon them to exhort and preach publicly in the camp. There is a great work of conviction among the men, and I hope that there are also some conversions.

They go after the strain of the Messrs. Wesley in England. If it were not too much trouble, I would be very glad to have your advice concerning our society, and the means whereby we may obtain and preserve the presence of God among us; and concerning myself. I greatly desire to hear of the healing of divisions, and of a reformation-work, both in heart and life, among high and low. O that that promise were made good! 'When thy judgments are in the earth, the inhabitants of the earth will learn righteousness.' (Isa. xxvi. 9.) Surely his judgments are in the earth now, and in some measure executed on our army. His hand seems to be lifted up against both nations and armies." *

When one goes forth in spring, and finds on the exposed hill-side the flowers and other indications of the advancing year, he naturally concludes that long ere now these must have appeared in the sheltered valley; and so might we also conclude, from what we have seen of the work of God even in the British camp. Scotland, with all its ecclesiastical wrongs and moral degeneracy, was comparatively a privileged land; the very sufferings which had been endured on the side of truth during the preceding century, had left behind them witnesses for truth, which, though like the works of God described by the psalmist, having no speech nor language so as to make their voice heard, had their line, nevertheless, going forth over the land, and with a meaning as intelligible as words. In very many cases, the men of this generation were the sons of persecuted fathers, whose prayerful instructions and high testimony for truth were not soon to be forgotten. The very oppression of an ecclesiastical majority, and domineering power of an irreligious age, increased the amount and intensity of *their* prayerful communings, who wept over the degeneracy of their times. A certain class of ministers, and a greatly larger class of the

---

* There are several other letters to the same effect, one addressed to the congregation at Marten, and published in the Monthly History, and another communicated by Mr. Halley of Muthil, in Perthshire.

people, were like the Simeons and the Annas of other days —the life of the church, and the hope of their generation. In such writings as the Memoirs of Boston, the Lives of the Erskines, and others of that age, we have laid open to us many of the hidden springs of a coming change; and in this there is much interest. There were general causes, otherwise so general a change would be unaccountable; but there were also special causes, and these lay hid in the circumstances of the different countries. From almost the very commencement of the century, there were in Scotland indications of returning power. The habitations of horrid cruelty abroad, and the abominations of immorality at home, being both glaring, began to engage the public mind. The country was not so far gone as not to feel, at least in many places, a want of gospel light and gospel warmth in the pulpit, and the tyranny of ecclesiastical moderatism in the church courts; and for a time the few strove against the many, in seeking to arrest the downward progress in both: the secession broke the strength of this reclaiming party within the church, and their attention was perhaps all the more directed to other and brighter scenes. Far in the west, beyond the Western Ocean, the Sun of righteousness seemed anew to arise—it was as if the apocalyptic angel had been seen to "fly in the midst of heaven, having the everlasting gospel to preach unto them that dwell on the earth, and to every nation, and kindred, and tongue, and people, saying with a loud voice, Fear God, and give glory to him, for the hour of his judgment is come; and worship him that made heaven and earth, and the sea, and the fountains of waters." (Rev. xiv. 6, 7.) So astonishing were the things seen and done, that many of the calmest and most philosophical friends of truth were of opinion, that what they then witnessed was to usher in the full revelation of the millennium. The minds of many in this country, wearied, as if labouring in the fire and for very vanity, were naturally drawn out to behold, and if possible to realize, some share in this coming glory.

But even in separate localities there were special preparations. Among other cases, Mr. Robe of Kilsyth speaks of providential events affecting that parish, and preparing the way for what followed, so early as 1733; and the direct means afterwards blessed, began to be used two years before the commencement of the revival. "In 1740," says he, "I began to preach on the doctrine of regeneration. The method I followed was, first to press the importance and necessity of it, from John iii. 3: 'Except a man be born again he cannot see the kingdom of God.' Next, to show the mysteriousness of the way and manner of the Holy Spirit, in effecting it, from John iii. 8: 'The wind bloweth where it listeth, and thou hearest the sound thereof, but canst not tell whence it cometh and whither it goeth; so is every one that is born of the Spirit.' Thirdly, to explain and apply the various Scripture views and expressions of it; as first, being born again, from John iii. 8; secondly, as a resurrection, from Rev. xx. 6, 'Blessed and holy is he that hath part in the first resurrection;' thirdly, as a new creature, from Eph. ii. 10, 'For we are his workmanship, created in Christ Jesus unto good works;' fourthly, as Christ's conquest of the sinner to himself, from Ps. cx. 3, 'Thy people shall be willing in the day of thy power;' fifthly, as the circumcision of the heart, from Ezek. xliv. 9, 'Thus saith the Lord God, No stranger, uncircumcised in heart, nor uncircumcised in flesh, shall enter into my sanctuary, of any stranger, among the children of Israel;' sixthly, as the taking away of the stony heart, and the giving a heart of flesh, from Ezek. xi. 19; seventhly, as the putting of God's law in the mind, and writing it in the heart, from Heb. viii. 10. I sometimes could observe," he adds, "that the doctrine of these sermons was acceptable to the Lord's people, and that there was more than ordinary seriousness in hearing them; yet I could see no farther fruit. *But now (1742) I find that the Lord, who is infinitely wise, and knoweth the end from the beginning, was preparing some for this uncommon dispensation of the Spirit, which we looked not for;* and that others were brought under convictions, issuing, by the power of the Highest, in their real conversion, and in a silent way." (See Mr. Robe's Narrative.)

Similar preparations were going on at Cambuslang for some time before the awakening broke out. But these will fall to be considered under a separate head.

CHAPTER III.

SOME ACCOUNT OF MR. M'CULLOCH OF CAMBUSLANG, CHIEFLY AS FURNISHED BY HIS SON, THE REV. DR. ROBERT M'CULLOCH, MINISTER OF DARSIE, AND PUBLISHED WITH A VOLUME OF SERMONS IN 1793.

THE late Rev. William M'Culloch, minister of the gospel at Cambuslang, was born towards the end of last century (the seventeenth), at Whithorn, in Galloway, where his father was the teacher of the public school. He received the rudiments of his education from his father, who, perceiving his studious disposition, sent him to the universities of Edinburgh and Glasgow. There he laid a good foundation; and in time acquired the character, which he always maintained among those that knew him, of extensive reading, good acquaintance with the Greek and Roman classics, and uncommon skill in Hebrew. His genius led him also to the mathematical sciences, particularly astronomy and geography, which he afterwards taught in Glasgow to numerous classes of young men, with great applause; and in subserviency to such studies, he constructed small globes with great accuracy. But his favourite study was theology, as contained in the Holy Scriptures; and being early called of God, by his grace, he determined to consecrate all his talents to the work of the ministry; and from that time forward no prospect, however alluring, could divert him from his steady purpose of preaching the unsearchable riches of Christ.

After attending the divinity colleges of Edinburgh and

Glasgow, he was licensed to preach the gospel by the presbytery of Wigton, in the year 1722. He resided mostly at Glasgow, where, in 1725, he was nominated to preach the annual sermon for the reformation of manners, which he published at the desire of the magistrates. This was the only sermon he ever published. Though at different periods of his ministry he was solicited to favour the public with some of his discourses, his modesty still prevented him. When he was a preacher, and had not yet received ordination, he lived some time in the family of Mr. Hamilton of Aikenhead, in the neighbourhood of Glasgow, where he acquired the esteem and friendship of that respectable gentleman and his family; for whom he always expressed a particular regard.

On the 29th April 1731, he was ordained by the presbytery of Hamilton minister of Cambuslang. This parish lies on the south side of the river Clyde, and about five miles east of Glasgow. It runs about three and a half miles south of that river, and nearly the same length east and west. At present the population is not much short of three thousand, but in 1742 it was only about nine hundred.

All the accounts we have seen of Mr. M'Culloch, unite in describing him as able, judicious, and faithful, yet no way distinguished as a popular preacher. "He was not," says his son, "a very ready speaker. Though eminent for learning and piety, he was not eloquent. Thoughtful and studious, he delivered the truths of God faithfully; but his manner was slow and cautious—very different from that of popular orators."

The sermons published by his son correspond with this description. They are in all thirteen, and are throughout clear, simple, and manly exhibitions of divine truth, but no way distinguished either for eloquence or unction.

In speaking of his habits, his son says: "He commonly rose about five in the morning, and excepting about two or three hours, which he allowed for relaxation, he was closely employed in study till about eight o'clock in the evening. His ordinary practice was to write out and commit to memory two sermons every week. He spent much time in secret prayer, waiting with humble patience for a favourable return. He greatly encouraged private Christians to meet for social prayer, *and particularly that God would revive his work everywhere.* He was often employed in reading and meditating on the Scriptures; and when his memory began to fail, he transcribed large portions of them, that he might impress them the more upon his mind. 'I never knew a man,' said one who had access narrowly to observe his conduct, ' that seemed to be more conscientious in remembering the Sabbath-day to keep it holy.' "

" In works of charity he was also singular. He was timorous in the extreme lest what he did in this way should be known. To mention a few instances: in 1752, he caused print, with the greatest privacy, three thousand copies of an exact and easy way of teaching children to read; to which he subjoined the Shorter Catechism, and the Proverbs of Solomon. These he dispersed throughout Scotland and America, for the benefit of young people of the poorer sort. This cost him about £12. In 1768, he purchased three hundred Bibles, which cost nearly £25, and secretly ordered them to be dispersed for the same benevolent purpose. About the same time, he employed one of his elders, in whom he could confide, to go to Edinburgh with £200 to the society for propagating Christian knowledge, with a strict charge that he should not tell any person by whom it was sent.

" Amidst the increasing frailties of age," his son goes on to say, " he continued his incessant labours in the gospel, and preached to his congregation till within a Sabbath or two of his death—even when, through weakness, he was obliged to be supported to the church by a person on each hand.

" About the 10th of December 1771, when he was beginning family worship in the evening, he was suddenly seized with the disorder that terminated his valuable life. During his affliction he was almost continually insensible. Recollecting himself one night, he said: 'The whole is shortly summed up in the words of Jesus Christ, 'He that believeth and is baptized shall be saved; but he that believeth not shall be damned.' On the 18th of December 1771, and in the forty-first year of his ministry, after some days of severe distress, he departed in peace from this life, to enter into the joy of his Lord. On the Saturday following his body was interred in the churchyard of Cambuslang, amidst the tears and lamentations of an affectionate people, who highly respected and loved him as their minister. On his grave-stone is this inscription: 'He was holy in his life, esteemed in his congregation, and honoured of God to be remarkably useful in preaching the gospel.'"

These biographical notices, though applicable perhaps chiefly to an after-period of life, are sufficient to bring before us *the man*, with his ordinary habits and constitutional tendencies. And it will now be seen, that there was nothing in these to account for the awakening which took place. There was, indeed, apparently the absence of what might otherwise have been regarded as a hindrance, especially pride of intellect, and a fondness for display; but there was really nothing on account of which the most observant could have said—God will yet employ that man in doing great things.*

* His son, the Rev. Dr. Robert M'Culloch, was recognised and respected by his cotemporaries, as a man of excellent talent, sound judgment, and evangelical views; and he is still favourably known as the author of Lectures on Isaiah, and two volumes of sermons. He was born in 1740, and died September, 1824. He is now represented by Mrs. Coutts, his daughter, and widow of the late Robert Coutts, Esq., Brechin.

CHAPTER IV.

MEANS AND CIRCUMSTANCES APPARENTLY EMPLOYED IN BRINGING ABOUT THE REVIVAL AT CAMBUSLANG.

It may be well again to recur, in a few sentences, to the proceedings of Whitefield, as apparently connected with what we have immediately to add. We last parted from him in Wales, which was in March 1739. In the August following he embarked for America, landed at Philadelphia, went from that to New York, and from this largely over the colonies; and he was thus thrown among the men who had been engaged in America as he had been in England. The field-preaching, begun among the colliers at King's-wood, was now practised in the colonies. He learned from the colonial brethren in some things, and they from him in others; and the work went on between them to the astonishment of all. Large districts of country were now ripened for the spiritual harvest. There was little spoken of but religion, and all who knew the truth were ever saying to their neighbours, "Know ye the Lord." Ministers, instead of preaching as if engaged in some professional task, dealt with men's souls in what they said; and hearers had their consciences so awakened, that they could not listen and remain indifferent. The power of God was everywhere felt, and the reports of what in this way occurred were spread everywhere, and especially in the mother country.

Now this was in 1740, and early in 1741 Mr. M'Culloch appears to have been in the habit of bringing the intelligence of these interesting events before his people. The following is the statement given of this proceeding in the last statistical account of the parish, and which, as regards this matter, was drawn up by the Rev. Dr. Clason, now of Edinburgh: "The kirk of Cambuslang being too small, and out of repair, the minister, in favourable weather, frequently conducted the public devotional services of the parish in the open fields. The place chosen was peculiarly well adapted for the purpose. It is a green brae on the east side of a deep ravine near the church, scooped out by nature in the form of an amphitheatre. At present it is sprinkled over with broom, furze, and sloe bushes, and two aged thorns in twin-embrace are seen growing side by side near the borders of the meandering rivulet which murmurs below. In this retired and romantic spot Mr. M'Culloch, for about a year before 'the work' began, preached to crowded congregations, and on the Sabbath evenings, after sermon, detailed to the listening multitudes the astonishing effects produced by the ministrations of Mr. Whitefield in England and America; and urged, with great energy, the doctrine of regeneration and newness of life." In a narrative drawn up in 1742, and approved by Mr. M'Culloch, it is said, "The minister in his ordinary course of sermon, for nearly a twelvemonth before this work began, had been preaching on those subjects which tend most directly to explain the nature, and prove the necessity, of regeneration, according to the different lights in which that important matter is represented in Holy Scripture."

This was the state of matters at Cambuslang during the spring and summer of 1741. But we must now again return to Whitefield, who, at this very juncture, appeared, and for the first time, in Scotland. In the month of March he had arrived in England, and soon after he was invited by many in this country to visit Scotland. Among these, Messrs. Ebenezer and Ralph Erskine, now separated from the establishment, and forming with their brethren of the secession the associate presbytery, were among the earliest and most urgent. Their wish was, that in coming to Scotland Whitefield should preach only in connection with their body, and so help forward the exclusive work in which they were engaged. To this he objected, regarding himself as an evangelist at large; and out of this difference many things that were to be regretted seem to have taken rise. But with these it is not necessary for us at present further to interfere. On the 30th of July he arrived in Edinburgh. He was urged to preach, but declined till he had seen the Messrs. Erskine; and he accordingly proceeded to Dunfermline. Writing on the 1st of August, he says: " I went *yesterday* to Dunfermline, where dear Mr. Ralph Erskine hath got a large and separate, or, as it is commonly termed, seceding meeting-house. He received me very lovingly. I preached to his and the town's people—a very thronged assembly. After I had done prayer, and named my text, *the rustling made by opening the Bibles all at once quite surprised me;* a scene I never was witness to before." The day following he returned to Edinburgh, accompanied with Mr. Ralph Erskine, and preached in the Orphan House park to a large and impressed audience. His text was, " The kingdom of God is not meat and drink, but righteousness, and peace, and joy in the Holy Ghost." (Rom. xiv. 17.) After sermon, a large company, including some of the nobility, came to bid him God-speed, and among others, a portly Quaker, a nephew of the Messrs. Erskine, who, taking him by the hand, said, " Friend George, I am as thou art; I am for bringing all to the life and power of the ever-living God; and therefore if thou wilt not quarrel with me about my hat, I will not quarrel with thee about thy gown." On Sabbath evening he preached in the same place to upwards of fifteen thousand; and on the evenings of Monday, Friday, and Saturday, to nearly as many; on Tuesday in the Canongate Church; on Wednesday and Thursday at Dunfermline; and on Friday morning at Queensferry. " Everywhere," says he, " the auditories were large and very attentive. Great power accompanied the word. Many have been brought under convictions, and I have already received invitations to different places; which, God willing, I intend to comply with." Writing on the 15th of August (that is, a week later), he says: "It would make your heart leap for joy to be now in Edinburgh. I question if there be not upwards of three hundred in this city seeking after Jesus. Every morning I have a constant levee of wounded souls, many of whom are quite slain by the law. God's power attends the word continually, just as when I left London. At seven in the morning we have a lecture in the fields, attended not only by the common people, but also by persons of rank. I have reason to think that several of the latter sort are coming to Jesus. Little children, also, are much wrought upon. God much blesses my letters from the little orphans. [Girls in the hospital.] He loves to work by contemptible means. O my dear brother, I am quite amazed when I think what God has done here in a fortnight. My printed journals and sermons have been blessed in an uncommon manner. I am only afraid lest people should idolize the instrument, and not look enough to the glorious Jesus, in whom alone I desire to glory. Congregations consist of many thousands. Never did I see so many Bibles, nor people looking into them, when I am expounding, with so much attention. Plenty of tears flow from the hearers' eyes. Their emotion appears in various ways. I preach twice daily, and expound at private houses at night, and am employed in speaking to souls under distress great part of the day. I have just snatched a few moments to write to my dear brother. O that God may enlarge your heart to pray for me! This afternoon I preach out of town, and also to-morrow. Next post, God willing, you shall have another letter. I walk continually in the comforts of the Holy Ghost. The love of Christ quite strikes me dumb. O grace! grace! Let that be my song. Adieu."

In this way he continued preaching very extensively over

the country; and early in September he arrived in Glasgow. On the 11th he began in the High Church-yard, and for five days in succession he preached there twice a-day—at an early hour in the morning, and again in the evening. The expectations were great, not only in Glasgow, but all around, and crowds flocked to hear him. Morning after morning, and evening after evening, that vast church-yard, almost paved as it is with tombstones, was crowded with living worshippers, trembling under the word. But not satisfied with hearing, the pen of the ready writer was from day to day at work, and each sermon was printed by itself, and put immediately into circulation. Eight of the ten are now before us in their original form. On comparing these with the sermons contained in the uniform edition of his works, only three out of the eight appear in that collection. Some of the remaining five will be found in the appendix, as true specimens of the kind of preaching which was so eminently blessed. In these there are specimens of preaching eloquence fitted to impress and to awaken; yet is there in them but little of the mere eloquence of intellect or of imagination. They are throughout characterized by great simplicity, as if the language of the preacher merely expressed what he felt; and yet is there so much earnestness and so much closeness of application, as in some measure to account for the effect produced—we mean in so far as that was human. All that we know of that wonderful man from his writings, confirms us in the impression that this was very much the character of all his ministrations; that with the advantage of a thrilling voice and an impressive manner, he was in the pulpit very much what Baxter was in the press. He spoke as a man realizing all that he said, and laying open the feelings of his own heart in addressing the hearts of others. And in this there is doubtless much of the power by which the sympathies of others may be awakened.

The impression produced by these sermons was very great, and they were blessed to not a few. Mr. Whitefield himself returned to England in the end of October, but many letters followed him, detailing the fruits of his labours in Scotland; and one of these was written by Mr. M'Culloch. This is important, not only as showing the interest which he took in Mr. Whitefield's first visit to Scotland, but also in making us acquainted with the views which he entertained concerning the effects produced. The following is an extract:—

"As it is matter of joy and thankfulness to God, who sent you hither, and gave you so much countenance, and so remarkably crowned your labours with success *here at Glasgow*, so I doubt not but the following account of the many seals to your ministry, in and about that city, will be very rejoicing to your heart, especially as the kingdom of our glorious Redeemer is so much advanced thereby, and as the everlasting happiness of souls is promoted. I am well informed by some ministers, and other judicious and experienced Christians, that there are to the amount of *fifty persons* already known, in and about Glasgow, who appear to be savingly converted, through the blessing and power of God on your ten sermons. And there are, besides these, several others apparently under conviction, but not reckoned, as being still doubtful. Several Christians, also, of considerable standing, were much strengthened, revived, and comforted, by what they heard. They were made to rejoice in hope of the glory of God, having attained to the full assurance of faith. Among those lately converted, there are several young people, who were before openly wicked and flagitious, or at best but very negligent as to spiritual things; and yet they are now in the way of salvation. Some young converts are yet under doubts and fears, but a considerable number of them have attained to peace and joy in believing. Several of those who were lately wrought upon in a gracious way, seem to outstrip Christians of considerable standing, in spiritual-mindedness, and in many other good qualifications; particularly in their zeal for the conversion of others, in their love to ordinances, and in their freedom from bigotry and party zeal. Those converted by your ministry have not been discovered at once, but only from time to time. A good many of them have been discovered only of late. Their convictions were at first less pungent, and through the discouragements they met with, in the families where they resided, as well as from their own feelings, they endeavoured for a time to conceal their state. These circumstances afford grounds for hoping, that there are yet others who may afterwards become known. Besides such as have been awakened through the power of God accompanying your sermons, there are others who have been since awakened, and who have been discovered in consequence of the change observable in their conduct. Young converts are very active in seeking to promote the conversion of others, especially their relations and connections. Sometimes this is done by conversations, exhorting them to flee to Christ, and sometimes by correspondence; and there are instances of such means being blessed. Such converts have all a great love for one another, and for all in Christ; and they have great sympathy with any who are in a state of doubt and fear. Such as have not yet attained to comfort, nevertheless of their deep concern and careful attendance on the means of grace, are sometimes useful to Christians of older standing, by the anxiety which they discover. These, dear brother, are a few hints concerning some of the most remarkable things, as to the blessing which accompanied your labours at Glasgow. May a rich and powerful blessing give a plentiful increase to them everywhere! —With great respect and esteem, I am, reverend and dear sir, your affectionate brother in the work of the gospel.

" WILLIAM M'CULLOCH."

It may be added here, that many of those who were afterwards brought under the power of the truth at Cambuslang, spoke of these sermons as among the first means of awakening them to concern. Instances of this will be brought out in the cases to be afterwards detailed.

CHAPTER V.

THE FIRST THREE MONTHS OF THE REVIVAL AT CAMBUSLANG.

We before saw the condition of this parish, as regarded the means of grace, some of which were special, and had a direct bearing on the existing state of religion. We have now seen that preaching of a very unusual kind had been brought to the immediate neighbourhood, and that Mr. M'Culloch had taken a deep interest in the work which ensued. It would have been strange indeed, if, nevertheless, the people of Cambuslang had remained *wholly unmoved*. On the contrary, we are informed, that towards the end of the year 1741, there was an observable change in the attention and apparent feelings of the congregation, under the ministrations of the word. Still there was nothing so remarkable as yet to warrant the term REVIVAL, in its ordinary acceptation: and as a narrative of the revival itself was drawn up and attested in May 1742, it will be best for us simply to copy the account given, and Mr. M'Culloch's attestation to its accuracy.

" *A narrative of the extraordinary work at Cambuslang, in a letter to a friend.*

" Sir,—As the report of the good work at Cambuslang, which has for several weeks engaged the attention of numbers in this city and country in the neighbourhood, is now spread over a great part of the nation, it is no wonder that one who lives at the distance you do should be curious to have a true relation of it. And as I would be glad of any opportunity to serve you, it is very agreeable to me to think that I can gratify you in this matter, especially in what concerns the people in that parish, and some other parishes near it; having had opportunity to converse fully with the minister of Cambuslang, and with many of the people there who are under this special exercise, and also with some other ministers who have several in their parishes that appear to be under the same happy impressions.

"There is one thing, in the entry, I must apprize you of, namely, that I am to confine myself to a simple narration of facts, as the evidences on which the opinion of many concerning the present happy change that is wrought on that people is founded; and this, without entering on any reasoning, but leaving it to yourself to draw proper conclusions from the facts, after comparing them with Scripture rules and instances.

"I must also acquaint you, as it was natural to expect, when, on a singular occasion of this sort, great numbers of people from adjacent towns and country came flocking to a place which became so remarkable, that, in such a promiscuous multitude, some counterfeits would readily appear. It was the early care of ministers, who interested themselves most in that matter, to enter into a strict examination of those who appeared to be under a more than ordinary concern; so as to obtain satisfaction to themselves whether the work was solid, being justly apprehensive that the powers of darkness would not fail to employ their devices to bring contempt on what might tend so much to the honour of the gospel.

"In those watchful endeavours, it must be owned that some impostors were found to have mixed with the sincere; but there is reason to bless God that, so far as yet appears, they have been very few; and, as these have been severely rebuked, so the most awful warnings have been given against all such insincere pretensions; which warnings, there is ground to believe, have had very good effect.

"Now, sir, to give you the short history of this matter:

The minister of the parish, in his ordinary course of sermons, *for near a twelvemonth before this work began*, had been preaching on those subjects which tend most directly to explain the nature and prove the necessity of regeneration, according to the different lights in which that important matter is represented in Holy Scripture. And *for some months before the late remarkable events*, a more than ordinary concern about religion appeared among that people. One evidence of this was, that about the end of January last, a petition was given in to the minister, subscribed by about ninety heads of families, desiring that a weekly lecture should be set up; which was readily granted, and the day fixed was Thursday, as the most convenient for the temporal interests of the parish.*

"On Monday, the 15th of February, there was a general meeting, at the minister's house, of the particular societies for prayer, which had subsisted in the parish for several years before. On Tuesday, there was another meeting for prayer in the same place; the occasion of which was a concert with several serious Christians elsewhere about solemn prayer relating to the public interests of the gospel. In this concert, only a small number of people in Cambuslang were engaged at first; but others getting notice of it desired to join, and were admitted. The people who met for prayer these two days apprehended that they had been so well employed, and found so much leisure for it, that they had a third meeting on Wednesday. But, on all these three days, they returned timeously in the evening to their own houses; so far is it from being true that they rushed from some of these meetings to the church, and continued for days and nights, as was reported.

"Previous to Thursday, the 18th February, they had weekday sermons only on Thursdays, according to the above-mentioned desire of the parish. And up to this time, though

---

* That the class with whom this movement originated may be known, it may be added, that the two men who went round for signatures, were Ingram More, a shoemaker; and Robert Bowman, a weaver.

several persons came to the minister under deep concern about their salvation, yet there came no great number together. But on that day (Thursday the 18th of February), after sermon, a considerable number of people, reckoned by some present to be *about fifty*, came together to the minister's house, under convictions and alarming apprehensions about the state of their souls, and desiring to speak with him.

"From this unexpected number coming in one evening in so great distress, and the necessity of the minister's exhorting them in general and conversing with them separately, you will easily perceive that he behoved to spend that night with them, as he had done most part of two or three more since this work began, *which is about twelve weeks.*

"After this, numbers daily resorted to that place—some to hear the word, some to converse with people who were under this remarkable concern, and others with different views. And the desires and exigencies of these were such that the minister found himself obliged, without any previous intimation, to provide them with *daily sermon*, a few days excepted, and after sermon usually to spend some time with them in exhortation, prayer, and singing of psalms; he being especially encouraged thereto by the extraordinary success with which God was pleased, from time to time, to bless his own ordinances, insomuch that, by the best information that could be had, the number of persons awakened to a deep concern about salvation, and against whom there are no known exceptions as yet, *has amounted to above three hundred.* And, through divine mercy, the work seems to be still making considerable progress every week, and more for some weeks of late than formerly.

"Of the number just now mentioned, the far greater part have already given, both to ministers and other serious Christians, a good account of what they have felt in their convictions and humiliation for sin, of the way of their relief by faith in the mercy of God through Jesus Christ, and of the change they feel in the prevalent inclinations and dispositions of their hearts.

" As to their devotion, with other parts of their practice, which is what chiefly attracts the attention and regard of this country, there are comfortable accounts given of it, by those who have the best and most frequent opportunities of knowing their daily behaviour.

" The parish of Cambuslang being of so small extent that most of the people live within a mile of the church, and some who have the best intelligence being almost every day with the minister, he and they have abundant opportunities of knowing the practices of such of the people as live within their bounds. And the account which they give is, that they appear to be in a very hopeful way; and the like good accounts are given by several ministers and others, of such as belong to other neighbouring parishes.

" Among the good fruits already appearing, both in Cambuslang and elsewhere, the following instances seem very encouraging: There is a visible reformation of the lives of some who were formerly notorious sinners, particularly in the laying aside cursing and swearing, and drinking to excess, among persons addicted to these practices;—remorse for acts of injustice and the violation of relative duties, confessed to the persons wronged, joined to new endeavours after a conscientious discharge of the duties previously neglected;—restitution, which has more than once been distinctly and particularly inculcated in public, since this work began;— forgiving injuries;— desirable evidence of fervent love to one another, to all men, and even to those who speak evil of them;—and among those people, both in Cambuslang and other parishes, more affectionate expressions of regard than ever to their own ministers, and to the ordinances dispensed by them;—the keeping up of divine worship in families, where it was often neglected by some, and entirely by others;—the setting up of new meetings for prayer, both of old and young, partly within the parish, where twelve such societies are now begun, and partly elsewhere, among the awakened;—and together with all of these, ardent love to the Holy Scriptures, vehement thirsting after the public ordinances, earnest desires to be instructed in private by ministers and others, with commendable docility and tractableness in receiving such instruction.

"This thirst after knowledge is remarkable among those who were formerly more ignorant than others. Some who cannot read, though old, are thus desirous that they may become better acquainted with God's word; and so they have resolved to learn to read; some of the younger having gone to school.

"These good impressions have been made on persons of very different characters and ages; on some of the most abandoned, as well as the more sober; on the young as well as the aged; on the illiterate as well as those better instructed; on persons of a slow as well as quick and more sprightly genius; and what seems to deserve special attention, on persons who were addicted to scoffing at sacred things, and at this work particularly, when it first began.

"The sum of all these facts is, that this work has been begun and carried on under the influence of the great and substantial doctrines of Christianity, pressing *jointly the necessity of repentance towards God, of faith in the Lord Jesus Christ, and of holiness in all manner of conversation;* that it came after such preparations as an extensive concern about religion, gradually increasing, together with extraordinary and fervent prayers in large meetings, and particularly in relation to the success of the gospel; that great and successful pains have been taken to discover and discountenance hypocritical pretences, and to warn people against what might have the least appearance of enthusiasm or delusion; that the account given by a very large number of people concerning their inward exercises and attainments, seems to agree with the Scripture standard; and that they are bringing forth in practice fruits meet for repentance, comprehending the several branches of piety, and of the most substantial morality, that can entitle men to the regard of the friends of religion and virtue.

"And now, sir, I have given you a plain and simple account of the most material facts relating to this extraordinary work at Cambuslang, and of such as were awakened there belonging to other parishes, together with the proper evidence by which these facts are supported; in all which I have avoided disputing, and studied brevity. I leave it with you to judge how far such facts make it evident that this work is from God; seeing that, to use the words of a pious divine, treating a subject of the same nature, 'He that was formerly a drunkard, lives a sober life; he that was vain, light, and wanton, becomes grave and sedate; the blasphemer praises God; joy is turned into heaviness, and that on account of the condition of the soul; the ignorant are filled with the knowledge of divine things; and the tongue that was dumb in the things of God, speaks the language of Canaan;'—seeing that secure sinners 'have been roused with a witness to care for the state of their souls, that those who were ignorant speak skilfully concerning religious matters, and that even the graceless increase in knowledge; that swearers stop their oaths and speak reverently of God; that vain persons, who minded no religion, but frequented taverns and frolics, passing their time in filthiness, foolish talking and jesting, or singing paltry songs, do now frequent Christian societies for prayer, seek Christian conversation, talk of what concerns the soul, and express their mirth in psalms and hymns and spiritual songs; that they who were too sprightly to be devout, and who esteemed it an unmanly thing to shed tears for the state of their souls, have mourned as for an only son; and that persons who came to mock at the lamentations of others, have been convinced, and by free grace brought over to such ways as they formerly despised.'

"I am, sir, yours," &c.

"May 8, 1742."

This letter was published without the name of the author,

but with the following attestation by Mr. M'Culloch himself:—

"May 8, 1742.

"I have perused the *following* short narrative,* *and can attest the facts contained in it;* partly from personal knowledge, and partly from the most credible information; but I think it a loss that it is not fuller. I have seen a large paper compiled by different hands; which, besides the facts related in this, contains several useful reasonings, tending to prove that the favourable judgment formed by many, and even by some who, through want of information, hesitated at first about this work, is supported by all that kind of evidence that things of this nature are capable of, in such a space of time; and consequently, that there is good ground to hope that, by the divine blessing, the confirmation arising from perseverance will be daily increasing, as hitherto it has been. The said large paper contained also a vindication of this work from various objections, and false and injurious aspersions thrown on it in print by some who have not yet appeared to own their accusations; which in justice they ought to do, or retract them. But though it has not been thought expedient to publish that large account at present, I understand the compilers of it can easily prepare it for the press, if it shall be thought needful afterwards. For my own part, I desire to join in hearty prayers with the people of God, that he may revive his work in the midst of the years, in this and all the churches, and make it to triumph over all opposition; and I conclude with the words of the prophet Zechariah (iv. 6, 7): 'Not by might, nor by power, but by my Spirit, saith the Lord. Who art thou, O great mountain? Before Zerubbabel thou shalt become a plain: and he shall bring forth the headstone thereof with shoutings, crying, Grace, grace, unto it.'

"WILLIAM M'CULLOCH."

We have not observed whether the large paper here referred to was published or not. But there is a collection

* This attestation was originally *prefixed* to the narrative.

of not fewer than nine attestations, nearly all by ministers whose nearness enabled them to judge, or who had themselves shared in the work. It is now unnecessary, and would be tiresome, were these to be all copied. But in several cases there is so much of what was actually observed by the writers, that extracts at least from their attestations can scarcely fail to be interesting. And they are all, it will be seen, attesting what had occurred during the same period, namely, the first three months of the revival.

The first which we shall copy is the attestation of Mr. Willison of Dundee, a name familiar among the pious as a household word. His letter is as follows:—

"Glasgow, April 15, 1742.

"Reverend and Dear Brother,—Seeing some are desirous to have my thoughts of the work at Cambuslang, I am willing to own that I travelled a good way to inquire and get satisfaction about it. And having resided several days in Mr. M'Culloch's house, I had occasion to converse with many who had been and were under convictions there. I found several in darkness and great distress about the condition of their souls, and with many tears bewailing their sins and original corruptions; and especially the sin of unbelief and slighting of precious Christ; some of whom had been in this state for several weeks past. Yet I saw nothing in any tending to despair; but, on the contrary, their exercise pointed still at the great remedy: for oft they would be breaking out in hopeful expressions, such as, 'Though He slay me, I will trust in him.' Others I found in a most desirable frame—overcome with a sense of the wonderful love and loveliness of Jesus Christ; they were even sick of love, and inviting all about them to praise him. I spoke also with many who had got relief from their soul-trouble, and in whom the gracious work of the Spirit of God appeared, according to my apprehension, in its fruits and effects. Such were ingenuous confessors of their former evil ways, professed hatred of sin, low and abasing thoughts of themselves, the renouncing the vanities of the world and all their own doings, and relying wholly upon Christ for righteousness and strength; expressing great love to Christ, to the Bible, to secret prayer, to the people of God, and to his image in whomsoever it might appear; and also love to their enemies, so that when they heard of some calling the work at Cambuslang a delusion, they showed no resentment, but wished their eyes might be opened; and they earnestly wished they could bring all their enemies and all the world to their dear Redeemer. I conversed with some who had been very wicked and scandalous, but who were now wonderfully changed. Some of them, who had before been rude and boisterous, had now the meekness of the lamb. When they spoke of their former ways, they blushed and wept, saying that none in all the country round had been so wicked as they; and they earnestly desired to exalt free grace. When I was cautioning them against new temptations, they showed a proper sense of their own weakness, and seemed on this account afraid of going near their old companions, though they would fain have had them brought to Christ. They would rather, they said, die than return to their old sins; and that if ever they should be so left to themselves as to fall into any of them, they would rather leave the country than bring dishonour on the cause of God. Though I conversed with a great many, both men and women, young and old, I could observe nothing visionary or enthusiastic about them. Their conversation was solid, their experience scriptural, and the comfort or relief they had got still came to them through some promise or word of Scripture cast into their minds. And it was pleasant to hear them mention so great a variety of these, up and down the Bible. Some who could not read repeated their words of consolation without knowing well whether they were words of Scripture or not; and on finding that they were, they greatly rejoiced. I had heard much of this surprising work by letters, and from eye-witnesses, before I came; but all that made slight impressions on me when compared with what I saw and heard for myself. On the whole,

I look upon the work at Cambuslang as a singular and marvellous outpouring of the Holy Spirit; and I pray that it may be a happy forerunner of a general revival of the Lord's work in this poor decayed church, and a blessed means of union among all the lovers of our dear Lord.

"JOHN WILLISON."

A somewhat similar account is given by Mr. Matthew Connel, minister of East Kilbride, a neighbouring parish; but as it does not contain much additional information it may be omitted. The third is by Dr. John Hamilton, minister of the Barony parish of Glasgow, and who was himself also honoured of God. He speaks in his attestation of some who belonged to his own parish, and who had been benefited at Cambuslang. We shall, therefore, communicate an abstract of his statements. Writing on the 20th of April, he says: " I understand it to be expected that I should declare my sentiments concerning the extraordinary work at Cambuslang, especially as a good many of my parishioners have lately been awakened there to a great concern about their souls. As soon as I was informed of their condition, I made it my business to wait on them. And I found a good many persons under the deepest exercise of soul, crying out most bitterly of their lost and miserable state, by reason of sin; of their unbelief, in despising Christ and the offers of the gospel; of the hardness of their heart; and of their gross carelessness and indifference about religion. And though some of them said that they had regularly attended the preaching of the gospel, yet they acknowledged with much regret their misimprovement of it; that they had heard many sweet sermons without benefit, and had come to church only to see and be seen. I have heard them express great sorrow for these things, and seemingly in the most serious and sincere manner, and this not so much, as some of them told me, from fear of punishment as from a sense of the dishonour done to God and the blessed Redeemer. Though I have seen some of them in great distress, I could never observe any disordered in mind, and their complaints were always suited to their circumstances. Neither did I observe any of them in a state of despair, but all of them seeking relief according to the gospel method of salvation—through an interest in Christ. When speaking of prayer, they have told me how much they had formerly neglected that duty, and how coldly and lifelessly it had been performed. But now they had much sweetness in it. Their love for the Scriptures was great. They spoke of them as very precious, and as an invaluable treasure. They seemed surprised how they could have so slighted them before, and they wondered at the discoveries which they were daily making in them. They had great love for the public ordinances, and felt unwilling, they said, to retire even when they were over. They are also very desirous of being instructed in private. Some of them came to my house; and I never saw persons more docile. Some were at first but little acquainted with doctrinal knowledge; but their progress was rapid. I have been surprised to observe how readily and even judiciously some, who had but lately been ignorant and unconverted, spoke concerning the most important points of practical religion, and with how much facility they adduced passages of Scripture suited to the subject in hand. I have often heard them express very strong desires for the conversion of others; and they discover great love to as many as are in Christ. The persons I conversed with had been different from one another in their previous character and conduct. Some had all along been sober and regular, and in the habit of attending public ordinances; whereas others had been careless, and addicted to many sins. But even the more blameless declared, that till now, their hearts had never been touched with the word; that they had never till now felt the influence of religion, but were altogether unconcerned."

Other attestations are afforded by the Rev. William Hamilton, at Bothwell; the Rev. William Hamilton, at Douglas; the Rev. John M'Laurin of Glasgow, whose name is in all the churches, and others in the neighbourhood; but passing over these, we shall further quote only from a letter by the Rev. William M'Knight, minister of Irvine, and father of Dr. M'Knight, well known as a critical commentator. And we furnish an abstract of his letter all the rather that, like Mr. Willison's, it describes the impressions produced on his own mind when at Cambuslang. Writing on the 6th of May, 1742, he says:—

"As I had, by information from letters, conceived a good opinion of the extraordinary and surprising work at Cambuslang before I went thither, so my opinion has been much confirmed by what I saw and heard. While I joined with your congregation in public worship, I observed among the vast number assembled to hear, not only serious looks, grave deportment, and close attention, but also weeping eyes, and other indications of deep distress. In conversing with some after the public services were over, I found that their convictions were deep touching the evil and demerit of sin, both original and actual, particularly that of unbelief. On directing them to the words of Paul, as addressed to the Philippian jailer, 'Believe on the Lord Jesus Christ, and thou shalt be saved, and thy house' (Acts xvi. 31), their answer was, 'Lord, help me to believe; gladly would I believe, but I cannot.' Yet I observed that, even in these circumstances, they expressed ardent desires after Christ. I conversed with others, who had been under deep and piercing convictions of sin, but who had also found in the blood of Christ a sufficient remedy; and these were ever exalting free grace, saying, with the apostle Paul, 'It is by grace that we are what we are; and blessed be the God and Father of our Lord Jesus Christ, who hath blessed us with all spiritual blessings in heavenly places in Christ.' When I conversed with them, they declared distinctly how their convictions began, and wrought, and how they got relief. They discovered, also, how gracious that work was, in their confession of sin with shame, sorrow, and blushing; in their professing so to hate it as to loathe

themselves on account of it; crying out, 'Behold we are vile; we abhor ourselves, and repent in dust and ashes:' also in their love to God and his ordinances, in renouncing their own righteousness, and relying wholly on Christ for righteousness and strength; in their high esteem and ardent love for their dear Redeemer; in their charity and love for one another, and for all who are Christ's; in their affectionate concern for such as fall under distress and anguish of spirit on account of sin; and in their endeavours to relieve them, whether by suitable exhortations, or by comforting with the consolations wherewith they had themselves been comforted. These are a few of the good fruits which I observed among some of those with whom I conversed at Cambuslang. "WM. M'KNIGHT.
"Irvine, May 6, 1742."

These attestations are, we doubt not, sufficient, and therefore we shall now only add the account which Mr. M'Culloch himself gives of what had taken place. Writing to Mr. Whitefield, on the 28th of April 1742, he says:—

"Rev. and very Dear Sir,—I have been so much employed daily for so long time in the Lord's work in this place, that I have not had leisure to write to you half so often as I inclined; but I cannot forget you one day, and would gladly hear more frequently from you, if your more important work will permit you now and then to employ a few minutes that way. It is matter of great joy to hear that our Immanuel is making such quick and amazing conquest in New England, and that his work still goes on and prospers with you. May he continue more and more to strengthen and furnish you for that great and extraordinary work to which he hath called you; and may he abundantly bless and promote your labours for the good of multitudes of souls, who may be as so many jewels in that crown of glory that our Lord will give you at his appearing! For my part, I cannot but often cry out, with wonder and astonishment, Whence is this to me, that the great God our Saviour should put so great and extraordinary a work into my hands—a work relating to the interests of his kingdom, and the bringing of souls to him—and that he should give any countenance at all, especially to the worthless endeavours of such a poor sinful creature in this work? How well does it become me often to say and to sing, 'Not unto me, O Lord, not unto me, but unto thy name, O Lord, be all the glory, for thy mercy's sake, and for thy truth's sake!'

"Help us, dear brother, to praise him for his goodness, and for his works of mercy to perishing sinners, that are everywhere made to taste of his distinguishing goodness, and particularly in this place of late. To the praise of his own mercy and grace be it spoken, I believe that, in less than three months past, *about three hundred souls* have been awakened and convinced of their perishing condition without a Saviour, *more than two hundred of whom are, I believe, hopefully converted and brought home to God*, and have been at times filled with joy and peace in believing; and the rest are earnestly seeking for Jesus, and following on to know the Lord.

"We have had several glorious days of the Son of man since this work began. Last Lord's-day was a remarkable day of divine power amongst us. The Lord was with us of a truth. The arrows of conviction flew thick among my people, and though there were but a dozen persons that had been awakened that day, who came to my closet to talk with me at night after sermon, yet I am informed that a considerable number besides these were wounded in spirit, and either could not get into the house for the crowd, or went away wishing to conceal their distress as long as they could. Some have computed the number present hearing, the last two Lord's-days, at nine or ten thousand. Mr. Willison came from Dundee about three weeks ago, to see the Lord's work here, and he returned much pleased. I believe his sermons, while here, were blessed to many. Our dear brother, Mr. L——n, has been very assisting and encouraging to this work. We continue still to have a sermon here every day. I long much to see you here. Let me know by the first opportunity when you think to be with us. Cease not, dear brother, to pray for the continuance and spreading of this blessed work, and for your poor and unworthy, but affectionate brother in the Lord, Wm. M'Culloch."

After hearing so much of the power experienced at Cambuslang, one naturally feels desirous of having some specimen of the preaching, and especially of Mr. M'Culloch's. Eleven of his discourses were published by his son. But they had generally been revised, remodelled, or, it may be, in some cases written out for the first time, after they had been delivered. During the pressing season of special duty, his discourses were, it may be, generally rather the fruit of meditation than of written compositions, and not therefore to be had. Two only of the eleven published sermons, however, are said to have been delivered during the revival, and one of them during the period just reviewed. But even these, though faithful manifestations of divine truth, were not the actual sermons, as delivered on the occasions referred to. Of the one, his son says: "The sermon which he preached, he afterwards altered, particularly in the improvement, when, about *twenty years after*, he again wrote and preached on the same text." It would, therefore, lead only to mistake, were these to be given as actual specimens of the preaching so eminently blessed. Many of the passages remembered by the awakened, as having been the most effective, are not likely ever to have been written, but spoken, in addressing the persons whose hearts had thus been touched and awakened.

CHAPTER VI.

THE FIRST COMMUNION.

WE have already been carried forward to the month of May, and as the usual period for observing the communion appears to have been in July, it was to be expected that some further progress would be contemplated. It is through the gospel that God especially calls sinners. But there must be more than calling—there must be answering. "When thou saidst, Seek ye my face, my heart said unto thee, Thy face, Lord, will I seek. O Lord, truly I am thy servant; I am thy servant, and the son of thine handmaid; thou hast loosed my bonds." (Ps. xxvii. 8, cxvi. 16.) These are sayings of the heart, and may be addressed to God in private: but it is at the Lord's table that they are fully and solemnly said. There, such as can use this language have a seat among the children; there they have to accept of the bread and the cup *personally;* there they profess to accept of Christ as set forth in these—of Christ as having made an atonement for them—of Christ as their loving and beloved Lord, reigning in them, reigning over them, and reigning for them. The hundreds already converted at Cambuslang must, therefore, have desired greatly such an opportunity as this. And, accordingly, we are told that when it was said to them, "Let us go into the house of the Lord," they were glad. Their prayers and conversation all looked forward to this holy meeting. Many spoke of seeing "the King in his beauty," and many hoped to have their bands loosed—each of these trusting that he might be released at this New Testament feast.

On the 3d of June, Mr. Whitefield again arrived at Leith; and the impression produced everywhere by this, his second visit to Scotland, was greater than during the first. He began in Edinburgh, but had pressing invitations to visit the west, which was by this time very generally in an excited state, whether from one cause or another. He complied; and on returning to Edinburgh, wrote as follows concerning what he had witnessed : " I arrived here last Saturday evening from the west, where I preached all last week. On Monday, I preached at Paisley; on Tuesday and Wednesday, thrice each day at Irvine ; on Thursday, twice at Mearns ; on Friday, thrice at Cumbernauld ; and on Saturday, twice at Falkirk, on my way back. In every place, there was the greatest commotion among the people that was ever known. Their mourning, in most of the places, was as for a first-born. The auditories were very large, and the work of God seems to be spreading more and more. Indeed, I have seen and felt such things as I never saw and felt before. I never before was enabled to preach so powerfully as I have been whilst in the west. I purpose going to Cambuslang to-morrow, in order to assist at the communion."

Besides Mr. Whitefield and some of the ministers in the neighbourhood of Cambuslang, Mr. Alexander Webster of Edinburgh was present on this occasion, and took part in the interesting services of the week.

It was in these circumstances that the first communion after the commencement of the revival was observed at Cambuslang; and some accounts of it cannot perhaps be better introduced than in the unstudied notice which Whitefield gives of what he himself observed on that occasion. The communion was fixed for Sabbath, the 11th of July; and he is, in the extract to be made, speaking of the preceding Tuesday : " Yesterday morning, I preached at Glasgow to a very large congregation. At noon, I came to Cambuslang, the place which God hath so much honoured. I preached at two, to a vast body of people; again at six in the evening; and afterwards at nine. Such a commotion was surely never heard of, especially about eleven o'clock at night. It far outdid all that ever I saw in America. For about an hour and a half there was such weeping, so many falling into deep distress, and manifesting it in various ways, that description is impossible. The people seemed to be smitten by scores. They were carried off and brought into the house like wounded soldiers taken from a field of battle. Their agonies and cries were deeply affecting. Mr. M'Culloch preached after I had done, till past one o'clock in the morning, and even then the people could scarcely be got to retire. Throughout the whole of the night might the voice of prayer and praise be still heard in the fields."

On Friday night, Mr. Whitefield returned again to Cambuslang, and remained till Monday. And writing on the Thursday following, he says: " On Friday night I came to Cambuslang, to assist at the blessed sacrament. On Saturday, I preached to above twenty thousand people. Two tents were set up (for the Sabbath), and the sacrament was administered in the fields. When I began to serve a table, the power of God was felt by numbers; but the people so crowded upon me that I was obliged to leave the tables to be served by some of the other ministers, and to go myself to preach at one of the tents. God was also with them and with his people. There was sermon all day by one or another; and when the table services were over, I preached to the whole congregation, this being at the request of the brethren. I preached about an hour and a half. Surely it was a time much to be remembered. On Monday morning, I preached to nearly as many, but so general a stir I never saw before. The motion passed swift as lightning from one end of the audience to the other. You might have seen thousands bathed in tears, some wringing their hands, some almost swooning, and others crying out and mourning over a pierced Saviour. In the afternoon the concern was also very great. Much prayer had been previously offered up, and during the whole night, you might have heard the different companies praying and giving praise to God."

This account is very striking, but it is mainly confined to what concerned Mr. Whitefield's own labours. It will, therefore, be gratifying to see what Mr. M'Culloch himself says. His letter, detailing what took place, was written on the Wednesday following this communion, and therefore, at a time when every thing must have been fresh upon his mind. It is as follows: " Our glorious Immanuel is still going on to make numerous conquests in this place. It is not quite five months since the work began, and during that time, I have reason to believe *that upwards of five hundred souls have been awakened, brought under deep convictions of sin, and a feeling sense of their lost condition. Most of these have also, I trust, been savingly brought home to God.* I do not include in this number such as have been found to be mere pretenders, nor such as have had nothing in their exercise beyond a dread of hell, which, as you know, may never issue in any saving change. There have been some of both classes, but, blessed be God, the number has not been great, so far as I have been able to ascertain. I do not include in this number, either, such as have been awakened by Mr. Whitefield's sermons; because I cannot pretend to compute them. He has been much here. He has preached not fewer than seventeen times during this, his last visit to Scotland. He and Mr. Webster of Edinburgh, as well as others from the neighbourhood, assisted at the dispensation of the Lord's supper here last Lord's-day, and they were also with me on the Saturday and the Monday. Both were much assisted and countenanced in their Master's work. There was also a more than ordinary concern among the people throughout all the services, but especially under Mr. Whitefield's sermon, which was preached on the Monday. Under it there was great weeping and mourning. The meetings also were very great. On Sabbath, it was reckoned that there could not be fewer than thirty thousand present; but Mr. Whitefield, who has been accustomed to large meetings, estimated them at twenty thousand. The tables were placed below the brae. The whole work was conducted in the open air. There were two tents, and two ministers employed in these all day, except in the evening, when Mr. Whitefield preached to the vast multitude who remained. The number of services was seventeen, and each table, except the last, contained about a hundred, or rather more; and the issue of tokens shows that upwards of seventeen hundred must have communicated. It was, I am persuaded, a blessed time to many; and yet I am hopeful that we shall see and hear of far greater things than these. May the Lord send a plentiful rain to Glasgow, his ancient heritage, whereby multitudes in it may be made to look to Him whom they have pierced, and mourn!

"WILLIAM M'CULLOCH."

It will be observed, that in none of these accounts is there any notice of the texts from which so many impressive discourses were delivered. We have not the means of supplying any regular list of these. But we have observed, from references in some of the manuscript cases, that the action sermon, preached by Mr. M'Culloch, was from the Song of Solomon v. 16 : " His mouth is most sweet; yea, he is altogether lovely. This is my beloved, and this is my friend, O daughters of Jerusalem." And that the sermon preached by Mr. Whitefield on Sabbath evening, was from Isa. liv. 5 : " Thy Maker is thy husband; the Lord of hosts is his name." The sermon preached from this text has more references to it, as having been blessed to individuals, than any other of all that great man's addresses. It is printed in the first edition of his works, and in the more recent collections of his sermons. But no one can obtain from these publications a correct impression of the sermon as delivered. We have been able to trace the same discourse as delivered in four or five places of the west, not very distant from one another, during the same season, and have seen reason to believe, that his ordinary practice was to adhere to a common outline which had been prepared, but to fill it up variously in different places, as his own feelings and a sense of duty prompted. It was in this way that he secured regularity in his general method and trains of reasoning, and yet gave all the freshness of originality, and all the directness of an immediate appeal to his addresses. Different men have different methods, as they ought, and different circumstances lead to changes even in these, which would not otherwise be advisable; but it is instructive to observe how a man of so much labour, so much eloquence, and who was so much blessed, conducted his discourses.

Some of the details occurring in this and other parts of the narrative, may require explanation. These outcries and faintings, it is said, do not look well. Revivals, accompanied with exhibitions such as these, are not desirable. They ought not to be encouraged. Well, even if it should turn out so, let us first see how the matter stands. It is not alleged, then, be it observed, that there is any virtue in such bodily manifestations. It is not wished that anything should be done for the purpose of promoting these. It is admitted that the demand put forth in the gospel is not, My son, give me thy tears, or thy groaning, or thy fainting, or thy bodily suffering of whatever kind; but, "My son, give me thy heart." These are regarded merely as effects; and it is alleged that, as such, there is not in them anything contrary either to reason or Scripture. The mother weeps, and, it may be, faints over the loss of a beloved child; the mercantile adventurer is distracted on hearing of some heavy and overwhelming loss; and the condemned criminal is removed from the bar agitated and convulsed; and is there anything unnatural in the tears, or even in strong bodily agitation on his part, who has just been brought to see that his soul, as well as his body, is in a lost, and, as appears to him, a hopeless condition? Then, every one conversant with the common sympathies of our nature must be aware how much our feelings, whether of joy or of sorrow, are heightened by the sight and the hearing of others in like circumstances; and it will from this be seen how much of the things observed at Cambuslang must have been owing to the vast concourse of people assembled, and to the intensity of the impressions produced. And if we now turn to Scripture, there must surely be something of this kind conveyed in such a passage as the following: "They shall look upon me whom they have pierced, and they shall mourn for him as one mourneth for his only son, and shall be in bitterness for him as one that is in bitterness for his first-born." (Zech. xii. 10.) And it is difficult to conceive of the multitude who heard Peter on the day of Pentecost, otherwise than as resembling the meeting at Cambuslang. Peter's audience, as well as Whitefield's, must have consisted of many thousands. This vast assembly were pricked in their hearts, and cried out, as men who saw themselves lost, "Men and brethren, what shall we do?" and not fewer than three thousand found peace under that sermon, and were saved. It is true we are not told of bodily agitations; but this was not to be expected in so brief a history, nor was it necessary, as these are merely the natural effects of such feelings as are here expressed.

But why, say some, have so many sermons and so many preachers, as if to awaken and keep up such excited feelings? Simply because they were found necessary. Men's minds are usually so thoroughly engaged with the things of this world, as to require all that can be done to bring them into a state even of proper concern about their eternal well-being. The common feeling is, that men require only to be *informed* on the subjects brought before them. But why, then, was it that, "in the last day, that great day of the feast, *Jesus stood and cried*, saying, If any man thirst, let him come unto me and drink?" (John vii. 37.) Was it not just because of the little interest which they had been taking in his previous teaching, and because of the sense which he had of their condition? And the same thing is true in such circumstances as these under consideration. The saying of our Lord has need to be often repeated and considered: " Martha, Martha, thou art careful and troubled about many things, *but one thing is needful.*"

But it is the opinion, we know, of some who sympathize with all this, that such gatherings on sacramental occasions are not advisable. Without offering anything controversially on this subject, it is well that we do not shut our eyes on purposes actually served by such meetings. It is of itself an important fact, that most of the remarkable revivals which have occurred in Scotland have been more or less in connection with these—have been eminently forwarded by them. They have also served the important purpose of extended fellowship among God's people connected with different congregations, and even different parts of the country. In consequence of this intercourse, these were often the means of opening communications between different places, and of promoting the work of God in these. Refreshed by what they heard, and saw, and felt, each little company returned to their own locality; and, in very many cases, their knowledge of each other, their intercourse when brought together in such solemn circumstances, and their opportunities of meeting afterwards, led to the employment of means which would not otherwise have been thought of, and, through these, to the revival of God's work in their own neighbourhood.

It is also to be observed, as regards the number of ministers brought together on such occasions, that the various gifts thus employed, no doubt, contributed to the effects produced. Different men, all excellent in their own way, are nevertheless very differently endowed. Some are fitted to awaken, some to melt, some to comfort, some to lay open the deceitfulness of the heart, some to solve difficult questions, and some to unfold the mysteries of the gospel. These and other gifts are really wanted, and hence another reason why greater effects have been experienced on such occasions than under the ordinary ministrations of some one instructor. And perhaps we should add, that there is really a blessing in Christian fellowship, which comes to be greatly more felt when its feelings traverse their usual limits, and bring together, as of one family, many otherwise strangers, or known only by report.*

* We have been very much struck with the fact observable in Scottish revivals, that the services of the *Monday* after the communion were usually, more than those of other days, eminently blessed. Livingston, when on his death-bed, said that the only sermons he had ever preached, and which he wished to see written, were preached on the Mondays after communion Sabbath, one at the Kirk of Shotts, and another at Holywood, near Belfast. And the readers of this volume will find many notices of special blessings attending Monday sermons.

CHAPTER VII.

THE SECOND COMMUNION.

The excitement produced by the first communion was very great. Frequent mention of this is made in the manuscript cases. Some had been disappointed at not being able to attend the former; some who were present had been so distracted with a sense of their condition, that they dared not to venture; and such as had been forward, and found Him whom they so much loved, eagerly panted for a renewed opportunity of the same enjoyment. But besides these personal feelings, there were extraordinary reports carried into all parts of the country. The meetings had been large, and many of those present were from a distance, and had never seen any thing of the kind before. They went, therefore, to their own places, proclaiming to all the things which they had seen and heard; and the effect was an extraordinary desire that a renewed opportunity of witnessing something similar should be afforded; many who had not been present on the former occasion, resolving that in these circumstances they also would attend.

But long before these desires could be learned, a proposal to this effect had been suggested, and was at this very time under consideration. But this cannot be better explained than in a letter written by Mr. M'Culloch himself. This letter contains an account of the communion, and although it wants the date, it must have been written very soon after that solemnity, for it was published in the 39th number of the "Glasgow Weekly History," which would fall due about the end of September. It is addressed to a brother minister, but his name is not given, and is as follows :—

"Rev. and Dear Brother,—You know that we had the sacrament of the Lord's supper dispensed here on the 11th of July last. It was such a sweet and agreeable time to many, that a motion was made by Mr. Webster, and seconded by Mr. Whitefield, that we should have another such occasion again in this place very soon. The motion was very agreeable to me, but I thought it needful to deliberate before coming to a resolution. The thing proposed was indeed extraordinary, but so had the work in this place been for several months past. Care was, therefore, taken to acquaint the several meetings for prayer with the motion. They relished it well, and prayed for direction to those concerned in determining this matter. The session met next Lord's-day, and taking into consideration the divine command to celebrate the ordinance often, joined with the extraordinary work that had been here for some time past; and understanding that many who had met with much benefit to their souls at the last solemnity, had expressed their earnest desires of seeing another in this place shortly; and hearing that there were many who intended to have joined at the last occasion, but were kept back through inward discouragements, or outward obstructions, and were wishing soon to see another opportunity of that kind here, to which they might have access; it was therefore resolved, God willing, that the sacrament of the Lord's supper should be again dispensed in this parish on the third Sabbath of August then next to come, being the 15th day of that month. And there was first one day and then another, at some distance of time from that, appointed for a general meeting of the several societies for prayer in the parish, at the manse. They accordingly met on the days appointed, with some other Christians from places in the neighbourhood. And when the manse could not conveniently hold them, they went to the church; and at one of these meetings, when light failed them in the church, a good number, of their own free motion, came again to the manse, and continued at prayers and praises together till about one o'clock next morning.

"The design of these meetings, and the business which they were accordingly employed in—besides singing of psalms and blessing the name of God together—was to ask mercy of the God of heaven to ourselves; to pray for such as unhappily opposed this work of God here and in other parts, that God would forgive their guilt in this matter, open their eyes, remove their prejudices, and convince them that it is indeed his work, and give them repentance to the acknowledgment of the truth; that the Lord would continue and increase the blessed work of conviction and conversion here and in other places, where it has begun in a remarkable measure, and that he would extend it to all the corners of the land; and that he would eminently countenance the dispensing of the sacrament of the holy supper a second time in this place, so as to make the glory of this latter solemnity to exceed that of the former. Much of the Lord's gracious presence was enjoyed at these meetings for prayer. Returns of mercy were vouchsafed in part, and are still further expected and hoped for.

"The second sacramental occasion did indeed much exceed the former, not only in the number of ministers, people, and communicants, but, which is the main thing, in a much greater measure of the power and special presence of God, in the observation and sensible experience of multitudes that were attending.

"The ministers that assisted at this solemnity were, Mr. Whitefield; Mr. Webster, from Edinburgh; Mr. M'Laurin and Mr. Gillies, from Glasgow; Mr. Robe, from Kilsyth; Mr. Currie, from Kinglassie; Mr. M'Knight, from Irvine; Mr. Bonar, from Torphichen; Mr. Hamilton, from Douglas; and three of the neighbouring ministers, namely, Mr. Henderson, from Blantyre; Mr. Maxwell, from Rutherglen; and Mr. Adam from Cathcart;—all of them appeared to be very much assisted in their work. Four of them preached on the fast-day, four on Saturday, on Sabbath I cannot well tell how many, and five on Monday; on which last day it was computed that above twenty-four ministers and preachers were present. Old Mr. Bonar, though so frail that he took three days to ride eighteen miles, the distance between Torphichen and Cambuslang, yet his heart was so set upon coming, that he would by no means stay away; and when he was helped up to the tent, he preached three times with great life, and returned with much satisfaction and joy. Mr. Whitefield's sermons on Saturday, Sabbath, and Monday, were attended with much power, particularly that on Sabbath night about ten o'clock, and that on Monday; several were crying out, and a very great but decent weeping and mourning was observable through the auditory. On Sabbath evening, while he was serving some tables, he appeared to be so filled with the love of God, as to be in a kind of extasy, and he communicated with much of that blessed frame. Time would fail me to speak of the evidence of the power of God coming along with the means, and I am in part prevented by what is noticed by Mr. Robe in his Narrative.

"The number of people present on Saturday and Monday was very considerable. But the number present at the three tents on the Lord's-day was so great, that, so far as I can hear, none ever saw the like in Scotland, from the revolution down, or even anywhere else, on a sacramental occasion. Some have called it fifty thousand, some forty, and the lowest estimate I hear of, with which Mr. Whitefield agrees, who has been used to great multitudes, and accustomed to form a judgment of their number, makes them to have been upwards of thirty thousand.

"The number of communicants appears to have been about three thousand. The tables were double, and the double table was reckoned to contain from a hundred and fourteen to a hundred and twenty communicants. The number of tables I reckoned at twenty-four, but I have been since informed, that a man who sat near the tables and kept a pen in his hand, carefully marking each service, declares that there were twenty-five double tables or services, the last wanting only five or six persons to fill it up. And this account seems the most probable, as it nearly agrees with the number of tokens distributed, which was three thousand. And some worthy of credit, and who had proper opportunities to know, gave it as their opinion, that there was such a blessed frame fell upon the people, that if there had been access to get tokens, there would have been a thousand more communicants.

" This vast concourse of people, you may easily imagine, came not only from the city of Glasgow, and other places near, but from many places at a considerable distance. It was reckoned, that there were two hundred communicants from Edinburgh, two hundred from Kilmarnock, a hundred from Irvine, a hundred from Stewarton, and some even from England and Ireland. A considerable number of quakers were hearing, and many formerly of the secession, some of whom communicated. A young man looking forward to the ministry, and who had been for some time under great temptation, as if the presence of God was to be no more enjoyed, either in the church or the secession, communicated here, and went home with great joy, and full of the love of God.

" There was a great deal of outward decency and regularity observable at the tables. Public worship began on the Lord's-day at half-past eight in the morning. My action sermon was, I think, reasonably short. The third or fourth table was a-serving at twelve o'clock, and the last was serving about sunset. When that was done, the work was closed with a few words of exhortation, prayer, and praise, the precentor having so much day-light as to let him see to read four lines of a psalm. The passages to and from the tables were kept clear for the communicants to come and go. The tables were filled so quickly, that oftentimes only four lines of a psalm could be sung between. The tables were all served in the open air, beside the tent and below the brae.* The day was temperate; no wind or rain sufficient to disturb. Several persons of rank and distinction, who were elders, most cheerfully assisted in serving the tables: such as the honourable Charles Erskine, advocate; Bruce of Kennet; Gillon of Wallhouse; Warner of Ardeer; and Mr. Wardrop, surgeon in Edinburgh.

" But the thing most remarkable, was the spiritual glory of this solemnity—I mean the gracious and sensible presence of God. Not a few were awakened to a sense of sin, and of their lost and perishing condition without a Saviour. Others had their bands loosed, and were brought into the marvellous liberty of the sons of God. Many of God's dear children have declared that it was a precious time to their souls—that they had been abundantly satisfied with the goodness of God in his ordinances, and filled with all joy and peace in believing. I have seen a letter from Edinburgh, in which the writer says, ' That having talked with many Christians in that city, who had been here at this sacrament, they all owned that God had dealt bountifully with their souls on that occasion.' Some who attended here have declared, that they would not for all the world have been absent. Others cried out, ' Now let thy servants depart in peace, since our eyes have seen thy salvation here!'† And there were who wished, had it been the will of God, to be removed while waiting on God in these ordinances, without returning again to the world or their friends, and so to be with Christ in heaven; which is far better.

" I thought it my duty to offer these few hints concerning this solemnity, and so to record the memory of God's great goodness to many souls on that occasion. And, now,

* One tent was placed at the lower extremity of the amphitheatre, and near the joining of the two rivulets, and here the sacrament was administered; a second tent was erected in the church-yard; and a third in a green field a little to the west of the first tent. (*Statistical Account.*)

† This we believe was the saying of Mr. Bonar, when taking leave to return home.

I suppose you will by this time find yourself disposed to sing the 98th psalm at the beginning, or the close of the 72d, or some other psalm of praise. May our exalted Redeemer still go on from conquering to conquer, till the whole earth be filled with his glory. Amen, so let it be. In him, I am yours, &c.

"WILLIAM M'CULLOCH."

Writing from Cambuslang on the 27th August, Mr. Whitefield says: "This day fortnight I came to this place to assist at the sacrament, with several worthy ministers of the church of Scotland. Such a passover has not been heard of. The voice of prayer and praise was heard all night. It was supposed that between thirty and forty thousand people were assembled, and three thousand communicated. The ministers were enlarged, and great grace was among the people. I preached once on Saturday, once on the Lord's-day in the morning, I served five tables, and preached about ten at night to a great number in the church-yard, though it rained much. There was a great awakening. On Monday at seven in the morning, the Rev. Mr. Webster preached, and there was a very great commotion; and also in the third sermon, when I preached. A very great and serious concern was visible throughout the whole solemnity. The Lord's people went home much refreshed."

We cannot better follow up this account of the second communion, than by extracting a few of Mr. Webster's remarks on the work at large, but written immediately on his return from Cambuslang, and pictures, no doubt, of what he had just witnessed. His letter is dated at Edinburgh, on the 30th of August 1742: "During the time of divine worship, solemn, profound reverence overspread every countenance. They hear as for eternity, and not knowing but the next moment they must account to their great Judge. Thousands are melted into tears. Many cry out in the bitterness of their soul. Some of both sexes, and all ages, from the stoutest man to the tenderest child, shake and tremble, and a few fall down as dead. Nor does this happen only when men of warm address alarm them with the terrors of the law, but when the most deliberate preacher speaks of redeeming love. Bring them to Mount Sinai, where the thunder roars and lightnings flash, and this may occasion greater outcry; but lead them to the consolations that are in Jesus, and then vastly greater numbers fall under the most kindly impressions. Talk of a precious Saviour, and all seem to breathe after him. Describe his glory, and how ravished do many appear! how captivated with his loveliness! Open the wonders of his grace, and the silent tears drop from almost every eye. Such eternal, such glorious themes, seem the delight of their souls, and reign triumphant over each power and faculty.

"These, dear sir, are the visible effects of this extraordinary work during the time of divine worship. Upon conversing with the subjects of this work, after public service was over, they gave a distinct and scriptural account of the temper of their minds, and of the various springs whence their tears of sorrow or of joy flowed. Those struck in the most awful manner, when recovered from the violence of the shock, mentioned the quick and affecting sense which they had of divine wrath, before they were so affected. They condescended on the particular part of the sermon or Scripture which occasioned such views of their guilt and misery. They described the gradual opening of their minds, till, led back to the rock whence they were hewn, they saw that they had been conceived in sin, and brought forth in iniquity, and humbly acknowledged that they had been transgressors from the womb. They spoke under a painful sense of sin, not only as the ruin of the creature, but as dishonouring to a kind and loving Saviour. Unbelief in a particular manner cuts them to the very heart. They cannot bear the thought of having so long rejected the Son of God, and despised his endearing calls, as set forth in the gospel. Being persuaded that he is the only Redeemer of a lost world, they breathe after him under every character and in every relation; as a king upon his throne, clothed with authority to reign, as well as a priest on the cross, endowed with ability to save. Willingly would they part with all for an interest in Jesus, and they desire nothing more than to be taught of him as their great prophet. Sensible of their utter inability to believe, how earnestly do they pray, ' Open the everlasting doors of our heart: Come in, thou blessed of the Lord: Be our God and portion!'

"Those who have attained comfort readily give a reason of the hope and joy which are in them with meekness and fear, declaring, to the praise of divine grace, how the Holy Ghost, formerly a convincer, proved also their comforter, by discovering to them their warrant to lay hold on Jesus the Saviour, and happily determining them to embrace a whole Christ as freely offered in the gospel: ' Whom, having not seen,' say they, ' we love; in whom though now we see him not, yet believing, we rejoice with joy unspeakable and full of glory.' Sensible of the blessed change which has passed upon their minds, they rejoice that old things are done away, and all things become new.

"It is not pretended, nor can it indeed be supposed, that all should, on being first awakened, give such distinct accounts of the working of their minds; or that all who have fled for refuge to the hope set before them, have attained to so joyful a faith; *but I have honestly described the condition of the generality as I had it from themselves.*"

But before concluding our account of this second communion, there are certain interesting memorials to be noticed. Mr. M'Culloch furnishes a list of the ministers who preached on the occasion, and of their texts, except those who preached at the tents during the table services. And it cannot fail to be interesting to have some memorial of these, and of the men who were so much honoured of God.

On Tuesday, the fast-day,—

1. Mr. Adams preached from Ps. cxix. 59: " I thought on my ways, and turned my feet unto thy testimonies."—(1.)

2. Mr. Robe from Isa. liii. 10: " He hath put him

to grief; when thou shalt make his soul an offering for sin, he shall see his seed, he shall prolong his days, and the pleasure of the Lord shall prosper in his hands."—(2.)

3. Mr. Henderson from Rom. viii. 33, 34: "Who shall lay any thing to the charge of God's elect? It is God that justifieth: who is he that condemneth? It is Christ that died, yea, rather that is risen again, who is even at the right hand of God, who also maketh intercession for us."—(3.)

4. Mr. Currie from John iii. 29: "He that hath the bride is the bridegroom; but the friend of the bridegroom, which standeth and heareth him, rejoiceth greatly because of the bridegroom's voice. This my joy, therefore, is fulfilled."—(4.)

On Friday evening,—

Mr. M'Culloch from Isa. liii. 11: "He shall see of the travail of his soul, and shall be satisfied."—(5.)

On Saturday,—

1. Mr. Whitefield from John xiii. 8. "If I wash thee not, thou hast no part with me."—(6.)

2. Mr. Webster from 1 Pet. ii. 7: "Unto you, therefore, which believe, he is precious."—(7.)

3. Mr. Robe from his former text, Isa. liii. 10.—(2.)

4. Mr. Bonar from the Song iii. 3: "Saw ye him whom my soul loveth?"—(8.)

On the Lord's-day,—

1. Mr. M'Culloch preached the action sermon from 1 John iv. 10: "Herein is love, not that we loved God, but that he loved us, and sent his Son to be the propitiation for our sins."—(5.)

2. The sermons at the tents during the table services are not given.

3. Mr. Whitefield exhorted in the evening after the other services were over, but without a text.—(6.)

On Monday,—

1. Mr. Webster at seven o'clock A.M., from Luke xii. 32: "Fear not, little flock; for it is your Father's good pleasure to give you the kingdom."—(7.)

2. Mr. Hamilton from 1 Thess. v. 17: " Pray without ceasing."—(9.)

3. Mr. Whitefield from the parable of the marriage supper, Matt. xxii. 2–14.—(6.)

4. Mr. M'Knight from Matt. xv. 28: " O woman, great is thy faith: be it unto thee even as thou wilt."—(10.)

5. Dr. Gillies from Job xxii. 21: " Acquaint now thyself with him, and be at peace; thereby good shall come unto thee."—(11.)

Notices concerning the above ministers.

1. Mr. George Adams was at this time minister of Cathcart, and was esteemed of all as a man of piety, and faithful in the discharge of ministerial duties: he afterwards fell into the sin of fornication, and was deposed from the office of the ministry. The signs of his repentance, however, were so evident to all, that application was made by the session, by the whole of the heritors, and by many of the parishioners, for his restoration. The presbytery, after a course of discipline, before the congregation and otherwise, were proceeding to replace him, when the commission, in November 1747, ordered them to desist, till the advice of the assembly had been obtained. The presbytery accordingly referred the case to the assembly, in May 1748; and, under the circumstances, the assembly allowed the presbytery to proceed, and he was re-instated in his former parish, on the 17th of August following. It is said by local tradition, that as often as he had discipline to administer on others for a like offence, his reference to his own case was so touching as greatly to affect all present.

2. Mr. James Robe was minister of Kilsyth, and a son of Mr. Michael Robe, minister of Cumbernauld before the revolution, probably as an indulged minister under the act of 1687, and after it as parish minister. His son, Mr. James, was inducted at Kilsyth in 1713, and died in 1755. His Narrative of the Revival shows much of his character and labours. His " Monthly History" contains much that is

not to be found in any other original work. His controversial pamphlets discover talent as well as zeal. His sermons, of which there are several volumes, are simple, full of gospel truth, and worthy of a place among other works of practical divinity. And there are still traditional anecdotes strongly illustrative of his character, as a holy and conscientious servant of Christ.

3. Mr. Henderson was minister of Blantyre, a parish in the immediate neighbourhood of Cambuslang; but we have not met with anything concerning him worthy of notice.

4. Mr. John Currie was minister of Kinglassie, in Fife. He was settled in that parish in 1705, and died in 1755. He was distinguished as an able, faithful, and laborious gospel minister. As he and Mr. Ebenezer Erskine were friends in early life, and their parishes adjoining, they lived as brothers, sharing each other's counsels, and striving together in the cause of their common Master. But when the secession took place, they parted. Mr. Currie became one of the leading defenders of the establishment, or rather of his own conduct and that of others in not seceding. Mr. Wilson of Perth was his principal opponent, as an author. And when the revivals broke out, Mr. Currie wrote in their defence, and was engaged in controversy with others of his former associates.

5. It is not necessary to add anything to the biographical notice already given concerning Mr. M'Culloch. His son, as already noticed, was minister of Dairsie, in Fife. He was highly respected in his day as an able and evangelical minister; and a daughter of his, Mrs. Coutts, is now resident in Edinburgh, a living example of the piety and benevolence of her ancestors, and warmly attached to the principles of the Free Church.

6. It may not be known to the reader, that Mr. Whitefield wrote his own life, up to the time of his obtaining ordination. In it, he freely exposes his own early sins, as well as acknowledges the grace which he had received. Dr. Gillies of Glasgow wrote the life which ac-

companies his works; and it is drawn up with great judgment. There is a curious fact connected with this, which may, like many similar facts, touch some of the hidden springs in providence, now at work. A Mr. William Burns of Falkirk or the neighbourhood, became so attached to Mr. Whitefield, as to follow him across the Atlantic, and after returning, to devote himself to the ministry. He never received any appointment, but continued to preach as opportunity occurred, so long as he was able. And as a memorial of his regard for Whitefield, he published an edition of his life by Dr. Gillies, with a preface written by himself. This Mr. William Burns was the uncle of the late Mr. James Burns of Brechin, of Mr. William Burns of Kilsyth, Dr. Robert Burns, formerly of Paisley, now of Toronto, and of Dr. George Burns of Corstorphine, with their numerous clerical descendants and connections, including Mr. William Burns, junior, who, like Whitefield, is properly an evangelist—all, so far as we recollect, of the Free Church.

7. Dr. Alexander Webster was one of the most distinguished men of his day. His father was Mr. James Webster of the Tolbooth Church, Edinburgh. The father had lived and suffered in troublous times. He was repeatedly imprisoned on account of his adherence to right principle, and his health was in consequence impaired. He received license from the persecuted church, and seems to have been for some time at Craigmillar, near Edinburgh, as an indulged minister. After the revolution, he was settled first at Whitekirk, and about 1693, in the Tolbooth Church, where he laboured till his death, which was in 1720. He was beloved by his people, and was one of the few who stood boldly up to stem, if it were possible, the rising tide of corruption in the church. In this capacity, he incurred much odium with many, but was honoured by the godly in presenting himself as the libeller of professor Simpson at Glasgow, on account of heresy. His son, Alexander, was but a boy when his father died. He was first ordained

at Culross, but in 1737, he was inducted to the Tolbooth Church, where his father had been minister. He was received with the love due to the son of a beloved pastor, and with high expectations as to his own merits. These expectations were not disappointed. He proved one of the most popular and influential ministers of the age, and his talents and influence were always on the side of gospel truth. Among the many important undertakings which engaged his attention, one was the establishment of the Ministers' Widows' Fund—an acknowledged monument not only of benevolence, but also of talents and influence. Mr. Whitefield saw him and other friends on first arriving in Edinburgh in 1741. Notwithstanding Mr. Webster's connection with the Erskines—for one of his sisters was the wife of Mr. Ebenezer Erskine—he remained the firm friend of the work of God in the establishment, after they had set themselves against it. One of the ablest defences of that work was written by him, and is entitled "Divine Influence, the True Spring of the Extraordinary Work at Cambuslang, and other places in the West of Scotland."

8. The Rev. John Bonar was educated at St. Andrews previous to the revolution settlement. Here he had trials to endure even as a student, on account of his adherence to presbyterian principles. In 1692 he was licensed; and in 1693 he appears to have been settled at Torphichen. In 1721 he was one of the twelve good men who joined in a representation to the assembly because of the injury done to truth in the censure pronounced on the "Marrow of Modern Divinity." He afterwards took part with those who, in defence of truth, prosecuted professor Simpson for heresy. Being thus allied with the little band of witness-bearers for the honour of Christ, he was deeply grieved at the harsh treatment which some of them received; and although he did not see it to be his duty to secede, he retained for such as did great esteem and affection, which they also cherished for him. In his own parish he manifested all

that personal piety and zeal for evangelical truth, which his public conduct would lead us to expect. Many serious persons from other parishes into which hirelings had been intruded attended his ministry, and especially on communion occasions, when he usually had assisting him men of a like spirit. When the revival at Cambuslang first broke out, he was greatly delighted, and anxious to hear all about it. Two of his letters, addressed to Mr. M'Culloch in the months of March and April, 1742, are still extant. But not satisfied with correspondence, he resolved, though now so frail as to take three days in riding eighteen miles, to witness with his own eyes what was doing. And so, as we have seen, he attended the second communion. There is another letter of his, addressed to Mr. M'Culloch the year following, which is so tender and touching that we give it entire: " Rev. and very Dear Brother,—I had your very desirable letter of the 25th August, by two of your elders, Archibald Fyfe and Ingram More, to whom I gave what tokens you called for to your Cambuslang people. It was on account of my bodily frailty and weakness that I was afraid to think of a communion, but was truly importuned both by strangers and our own people, making use of this weighty argument, that they apprehended it would be the last they should have with me. But even amidst all their pressing desires, they evidenced their fear that I should not be able to go through with it. At last I yielded to them, not knowing what might be in the womb of Providence; but so much I think we can now say, that it was begun, carried on, and completed by prayer. Sure I am that God did manifest himself as a prayer-hearing God. He sent to us very agreeable assistants with the fulness of the blessing of the gospel, and perfected strength in my weakness; so that I was carried through all the parts of my work to the admiration of many. *The Lord was here in a remarkable manner, so that his people were both fed and feasted, and several who knew nothing of religion were awakened, both of our own people and strangers.* O that I could with my soul and all that is within me magnify his holy name for what he hath done for us! And I hope, my dear brother, as I believe you joined in wrestling for a blessing to us, so will you join me in ascribing the glory and praise that is due to our exalted Redeemer, for his wonderful love and grace, manifested to unworthy me and my flock.

"It was refreshing to hear that the Lord continues to build up his own among you in holiness and comfort, and of your two desirable sacramental occasions this year. May the Lord prosper his work in your hands, and spare you long as an instrument of doing him much service! Our dear Lord has been riding prosperously this year in the chariot of his salvation; may he continue so to do, in this our land, and in those happy places which he hath so remarkably countenanced abroad! May the glorious work spread from nation to nation, till it fill the length and breadth of thy land, O Immanuel! As for me, my work seems to be near an end; and now my desire is, that before I go off the stage, God would give me some new seals of my ministry, and make me see glorious days of his power and grace in this place, where I have laboured these *fifty years*. I must now go the way of all the earth: may God be with you and my other brethren, whose years promise a longer time in the vineyard! Be valiant to fight the Lord's battles: let no opposition, though even from the pretended friends of Jesus, discourage your heart or weaken your hands. The Lord sits king upon the floods; yea, our God shall reign for ever and ever. He will make even the wrath of man to praise him, and the remainder thereof shall he, in his own time, restrain.

"Remember me in my distress at a throne of grace. I join my wife and grandson in affectionate service to yourself and Mrs. M'Culloch.—I am, Rev. and Dear Brother, your most affectionate brother and servant in the Lord, J. Bonar.

"Torphichen, September 20, 1743."

Four years after the writing of this letter, he appears to

have entered into his rest, namely, in 1747; leaving behind him an impression of guileless zeal and devotional earnestness, which died only with the last of the generation to which he belonged. And now, that several generations have succeeded, his memory is still preserved in a long line of honoured descendants. He had a son, minister of Fetlar, in Shetland. John, his grandson, was first minister of Cockpen, and then of Perth; Archibald, his great grandson, first of Glasgow, and then of Cramond; John his great great grandson, first of Larbert, and now of Aberdeen; and with him, there are three other grandsons of the minister of Perth—Horatius, minister of Kelso; John, of Greenock; and Andrew, of Collace—all the four being of a like spirit with their common ancestor, and faithful to the same principles. They are all ministers of the Free Church.

9. Mr. William Hamilton was minister of Douglas, in the upper ward of Lanarkshire, and one of those who attested the Narrative; but we have not otherwise observed any thing remarkable concerning him.

10. Mr. William M'Knight was minister of Irvine. He was a native of Ireland, and is said to have been in Irvine merely as a stranger—probably on his way to or from Ireland—when, after the demission of Mr. Warner, he was asked to preach, and gave so much satisfaction, as soon after to be settled in that town. This was in 1702, and he died in the same place in 1750. He was a popular preacher, and esteemed for his piety and uprightness. Dr. James M'Knight, the well-known commentator, was a son of his.

11. Dr. John Gillies was a son of the minister of Careston, in Forfarshire. He was born in 1702, and inducted to the College Church, Glasgow, on the 29th July 1742. His preaching at Cambuslang, must, therefore, have been only a few weeks after his induction, and is itself a strong proof of the estimation in which he was held, seeing that so many highly esteemed ministers were there as hearers. His labours in Glasgow were numerous, and few men of

that age did so much to advance the cause of practical godliness. Deeply serious, and of a very catholic spirit, he seems to have been continually seeking opportunities of doing good, and in every possible way. His writings, which are numerous and varied, are all characterized by an earnest, evangelical spirit. They all have reference to the realities of religion, rather than anything speculative or merely popular. As regarded correspondence with foreign churches and eminent servants of God, he and Dr. Erskine of Edinburgh were generally known on both sides of the Atlantic as the Scottish representatives. His first wife was a daughter of the celebrated M'Laurin, also of Glasgow, whose society he greatly enjoyed; and co-operating with his more aged relative, as Timothy with Paul, they, together, may be said to have given, for many years, the proper tone and character to the religious movements of that great city. When he had reached his eighty-fourth year, he was asked by a friend, how he felt? "You ask me," said he, in reply, "how old age sits upon me? I am now in my eighty-fourth year, and, thank God, enjoy tolerable health and spirits; though it has pleased our heavenly Father to lay me almost wholly aside from my work for many months past. I comfort myself with my favourite Milton's words—'They also serve, who only stand and wait.' I am waiting, I hope with patience, God's time, which is the best, for my dismission hence. Christ's lying in the grave, has sweetened the thoughts of it to all believers; and through his merits, we can have hope in death." This was written in autumn 1785, and on the 29th of March 1786, he fell asleep in Christ.

He left a son, Mr. Colin Gillies, who, after officiating for some time in the West parish of Greenock, was inducted to the Low parish of Paisley in 1781, where he died in 1810. He is said to have been a very tender and affectionate preacher, much esteemed by the more serious; and cases have been brought to the writer's knowledge of his having been also blessed in his labours.

CHAPTER VIII.

THE CONDITION OF CAMBUSLANG AFTER THE REVIVAL OF 1742 HAD SUBSIDED.

THERE was but one day of Pentecost at Jerusalem. There is no mention of so many as three thousand being converted under one sermon in the times which followed. But the work of God did not on that account cease. The number of such as believed was soon after reckoned at five thousand, instead of three. Moreover, many of the effects remained. Those who were thus born as in a day became the seed of a more numerous generation in the age which followed. It also gave a high tone to the religious character and devotedness of professors, to which they might not have otherwise attained. Who can tell whether, if there had been no Pentecost, there would have been, among other indications of high principle on the part of the converts, the devoting of their entire substance to the cause and service of God? (Acts ii. 44, 45) the only other occasion on which it is specially mentioned, being after a similar visitation. (Acts iv. 34- 37.) The revivals of the last century did not cease all at once. There were some precious years after 1742; and many precious seasons, holding a connection with these, were enjoyed in different parts of the country for many years after. We do not think it impossible even to trace a connection between these and the missionary spirit which broke out at the end of the century, namely in 1795, 1796, &c. Some of the generation who took part in these movements spoke of a state of religion then fast waning, which was, however, even then, more intense, more devotional, and more closely associated with the habits of the revival period, than any other. Speaking of the west of Scotland, there were not a few, as we have been assured by some of themselves when old men, who travelled in the summer season upwards of twenty miles, that they might enjoy the privileges of a gospel ministry; passing, as they pursued their journey, several churches into which they felt as if they could not profitably enter. There were common mechanics, and others of similar standing in society, who were in the habit of travelling ten or twelve miles, once a week or once a fortnight, to attend fellowship-meetings. And on sacramental occasions, it was quite common for the pious of one place to lodge with those of another for several days, so that there would be in the same house some belonging to places twenty or thirty miles asunder; and while together, they were either hearing the gospel, or conversing on matters of religion, or engaged in devotional exercises. In country places, the barns were for this purpose fitted up as barrack-rooms, and those who had such accommodation waited after divine service, especially on the Saturday, to invite their guests. In some places, public intimation was usually made from the pulpit, instructing strangers how to find the necessary accommodation. Some of these practices existed probably thirty years ago; and there are persons still living who are able to recollect, not the forms merely, but the spirit by which these had been animated at an earlier period. Nor can any of us tell how much we are even now indebted to what God did in this country upwards of a hundred years ago. It is in early life, and under the influence of parental example and parental instruction, that we commonly acquire those habits and form those tendencies which afterwards appear in public conduct. And among those who are now active, and others who may have been active at a somewhat earlier period, there doubtless are some whose boyish musings were first nursed under the lingering influence of an earlier state of religion. Due attention, moreover, is not usually given to the importance of merely awakening to inquiry a comparatively dead and worldly generation. Apart altogether from the immediate work of conversion, there is much in disturbing the slumbers of a Laodicean church; and this end is, in some measure, served by the very peculiarities of a revival. There is a voice in spring as well as a hidden power; and so is there in a revival of religion.

But as regards Cambuslang, we have much more direct and satisfactory information. In 1743 and 1744 special days of thanksgiving were appointed by the session, and observed. In 1751—that is, nine years after the special season of revival—Mr. Robe of Kilsyth was about to publish certain attestations, and Mr. M'Culloch prepared a review of the fruits of the revival at Cambuslang. The account is somewhat long, containing a practical exposition and application of the parable of the sower; it being the object of the writer to show cause for the falling away of some who had at first given promise of better things. But as regards a mere statement of facts, the expositions introduced rather mar than promote the communicating of a distinct impression. The piece will be found entire in Robe's Narrative, which was lately republished, but we shall merely embody the facts, with so much only of the exposition as seems necessary.

"Cambuslang Manse, April 30, 1751.

"Rev. and Dear Brother,—Hearing that you are very soon to publish some attestations to the fruits of the revival of religion in this country in the year 1742, at the desire of some ministers, I drew up, and herewith send you, my attestation, relating to the effects of the extraordinary work here in 1742, which you may publish along with your own attestation and that of others. When the God of all grace is pleased, in infinite mercy, to send a revival of religion to a church, or any particular corner in it, among other artifices whereby Satan and his instruments endeavour to obstruct its progress, a very usual and successful one is, to raise prejudices against it in people's minds, by suggesting and alleging that, though the like awakenings and promising appearances formerly obtained in as high, or even a higher degree elsewhere, yet there was no good that followed, but a great deal of evil.

" In order, therefore, to set this matter in a clear light, and that I might be able to give a brief but just account of a work that happened in a parish whereof I have the pastoral inspection and charge, and which I cannot but look upon to have been a glorious work of God's grace, I thought it my duty to make a particular inquiry concerning the behaviour of the known subjects of the work at Cambuslang in 1742; that is, of those persons not only living in the parish of Cambuslang, but who came from many other places, near or more remote, and who, upon resorting to Cambuslang in 1742, are known to have there fallen under awakenings, convictions, and a deep concern about their eternal salvation, for the first time, or, at least, the first time that their convictions and concern seemed to prove effectual, and to come to a gracious issue.

" I do not propose to speak, except in a few words, of those who resorted hither in 1742, and who were true Christians before that. Of these there were many hundreds, I may say thousands, from places near and far off, who then flocked hither and joined in hearing; and great numbers of them, *upon producing sufficient testimonials*, were admitted to partake of the sacrament of the Lord's supper; and thereby the number of communicants, which here used to be about four or five hundred, previous to 1742, came to be greatly increased in that and the following years. At the first sacrament in 1742, the number was upwards of seventeen hundred; at the second sacrament, in 1742, the number was reckoned at three thousand; in 1743, it was about two thousand; in 1744, it was about fifteen hundred; in 1745, it was about thirteen hundred; in 1746, it was about twelve hundred; and down to this year (1751), it has continued to be greatly more than it was previous to 1742.*

"The unweariedness of the Lord's people in religious exercises at these times, especially at the sacramental occasions in 1742, 1743, and 1744, was wonderful. What eager attention in hearing the word—all upon the stretch, and as for eternity! What a serious, solemn air in the manner of their worship! What vehement workings of joy and sorrow and other feelings in their looks! What attendance on God in his ordinances! hearing three sermons on each of the three days, Thursday, Saturday, and Monday—double the number on the communion Sabbath; besides partaking of the sacrament, joining in public prayers and praises, spending almost the whole of Saturday and Sabbath nights in praises and prayers with others, or apart by themselves.

"And their attainments were answerable to their exercises. This was the case, at least with many of them, according to the account which they gave to me or to others from whom I had it, and whom I could entirely credit. Many attained to the full assurance of faith, had a sense of God's love to them, and an exercise of ardent love to him; and who, after believing in Christ, were sealed with the Holy Spirit of promise. Some eminently pious ministers, who assisted here, testified that they had never seen so much of heaven on earth. A very aged and worthy minister, at going away from this, cried out, at the stair-head in the manse, 'Now, Lord, lettest thou thy servant depart in peace; for mine eyes have seen thy salvation.'† Others, after reaching home, wrote that they would not on any account have been absent, or missed what of God they had enjoyed at Cambuslang.

* In 1836, instead of 900, there was a gross population of 2,705, of whom 2,016 were professedly connected with the establishment, and yet the number of communicants was only 245; and the average attendance at church 400 in summer, and 300 in winter.

† This, we have little doubt, was Mr. Bonar, who had by this time been nearly fifty years a minister, and who was so frail as to require help in ascending the place where he had occasion to preach.

"It must be owned, that there is a considerable number of those who were hearers here in 1742, who have since appeared to be but as the way-side hearers, the stony-ground hearers, or the thorny-ground hearers, described in the parable of the sower. (Matt. xiii. 1–9.) There are of these who are still going on in their defection and apostasy, enlarging the breach between them and God; but, blessed be his name, there are some even of these who seem to be greatly humbled, and whose souls are responding to the Lord's call, as addressed to backsliders. They are virtually saying, 'Behold we come unto thee, for thou art the Lord our God.'

"Speaking of these different classes, there is no doubt that a considerable number of thoughtless persons came here for fashion's sake, without either preparing their hearts so as to profit, or seriously attending to what they heard. Some also were gross counterfeits, who crowded in among the really distressed, and observing and imitating their manner, pretended to be in a like condition. But these were soon detected, and their number was never large. There were also many idle boys from Glasgow, some of them apprentices, who, pretending or seeming to be under concern about their souls, came often to Cambuslang to hear and to join together in prayer, in the fields, as they pretended. But these appearances generally came to nothing, and they brought much reproach on the work, by their neglecting so often their masters' work, and strolling about in the fields. Some also came here in 1742 for diversion, or to cavil at what they saw, and to mock such as were in spiritual distress. The bands of such mockers were, no doubt, generally made stronger, by their coming here and behaving as they did; yet some of them were made monuments of victorious grace and sovereign mercy. In a letter which I had from an aged and experienced Christian, worthy of all credit, the following testimony is offered: 'I have to say, for my own part, that I am able to go to death with it, that the Spirit of God was so powerfully at work in Cambuslang, that not only sinners, who knew nothing of God before, were reached both by conviction and conversion, but even saints themselves were enabled to attain what they never before could reach in matters of religion. I am able, if time would allow, to give a most satisfying account of not a few, both men and women, who will, I hope, bless God to all eternity for that happy time. There were, among others, two young men living not far from me, who went over to you in 1742, purposely to mock the work; and as they had been formerly horrid cursers and swearers, the one swore to the other that he would go to see the falling at Cambuslang, asking his comrade if he would go with him. The other swore that he would, and that they should not make him fall, for that he would run for it. But after going, they were both caught the same day, and for a quarter of a year after they continued under deep convictions. They have ever since attended fellowship-meetings weekly; and I have been sometimes with them, and have heard them both pray and converse on matters of Christian experience to my great satisfaction.'—These young men, instead of being able to run away, fell both under awakenings nearly at the same time, as is well known here. They were glad to get into a stable which was at hand, and there, on their knees, among the horses, to betake themselves to prayer. The greater part of those who afterwards fell away, might be said to resemble the stony-ground and thorny-ground hearers.

" There were many, in 1742, who, in time of sermon, fell under various bodily agitations and commotions, such as crying aloud, fainting, falling down as dead, &c. Concerning such bodily effects, we cannot certainly conclude that the persons so affected are under the influence of the Spirit, whether convincing, comforting, or sanctifying; because, for aught we know, they may proceed from the mere power of the imagination, or from some bodily disorder. Neither should any one suspect himself, merely because he has not experienced such effects. Some are brought truly under a sense of their lost condition with fewer terrors than in other cases, and are brought home to Christ in a more gradual and gentle manner; they are allured by the love and loveliness of Christ, and are sweetly drawn to him, and bound to him with cords of love, and bands of a man. But neither are we to infer, from the presence of such effects, that the cause is not divine. So close is the union between the soul and the body, that when anything greatly affects the one it reaches also the other. This is often seen in the ordinary occurrences of life. Suppose tidings to reach some family of the death of a beloved son, who had been abroad, would not all be deeply affected, and would not this appear in outward signs? Or, suppose that, after he had been thought dead, news were to come of his being alive, would not opposite emotions, scarcely less strong, discover themselves? These also would differ according to the constitutional differences of individuals. And why, upon the same grounds, should it be thought strange that a sense of being lost, and afterwards of having obtained mercy, should have similar effects? and that these should appear differently in the case of different individuals?

" Yet, from all that I can hear or observe, there are more of those who, in 1742, were brought under concern without these bodily agitations than of such as were so affected, that seem to persevere in gospel holiness. There are, indeed, some of both sorts, whose convictions have led to a gracious issue; yet are there many more of the former than of the latter. Some were led, under a sense of the dishonour done to God, as an infinitely holy and gracious being; while others were so brought under the terrors of the law, seeing themselves ruined for ever, that they cried aloud, trembled, and fell down. But when there was nothing more, these fears wore away—they returned to a state of security and to their wonted habits of sin. Their state was now worse than at the first. There were also some who, after a short time, were all at once filled with transporting joys, even to their crying out in the congregation, and who, upon examination, seem really to have had manifestations of the love of God made to their souls. even such as are described in the gospel; and these, so far as I know, persevere, bringing forth fruits of holiness. But there were others who, like them, had sudden transports of joy, who have since fallen away. These last, often on hearing some one saying or reading a portion of Scripture. did all at once assume its application to themselves. They had, therefore, for the time the joy of something real : whereas the grounds of that joy were altogether imaginary. When the heart has not been humbled, the soul united to the Saviour, and made one with him in all things, outlets from distressing terrors, and sudden joy, though apparently conveyed by Scripture promises, are always to be suspected, and often not to be regarded otherwise than as the joy of the stony-ground hearers. And of this class, we had several instances in 1742; some of them still maintaining a blooming profession in 1743. They fancied that now the bitterness of death was over; whereas unsubdued pride, a worldly spirit, and other corruptions, obtained such mastery over them, that they took offence at the requirements of a holy, self-denied life, and so fell away and relapsed into sensual indulgences.

"As to crying out in the time of divine worship, it is best to avoid extremes. On the one hand, hearers should not give way to these, if they can, as they disturb the attention of others, and interrupt the service of God. And ministers should beware of doing anything purposely to promote such expressions of feeling; but they ought to set forth the terrors of the law and the unsearchable riches of Christ fully and unrestrainedly, leaving it to God to take his own way in whatever might follow; and He is able, as happened in some cases here, to employ the outcries of some to contribute to the awakening of others. It is due, also, to remark, that hearers ought not to be censorious, as if all who cried out were to be blamed; and neither ought ministers too severely to rebuke such. Although there may be pretensions in some cases, in others there is necessity. Some who in 1742, endeavoured to restrain themselves, fell a-bleeding at the mouth and nose, and continued so for a considerable time, to the injury of their health and the alarm of all near; real violence having been done to nature.

"Meantime, we see in some things the malice of the wicked one. When he saw a number under deep convictions, that were likely to issue well, as these appeared towards the end of 1741 and the beginning of 1742, he taught certain of his wretched bondsmen to mimic them, crying out, falling down as dead, and afterwards reporting dreams and visions, making a high profession—some for weeks, some for months, and some for years; and when this was ended, they were driven on in evil courses—some falling into habits of uncleanness, some of drunkenness, some of lying, some of cheating, and some of other abominations—utterly casting away from them all respect for religion.

"But this leads us to speak of such as resembled the good-ground hearers, and who are as epistles of Christ, known and read of all men. Glory to God, setting aside all who have remarkably backslidden, whether persisting in it still, or whether they have returned from it, there is a considerable number of such as were awakened in 1742, who appear to bring forth fruits of righteousness. I do not speak at random or loosely, but from a writing which I have now before me, dated 27th April, 1751; and which contains a list of *about four hundred persons, who were awakened here in* 1742, and who, from that time to the time of their death, or till now, have been enabled to behave in a good measure as becometh the gospel. This I state on what I have myself observed, and on the best information I could obtain, whether by conversation or by writing, from persons of established character, and who knew those concerning whom they report. But under this head I must be more particular.

"And first, there are certain things which I do not say, and which, without explanation, I might be understood as saying. I do not say, then, that those of whom I am to speak have been in all things blameless; but that, with the ordinary allowance made for the infirmities common to man, they have, so far as I have been able to learn, been enabled in a good measure to walk worthy of their profession. Neither do I wish to be understood as speaking of these as if they alone had persevered. Some of these have been reported to me only of late; and many more, it is to be hoped, remain quite unknown. It will be recollected, that many of the subjects of that work have since deceased, only some of whom are reported; but these having finished their course consistently, and some of them triumphing in the full assurance of faith, their testimony is of all others the most valuable. Need I guard against having it supposed, that in speaking of what happened here in 1742, I am forgetting that it was all of God—of free, sovereign grace? The speakers were but as the rams' horns in overthrowing the walls of Jericho. The power was not in their words—it flowed through them. It is His to bear the glory whose temple the soul is, when prepared by his grace and Spirit. And last of all, I do not presume to say that all of whom I speak have been truly converted. A true believer may, without any extraordinary revelation, be infallibly assured that he is in a state of grace, though this is not the attainment of all, or perhaps even of the greater part; but this is not usually to be expected concerning others. The white stone and new name are fully known only by such as possess them.

" But so guarded, I now remark, that the evidence proceeded upon concerning these, would warrant a like judgment in as many other cases wholly unconnected with any special revival. Now, there are in other cases chiefly two grounds usually proceeded upon—a Christian profession, and a suitable walk and conversation. Confining ourselves, then, to these two things, we remark:—

" First, that all the persevering subjects of the work here in 1742, agree in professing faith in Christ as the mediator, through whose mediation alone we can come to God the Father as our God and Father in him, through the power and grace of the Holy Spirit. They all profess to hope for salvation through the gospel plan, namely, through the imputed righteousness of Christ entitling to eternal life, and all other covenant blessings; also through the sanctifying influences of the Spirit of Christ fitting for eternal life, and for all holy services and enjoyments, whether here or hereafter.

" And secondly, there is evidence as to their walk and conversation. I am not, at present, free to publish any of their names, or those of the attesters; but all the above number are severally attested either by ministers, elders, or private Christians of established reputation, who have known those whose characters they attest, and their manner of life, from 1742 down. And these attestations bear, not only that the persons they mention were awakened at Cambuslang in 1742, or were under convictions and remarkable concern there at that time, but that they have from that time till now, or till the time of their death, behaved as became their Christian profession, with such exceptions as must always be made in judging of imperfect creatures. But besides this general statement, the following particulars are submitted, either on my own personal knowledge or good and credible information.

" In practising justice and charity, relative duties, public-spiritedness, humility, meekness, patience, close and diligent attendance on gospel ordinances, heavenly-mindedness, watchfulness against sin, especially such sins as formerly more easily beset them, they adorn the doctrine of God their Saviour, glorify their heavenly Father, and excite others to do so on their account. Such as were given to cursing and swearing have laid aside the practice, learning to speak the language of heaven, and having upon them a holy awe of God and of things divine. Such as were accustomed to frequent taverns, to drink and play at cards, &c., till late, or it may be morning hours, have, for these nine years past, avoided all occasions of the kind, and kept at home, spending their evenings in Christian conference, in matters profitable to their families, and in secret and family devotion. He who was formerly drunken, accustomed to lie in bed till eight or nine o'clock in the morning, sleeping off his night's intoxication, has, for these nine years, been in the habit of getting up at three or four in the morning, of reading his Bible and other good books, of being engaged in prayer and meditation, &c., till seven or eight, when he calls together his household for family devotion; which is again repeated in the evening.

" Some wives, who, before 1742, lived at variance with their husbands, have, since that time, learned to put on the ornament of a meek and a quiet spirit; so that they now live with them in great peace and affection. Others, when their husbands' passions break out against them in boisterous language, run into another room and engage in prayer, asking of God for their husbands forgiveness, with a better temper; and for themselves, patience, and meekness; and after a while, they return with the law of kindness on their lips.

" Those who were formerly covetous and selfish, have acquired much of a public spirit, and of concern for the kingdom and glory of Christ, especially in the salvation of sinners. And with this view, they are not only exemplary in their conduct, but useful to all within their reach. They contribute cheerfully, and some of them beyond their ability, at collections for the interests of religion, or the relief of the distressed. They carefully observe seasons fixed for the concert for prayer, and join in earnest supplication for the farther spread of the gospel, and the outpouring of the Spirit on the churches.

"' As new born babes, they desire the sincere milk of the word, that they may grow thereby,' flocking with eagerness to hear in their different localities. The weekly lecture on Thursday, which was established in this place in 1742, has been continued ever since, summer and winter, even in harvest; only it is then held in the evening, and it is well attended. In harvest, the reapers come running from the fields, where they have been toiling all day. And as regards the rest of the year, some servants are known, of their own free choice, to sit up all the previous night working, that they may get time to attend the lecture next day.

"They are careful in their preparations for the Lord's supper, and frequent in the observance. Country parishes have the sacrament usually dispensed only once a-year, but ever since 1742 we have it here twice. And these have been indeed remarkable times for communion with God. Then especially, his people have seen the goings of their God and King in the sanctuary. They have been made to sit under Christ's shadow with great delight, and his fruit has been sweet to their taste. They have been feasted in the banqueting house, his banner over them being love; and meeting with like entertainment at other places, they resort to many such solemnities, especially during the months of June, July, and August, when these commonly occur.

"To conclude, they abound much in prayer, both secret and domestic, and also in the observance of fellowship-meetings. These are usually held weekly; and the exercises are, prayers, praises, and Christian conference. In 1731, when I came to this parish, there were only three of these; in 1742, they increased to a dozen or more. They have since been reduced to six. In every town or village almost in this country side, where there is any competent number of serious and lively Christians, and where religion is in a thriving state, meetings of this kind exist; and the persevering subjects of the work in 1742 are, if at all near, sure to form part of them. Common tradesmen, who are members, and who work for so much a-day, allow their employers to deduct so much for the time they are absent. Some of these meetings, besides, have also special seasons for fasting and prayer, on extraordinary occasions; such, for example, as on receiving news of heavy losses, or dangers occurring to any of themselves, or of what threatens the interests of religion; and on some of these occasions, they enjoy much of the divine presence, and much enlargement in prayer, though less, alas! than in former times.

"And now, in concluding, if this paper shall fall into the hands of any one concerned in the work of which it treats, and if he shall pervert anything here said, so as to encourage himself in pride or carnal security, counting himself among the persevering subjects of this work—to such I say, Perhaps it is not as you imagine; but suppose it be, what of that? was Judas the better for being in the list of the apostles? Men may approve, and yet God condemn. If thou valuest thyself merely on the approbation of others, thou art deluded, and the delusion will ruin thee. Be not high-minded, but fear. Those who have hitherto been enabled to persevere, and who may still hope to be enabled to go on in the ways of God, are the humble and lowly, the modest and self-denied; while the haughty, the presumptuous, and self-confident, have been suffered to fall, or have reason to fear that a fall is not far distant.

"Now to Him that is able to keep us from falling, and to present us faultless before the presence of his glory with exceeding joy, to the only wise God our Saviour, be glory and majesty, dominion and power, both now and ever. Amen.

"Upon the whole, I think I may say, 'The Lord hath done great things for us, whereof we are glad.' To Him alone be all the glory and praise, of whatever good was got or done in that remarkable work of his grace. Amen.—I am your affectionate brother, WILLIAM M'CULLOCH."

An attestation so full and minute as the above, can scarcely be strengthened by additional testimony; but there is also an attestation signed by the elders, after the above had been read over to them, and considered paragraph by paragraph; and as it is short, and contains certain additional information, it would be wrong not to give at least the substance of it.

ATTESTATION BY THE ELDERS.

"Manse, Cambuslang, April 30, 1751.

"We, the undersigned elders, members of the kirk-session of Cambuslang, having heard the foregoing attestation read to us by our pastor, and having maturely considered the same, paragraph by paragraph, do heartily join with him in said attestation; and hereby make it our own, being persuaded that it contains a just and true account of the extraordinary work here in 1742, and of the comfortable and abiding effects of it on many, *probably on more than the four hundred mentioned in the foregoing attestation*, and particularly as regards seventy of these, who lived in this parish in 1742, and from that time down, or till their death, and who lived, to the best of our knowledge, as becomes their profession. And to what is above said, we add the following general observations:—

" 1. The awakening in 1742, instead of leading to separation, as has been alleged, caused many who were at the point of leaving the church to remain, acknowledging that God was in the midst of her; and it greatly increased their regard for all true ministers.

" 2. Though most of such as had in their exercises a large mixture of fancy and imagination have fallen away, yet are there of these who persevere in their Christian profession, and who maintain a character for unblemished conduct.

" 3. The decrease in the number of meetings, from a dozen or more in 1742, to six as at present, has not been owing merely to backsliding. It has also been occasioned by the death of some, and the removal or altered circumstances of others. And where meetings were broken up, the remaining members joined other meetings.

" 4. The reason why we think that there are more than four hundred of such as were awakened here in 1742, who persevere. is because we have had no returns from the west country (Ayrshire and Renfrewshire), where we know very many of the subjects of the late awakening live, and of whom doubtless many are walking in the fear of God.

"5. And now, upon the whole, we, the undersigned, with the greatest freedom, after the most impartial inquiry for information, being all the elders of this parish, save one occasionally absent from this meeting, day and date aforesaid. do hereto subscribe our names.

"ALEXANDER DUNCAN, *Elder*.
ARCHIBALD FIFE, *Elder*.
INGRAM MORE, *Elder*.
CLAUD SOMERS, *Elder*.
BARTHOLOMEW SOMERS, *Elder*."

Dr. Robert M'Culloch, writing in 1793, says: " Though I cannot possibly have the least remembrance of anything that occurred at that period, yet, having spent about twenty years of my life in that parish, I had the best opportunity of strictly inquiring into facts, and of impartially examining the evidences of their truth and reality. After a careful investigation of the subject, and the circumstances and effects. I adopt, without the least hesitation, as clearly expressing my sentiments, the words of the late celebrated Dr. Alexander Webster." And after quoting a long passage from Dr. Webster, he adds: " All these happy fruits of the ministry of the gospel, and of the Spirit being poured out from on high, I have seen with pleasure, in many instances, in the place of my nativity."

There is only one additional testimony, which we shall very briefly subjoin. The late Dr. Robertson was inducted minister of Cambuslang towards the close of the last century, at which time some of the converts of 1742. or some of the following years, were still alive; and his testimony of them and theirs concerning the awakening went to confirm the foregoing attestations.

CHAPTER IX.

SOME ACCOUNT OF TWO MANUSCRIPT VOLUMES LEFT BY MR. M'CULLOCH, AND OF THE CASES WHICH THEY CONTAIN.

In preparing the preceding statement from Mr. M'Culloch's attestation, we purposely omitted an entire paragraph, because it stood isolated, and was originally meant chiefly as a notice of what is now to be introduced. It is as follows: " But besides what concerns a credible profession, and a suitable walk and conversation, some require that persons, who would have a place in their good opinion, should be able to give some account of their experience of the grace of God. And this also has been done by not a few. *Upwards of a fourth perhaps*, of the persevering subjects of the revival in 1742, gave me very particular accounts of God's dealings with their souls, as regards their first awakening, their outgates, their distresses, their deliverances, and their comforts in 1742, 1743, and 1744; and some of them continued their accounts down to 1748. I took down many of these from their own mouths, always in their true sense, and very much also in their own words. Many of the statements so prepared *have appeared, to competent judges, to whom they were submitted, and who perused them with care*, to be very rational and scriptural, and worthy of seeing the light; *which perhaps may be done hereafter*."

It is nearly a hundred years since this *peradventure* was put on record, and it is only now that it is to be realized.

Had the good man who so expressed himself, been able to foresee the condition of the church, when this saying was to be fulfilled, he would have been as much astonished in looking forward, as we are in looking back. And yet, in tracing the ordinary connection of moral cause and effect, it is not very difficult to see in the one a real, though remote issue of the other.*

Two quarto volumes, containing a hundred and five cases. are now before us. These were preserved by Mr. M'Culloch's family, and were, in 1844, presented by Mrs. Coutts of Edinburgh, a grand-daughter of Mr. M'Culloch, to the Free Church Library.

A considerable part of the whole are in Mr. M'Culloch's handwriting, particularly of those in the first volume; but some are in other hands, and a few seem to have been written by persons of only common education. They generally proceed so much on the same plan, as to suggest the idea of certain queries being put or submitted to all, and that the information was drawn up under these heads. These heads touch the original condition, education, and religious or irreligious habits of the individual; the means employed, under God, for his conversion; the changes which ensued, the progress made, and the grounds on which, at the time of writing, he concluded himself to be in a state of grace.

Generally speaking, the persons introduced appear to have been of the working classes. Many of both sexes were farm-servants. Married men were generally labourers or common mechanics, and married women were of the same rank. A few, both men and women, were of a higher rank, and had obtained more or less of a liberal education.

* Mr. M'Culloch seems to have contemplated a work in two volumes, consisting of a narrative and the cases; the whole forming a kind of continuation to Fleming's Fulfilling of the Scriptures. We have now before us a letter, containing the printer's terms, and also several letters from lord Grange; from which it appears that he had counted on the patronage of the noble family of Hamilton, hoping thereby to get the subject introduced to persons of rank. But in this he failed, and was advised greatly to alter his plan, and to publish only a selection of the cases.

Among these, there were magistrates, landed proprietors, and gentlewomen connected with families of a similar condition in life.

It is necessary to keep these circumstances in mind, in judging of the cases. The persons chiefly described were but imperfectly educated; many of them had previously been grossly ignorant, and some of them immoral. They had been but recently brought to a knowledge of the truth, and were therefore wanting in experience, and in those habits of thought and of conduct which rather grow out of such a condition as theirs, than form any large and ordinary portion of it. Theirs was like new wine, rather than wine resting on its lees; or, like the machine recently put in motion, and still tremulous and jolting from the unevenness of its moving surfaces, their experience was less equable and noiseless, than no doubt it afterwards became. They had very generally an undue dependence on their feelings—something like a superstitious regard for the suggestions of Scripture passages, which was indeed characteristic of their times; and in some cases, especially among the more ignorant and doubtful, there was a proneness to indulge in suggested thoughts, dreams, and visionary impressions.

We must take these considerations along with us, to avoid the dissemination of what was merely human, and associated with the errors and imperfections of humanity, under the character of its being of the teaching and influence of the Holy Spirit. The work was of God; but the subjects of that work were fallen, sinful, erring creatures, and for the most part, in circumstances unfavourable to proper discrimination. But the cases are not on that account the less valuable. There are two errors of judgment very common in the religious literature of the day. The one is, that religious biography should mainly consist of the lives of the more educated and exalted in rank; and the other, that religious experience should be as much as possible freed of doubts, misgivings, and fitful changes, though really incident in common life, because unsuitable, as elements of an example, to be held up to others. The former of these errors consists in overlooking the dependence of our sympathy on the similarity of our circumstances; and with this, the fact that our common people are as a hundred to one of the literary and reflective. Our fathers knew better than we do where the religious heart of Scotland lay, and hence their many touching rehearsals of what occurred in the cottage, and was experienced in the breasts of men covered with " hodden grey." And the latter of the two errors consists in also forgetting that such as particularly require instruction, are not those who have reached " the land of Beulah, where the sun shineth night and day;" but those who are looking despairingly on the slough of despond, or standing in fear and trembling at the wicket gate, or it may be, entangled in some of the snares which lie thick in the way even of the believer. It is a great comfort for the sorely tried, just to know that others have been in like circumstances; and it is not only instructive, but the instruction most wanted, to be told how they obtained relief, what they found to be errors and mistakes, and what also they found to be useful. And in both respects, many will, we trust, be interested and profited by the details which are now to be brought before them.

It is necessary, however, to add, that in consequence of the number, the sameness, and repetition of details in these cases, and because of passages containing unguarded statements, it will be advisable to publish only a selection, and sometimes to abridge even these, being chiefly careful, with the original compiler, to give always the true sense, and as much as may be the language, but still to study with these brevity and variety.

It may be interesting farther to add, concerning both volumes, that the names of ministers and others referred to in these cases, are indicated by numerals, which stand connected with the true names in a separate list. We have been able, in most instances, to identify the persons meant, and they will thus be embodied in the references. By a comparison of various lists, the names, and sometimes the condition of the persons described, may be also ascertained, and will be inserted.

And it is yet farther necessary to explain, that it will be advisable, unless otherwise stated, to give the cases of each volume separately—those of the first in the following chapter, and those of the second in the chapter succeeding it. Leaving, therefore, some of the peculiarities of the second volume to chapter xi., we shall here subjoin those of the first.

The first volume contains forty-seven cases, nearly all in the handwriting of Mr. M'Culloch, and bearing evidence of having been carefully examined by four "competent judges." These were Dr. Alexander Webster of Edinburgh; Mr. John Willison of Dundee; Mr. Thomas Gillespie of Carnock; and Mr. James Ogilvie of Aberdeen. Mr. Ogilvie examined the whole, wrote his criticisms, and returned the volume in August 1744. Dr. Webster had it next, and then Mr. Willison, who, writing in January 1745, says: " I read over the manuscript with much delight and edification. It gave me great pleasure to read *the Scripture texts* which the Lord blessed, and *the notes of sermons*, set down as accompanied with success." Mr. Gillespie examined it last. And the margins afford proof of the care which they all four bestowed on the volume. Some account, however, of these great and good men will now be added.

Dr. Alexander Webster of Edinburgh, has already been noticed in chapter vii., and no person would more readily occur as well qualified to advise in this matter. His distance from the locality, his general acquaintance with the religious world, and his sound judgment, would all of them suggest him as one of the very first.

Mr. John Willison of Dundee was probably born in 1680, was inducted minister of Brechin apparently in 1703, but being soon after translated, he is commonly known only as one of the ministers of Dundee. He took an active part in church matters, was sent as one of a deputation to London in 1734, to obtain, if possible, a repeal of the law of patronage, and in 1744 he published his Impartial Testimony, as a kind of ecclesiastical protest, representing the sentiments and feelings of a large and honoured minority. But it was as a minister of the gospel, and as a plain practical writer, studying the instruction of the many rather than the taste of the few, that he stood out among the men of his own and following ages. His " Mother's Catechism," his " Exercises of a Communion Sabbath," and his " Afflicted Man's Companion," have embalmed his memory amidst the domestic duties of a Sabbath evening, the anxious preparation of young professors, and the solemn stillness of sick and dying chambers. His " Treatise on Sabbath Sanctification" should be better known; and there is a proof of the early interest which he took in the revivals of the eighteenth century, in the preface to his " Balm of Gilead," which was written in January 1742. He there speaks of them as already commenced, and urges, especially ministers, to take part in awakening the slumbering churches. At this time, he must have been upwards of forty years a minister; and from his circumstances and qualifications altogether, he was just such a person as would be desired for giving an opinion concerning these cases. It was probably one of the latest of his special labours, for he died in 1750.

Mr. Thomas Gillespie, after finishing his studies in Edinburgh, went to England, where he was ordained among the Independents, Dr. Doddridge presiding at the ordination. This was on the 22d of January 1741; and, recommended by Dr. Doddridge and fourteen other ministers, he came to Scotland during the March following, and was soon after called and admitted minister of the parish of Carnock. Dr. Erskine says of him: " The fidelity and diligence of Mr. Gillespie in the discharge of the various duties of his pastoral office, and the remarkable success with which God was pleased to bless his labours for awakening and converting sinners, and for comforting and establishing Christians, is known to many, not only in the congregation under his charge, but in Edinburgh, *the west of Scotland*, Muthil," &c. He visited the west, and particularly Kilsyth, during the summer of 1742, and was one of those whose attestations were published by Mr. Robe. His labours, and the blessing which attended them, with his situation, might therefore point him out as an examinator.

But we can scarcely leave Mr. Gillespie, without noticing what soon after befell him. He had not taken any leading part in ecclesiastical matters, having given himself wholly to pastoral and evangelistic duties; but he was not on that account the less decided and conscientious in his convictions on the side of popular rights, and a free and unfettered preaching of Christ. And now, he was also to be driven forth of the church. In 1752 the general assembly, without a libel or any formal process, deposed him, on the grounds of his refusing to take part in a violent settlement at Inverkeithing. He meekly submitted to this most irregular and unjust sentence, retiring to the fields, where he preached for a year, without organizing either a session or congregation. In 1753, an attempt was made to have him restored, but the motion was lost; and he then formed a congregation in Dunfermline. And being joined by two other ministers, they formed themselves into a presbytery, taking as their distinctive title, " The Presbytery of Relief." And hence the origin of another separation from the establishment. Mr. Gillespie died in 1774, deeply regretted by many; his memory being held in esteem by all who knew him, and who loved the truth and the cause of evangelism in Scotland.

Mr. James Ogilvie was one of the ministers of Aberdeen. This city was not, during that day, or even that century, very well affected to a fully preached gospel. At this time, however, both Mr. Ogilvie and his colleague, Mr. Bisset, who, as sir Henry Moncrieff says, was the highest of the high, were both evangelical, though otherwise very opposite men. " Though colleagues of the same congregation," says Whitefield, "they are very different in their natural tempers. The one is, what they call in Scotland, *a sweet blooded man*, the other of *a choleric disposition*. Mr. Bisset is neither a seceder nor quite a true kirkman, having great fault to find with both. Soon after my arrival, dear Mr. Ogilvie took me to pay my respects to him. He was prepared for it, and pulled out a paper, containing a great number of insignificant queries, which I had neither time nor inclination to answer." Seeing Mr. Ogilvie was so situated, his zeal for advancing the cause of Christ must have been early and great, for, *several years before this*, he had been corresponding with Mr. Whitefield to get him to visit Aberdeen, hoping that some good might be done; and now he had succeeded even in 1741. Mr. Whitefield, in the letter already quoted, gives some curious proofs of Mr. Ogilvie's prudence as well as zeal. He was himself to preach on Sabbath forenoon in presence of the magistrates. He gave Mr. Whitefield his place. The congregation was large, and apparently much interested. Mr. Bisset, in the afternoon, preached against Mr. Whitefield by name. Mr. Ogilvie, without either consulting his friend or noticing the conduct of his colleague, stood up after sermon, and intimated to the congregation that Mr. Whitefield would again preach in about half an hour. The magistrates remained in the session-house, and the people hastened back, expecting to hear a reply. Mr. Whitefield, waiving as much as possible all controversial matter, preached Christ. The audience was silent, solemn, and deeply impressed. Next day, the magistrates apologized for their minister; and, as a mark of their own respect, presented to Mr. Whitefield the freedom of the city. The moral and religious effect of this visit to Aberdeen was great and beneficial, as Mr. Ogilvie explains in several letters, published in the "Weekly History," which seems to have been chiefly under Mr. M'Culloch's management. In these circumstances, grounds will be seen for selecting such a man to examine the cases, especially as he had himself been at Cambuslang.

By such men as these, then, were the cases which are contained in the first volume examined, and, so far as we shall have occasion to transfer them to our pages, also approved.

CHAPTER X.

A SELECTION OF CASES PREPARED FROM THE FIRST VOLUME,
AND APPROVED OF BY THE ORIGINAL EXAMINATORS.

1. William Baillie, a married man, about thirty years of age:—

"I was taught to read and write, and I got some part of the 'Shorter Catechism' by heart, when young; and to this day I retain much of it upon my memory, and also of the Scripture proofs. I also read the Holy Scriptures by themselves. By these and other means I attained to a competent knowledge of the principles of religion. My parents also set me to pray when I was young; but I often neglected this duty. Sometimes I thought myself serious, but usually I was not. On growing up, I was often made deeply sensible that it was both my duty and my interest to pray; yet was it uninviting, for I had no abiding impression of God, or of the concerns of my soul. I usually went to church and heard sermon, and sometimes I prayed, before going, that the Lord would prepare my heart for the due reception of his word; and now and then, after sermon, I have meditated on what I had been hearing, and have gone again to prayer for a blessing.

"About twelve or fourteen years ago I heard Mr. H. Cross preaching in our parish church; and as he spoke about the redeeming love of Christ, I became much affected. I was somewhat convinced of my own want of love to Christ, and for some time after I was more concerned about my salvation and more attentive to duty. But that impression wore off, and I became again cold and careless. I was not given to any open vice, and as I had a competent measure of knowledge, I was admitted to the Lord's table. About nine or ten years ago, when attending on a sacramental occasion, I thought it my duty to go forward. I was warned by my father to beware of unworthy communicating; but after some preparation, I obtained a token and went forward. I did not find Christ there: still for a time I walked more circumspectly than I had been doing; but this also fell into decay. Every year after this I communicated; and on such occasions I was accustomed to review my past life, seeing and confessing my shortcomings, and essaying to renew my baptismal covenant; but I cannot say that my repentance was of a right kind.

"About five years ago I married. In this I sought divine direction; and on becoming the head of a family I kept up a form of family worship once a-day, but I was less regular in secret prayer, allowing the other sometimes to stand instead. In this way I continued to go the round of external duties in religion, and I had a perfect abhorrence of injustice and oppression against whomsoever these were directed. I have also reproved others for cursing and swearing, and have felt something like remorse on account of heart sins. I therefore thought favourably of myself, and I continued to entertain this opinion till the winter of 1741.

"I had bought and read Mr. Andrew Gray's sermons on the 'Great Salvation' and other subjects; and from them, but especially those regarding the 'great salvation,' I began to see that I had all along been despising that salvation. This led me to plead for pardon, and especially on account of my having rejected Christ so long. But even that conviction wore off without any saving effect.

"After the awakening began at Cambuslang I heard various accounts about it; some calling it a work of God, and others a delusion of the devil. I went to prayer, pleading that if it was a delusion I might not fall under it, but that if it was of God, I might be made a subject of its power. I went thither about the beginning of May, and heard Mr. M'Culloch. From what I heard and saw, I thought it was a work of God. I went home and prayed that I and my family might obtain a saving benefit, and I continued to use this prayer for some time; and the Lord heard me—I and all my family come to the years of discretion, except a hired boy, were enabled to profit.

"With regard to the means of my own effectual awakening; I was hearing Mr. M'Culloch, and he was showing how far a sinner might go in the observance of external duties, and yet be a stranger to the life and power of godliness. From what he said, I became convinced that this was my state, and that I had yet to become a new creature, ere all old things would become new. This awakened new troubles, especially as regarded sin. I besought God to give me a full discovery of my state, and grace to enable me to mortify sin. The Lord heard me. My sins rose up before me when so engaged, and particularly that of unworthy communicating, and my many breaches of solemn vows made on such occasions. I saw, also, my original sin so heinous as to be enough to condemn me. I read much in my Bible, so as to obtain a more humbling sense of the evil of particular sins; and against these I resolved in the Lord's strength continually to watch. I was also enabled, in dependence on the righteousness and strength which are in Christ, to devote myself wholly to his honour and service. About this time, that saying of the prophet, 'Trust ye in the Lord for ever, for in the Lord Jehovah is everlasting strength' (Isa. xxvi. 4), came powerfully home to me, as it has often done since. I was, through it, enabled to look to God for strength to perform duty and overcome temptation. And I think it was about this time that a change was wrought upon my heart; for ever since I have had an abhorrence of all manner of sin, and when tempted I can go to God in prayer, and often in this way I obtain relief. One thing which greatly confirmed me in this, was a mark given by Mr. M'Culloch to this effect, that as many as were truly changed would curb sin in its first motions in the heart. This was now my experience, and it gave me comfort.

"When the first communion was intimated at Cambuslang, I resolved to prepare for partaking of that ordinance. I was enabled in some measure to review my past sins, and truly to humble myself before God; and at the table of the Lord I was also enabled, in some measure, to receive Christ anew into my soul by faith, and I was thereby strengthened for resolving on new obedience. In the evening I heard Mr. Whitefield preach from Isa. liv. 5: 'Thy Maker is thine husband: the Lord of hosts is his name.' From this text he set forth the articles of agreement between Christ and as many as are his. To all of these I freely consented, and was comforted by what I heard.

"During night a number of us were in a barn. Some were strangers and some were acquaintances, but we all united in spending the night singing psalms and praying. After several had been engaged leading these exercises, it was put upon me to do so next. I felt sadly abashed, and for a time refused, but recollecting what our Lord says about denying him or not owning him before men, I became ashamed of myself. And although I had great fear, yet the Lord so opened my heart as to give me great liberty in the duty; and the sweet frame which I then got in believing on Christ remained for some time with me.

"On Monday morning, after the *second* communion, I heard Mr. Webster preach from these words: 'Fear not, little flock; for it is your Father's good pleasure to give you the kingdom.' (Luke xii. 32.) He gave several marks of such as belonged to Christ's little flock; all of which I was enabled to apply to myself with much clearness.

"About Candlemas, I had a child to offer to God in baptism. In looking forward to this duty, I went often to God, pleading the promises, and particularly that he would be my God and the God of my seed; *and I was enabled to plead in faith, so that while my child was receiving the baptism of water, I was looking to God for the inward baptism of the Holy Ghost, and was enabled to believe that it would be so.*

"And now, as to the ordinary bent of my desires, since my first effectual awakening, I find, that whereas my heart before was ever running out, mainly after the world and its vanities, I now find it to be set upon those things which are above. Though I had no prospect of any reward beyond the present state, and no fear of coming wrath, I would far rather go on in the ways of holiness, than return to my former sins and follies. The pleasures of sin which I formerly enjoyed, were not to be compared with what I now enjoy in serving God. I have also been forecasting trials and sufferings for truth's sake, and although I can have no confidence in myself, yet I trust that, if the Lord call me to suffer, I shall be enabled to choose sufferings rather than sin, and that he will not permit me to fall away. My heart's desire and prayer to God also is, that all Israel, whether Jew or Gentile, may be saved, and that the Lord may visit every corner of the land with a reviving power. Sometimes I am led in prayer to desire even that I may be dissolved, to be with Christ, to be joined to the glorious company above, singing hallelujahs to Him that sitteth upon the throne, and to the Lamb."

There is, in this case, an example of how far a mere professor may go apparently in the ways of God, before entering in at the strait gate. And should any feel as if the evidence here required were greatly more complex than that which was admitted by the apostles, let them not forget that unconverted professors are all the while deceiving themselves, and that therefore the change wrought on such has a greatly more complex aspect. There is, in such cases, much to unlearn, and much to discover and overcome of the deceitfulness of the heart.

2. Janet Jackson, an unmarried woman, aged twenty-four:—

"In early life, I was very indifferent about religious duties.

As I grew up, I became more observant of these, but it was only because I saw others do so. I went to the kirk, but I paid little attention to what was said. I did not understand it, and I did not care whether I heard it or not. I was not grossly vicious. When I heard swearing, I was even afraid, and sometimes I reproved those who were guilty. But though outwardly sober, I had no love to God. I did nothing to please him—I was always provoking him; and yet I knew it not, my conscience being altogether asleep.

"Some years before the awakening, I was a servant in Mr. M'Culloch's family. He took a great deal of pains with me to have me instructed, and I attained to some measure of knowledge, had some concern about my soul, and was more attentive to duty. Still, I had no true sense of my condition before God. About five years ago, during a communion season, I observed some young people coming to my master about the concerns of their souls, and they seemed to be very deeply impressed. I wondered what it was that affected them, seeing I had no such feeling; but this reflection wore off when the sacrament was over. Next year (1739), when the communion came round, I began to think more of my state, saw more of my heart plagues, and I prayed to God with some earnestness. After much thinking and anxiety, I went to the Lord's table, but I cannot say that I was enabled to discern the Lord's body; only I resolved henceforward to serve God, and did reform my conduct in various respects. But my goodness on this occasion also was but as the morning cloud and the early dew. The year following, I was much impressed with the saying of a minister, whom I heard at Carmunnock serving a table. 'Only such,' he said, 'as had clean hands and a pure heart ought to sit down at that table.' I saw that I had no right there—I shed abundance of tears; yet were my convictions but shallow, only a concern about my condition remained with me all summer.

"In September 1741, I heard Mr. Whitefield, at Glasgow,

preach two sermons in the churchyard—the one in the morning, and the other in the evening. In one of these, he spoke frequently of those to whom God spoke not of peace. I felt concerned to know who these people were, and how they might be known. Afterwards, hearing of several who had been awakened hearing Mr. Whitefield, I fell into deeper concern about my own state. And seeing Elizabeth Jackson, a near friend of my own, who had been hearing him, I observed a great change in her. She now spent much of her time in prayer, and in reading her Bible and Mr. Whitefield's sermons. This showed me that she and I were not in the same state. I frequently also heard Jane Galbreath, one of my neighbours, speak of some who had been awakened at Glasgow, as greatly changed in their life and conversation. I now prayed more frequently, read more in my Bible and in Mr. Whitefield's sermons, and also the 'Weekly History,' after it began to be published; and I began also to think that my own minister (Mr. M'Culloch) *must now be preaching better than he used to do.* In the beginning of December 1741, he preached from 2 Cor vi. 1, 2: ' We then, as workers together with him, beseech you, that ye receive not the grace of God in vain.' He spoke of people who heard the gospel as if they heard it not, and felt but slightly. I felt this as addressed to me. I saw myself to be as those described, and I was so affected with the thought as scarcely to be able to restrain myself from crying out. And now my unworthy communicating, my heart wandering in time of prayer, and my slighting of ordinances, stared upon me as enemies. I went home deeply affected. Never before had I such a sense of the evil of sin; and yet, I do not remember that I had with this any fear of hell. What I felt was the provocation I had given to God. I was now more deeply engaged in prayer, but I did not discover myself to any one. For several Sabbaths after this I felt as if the minister was preaching to me, and me only, and I was getting fresh discoveries of the evil of my ways from day to day, so that

I now saw sin to be something wholly different from what I had ever taken it to be. I found in the very corruption of my nature, and the unbelief of my heart, the causes of my other evils; and knowing that till these were removed I could not be saved, I began to fear that God would let me alone. My friend, Elizabeth Jackson, left the place for some time, and this added to my despondency, for it seemed as if she had been removed from me because of my sins. My convictions were every day deepening, and becoming more and more cutting; yet I kept all my feelings to myself, working my work, and even forcing myself to eat my meals, that my state might not be discovered. But often my sleep went from me. Sometimes my night thoughts were sweet, so that I blessed God for the comfort which I found in the passages which passed through my mind.

"About the 12th of February 1742, I heard Jane Galbreath tell my father (James Jackson) that several in the parish had been awakened, and I felt keenly, even as if God was to show mercy to others and leave me in my sins. The same night my father read from 'Guthrie's Trial of a Saving Interest in Christ,' which so increased my convictions as very nearly to force me to cry out before all present. I went to the door to conceal my state, when that saying—'A broken and a contrite heart, Lord, thou wilt not despise,' burst in on my soul and relieved me. After this relief, I went to see an acquaintance and to converse with her a little. Our conversation turned on the case of a relation of hers, who had obtained an outgate. This touched my tender part. I fell a-weeping, though I concealed the cause. Next day, I went to Jane Galbreath, who had experienced what I now felt. She saw what was the matter, and charged me not to conceal from her the cause of my distress. I could not reply, but hastened home and sat down to my wheel, in my father's house, reading, with the Bible on my knee, and shedding many tears. These words were, however, supporting: 'The prayer of the destitute he surely will regard.' I spent a portion of the day with a comrade, and Catherine Jackson, a relation of mine. But we were all three in such a state of trouble as to be of little service to one another. Next day being Sabbath, I went to the kirk, which was so full that I could not get a seat, and stood with great difficulty. It seemed as if everything said were levelled at me. ' Some of you,' said the minister, ' are perhaps grieved that God should gather others to himself and not you, and ye may on this account be murmuring against him.' This, I said, is exactly my case. I was made to see the evil of this, and to be satisfied that God might in justice pass me by, and suffer me to perish in my sins, and that it was an act of pure, sovereign mercy on God's part that he should save any; and my heart became thus humbled, because of my rebellion against God. I think it was on this occasion, also, that the minister explained to us the difference between mere concern and real convictions of sin. This I had not before understood. Now I saw it, and was glad to find that my trouble was more than concern; yet did all this deepen my sense of sin and sorrow on account of it.

" Catherine Jackson was this Sabbath so overcome with the power of her convictions, that Ingram More, one of the elders, had her removed to the minister's room. He knew not my state, and left me behind; yet was I sorely affected with this. It seemed as if I were despised of all. I nevertheless went with them. During Catherine's great agony, I remained in a kind of stupor; but when she obtained an outgate, and was commending the grace of God to others, and came and addressed herself to me, I felt as if there remained for me no mercy. Yet the Lord saved me from despair, sending home to my heart these words, ' I will draw thee with the cords of love and the bands of a man' The moment these words entered my heart, I found myself drawn out in love towards God. And other passages followed with similar effect, especially Matt. xi. 28, and Isa. xl. 4. The next day, James Miller a young man of my acquaintance,

I

asked me what ailed me, and whether I was in fear of hell; for, said he, 'I have a brother in great fear of hell.' I told him that such was not the case with me. ' What, then,' said he, ' makes you so concerned?' 'Because,' said I, ' of the dishonour I have done to God by my sins.' He advised me to take courage, and to hope in God. That evening, I went to Jane Galbreath's, and found there eight or nine young people who had fallen under trouble of mind, and with them was Mr. Duncan, a preacher, an elder, called John Bar, and a man who had been awakened by hearing Mr. Whitefield the harvest before. Mr. Duncan exhorted us not to read any book so much as our Bible, as it was fittest for persons in our condition; and from this I saw that I had been wrong in reading more of other religious books than of my Bible. Next morning these words came with power upon my soul, ' Believe in the Lord Jesus Christ, and thou shalt be saved.' (Acts xvi. 31.) This led me to see in faith the way to peace. Still I wanted that joy and love experienced by my friend Catherine Jackson. And that very evening, Elizabeth Jackson had her heart kindled, and her tongue loosened to proclaim the love of God, and to praise him. She wished all the people in the place to be brought to her, that she might tell them how good and gracious God is. This again cast me down, and led me to suspect my state.

" On the 18th of February, I heard that sermon under which so many were awakened. It was from Jer. xxiii. 5: ' And this is the name whereby he shall be called, The Lord our Righteousness.' I thought that sermon to be as a kind of new gospel to me. I had great satisfaction in hearing it, although I do not recollect that I could freely say, ' The Lord is my righteousness.' I went into the minister's room, was glad to see so many in an awakened state, and so many obtaining relief and commending Christ to others, and I was even myself enabled to offer a word to one in distress. Still my state, when compared with that of others who were so full of joy, caused me to fear, especially when, the day following, I heard a young man, James Miller, speak of his experience in a way greatly beyond my reach. I thought I would do anything to enjoy as they did. About the 11th of April, the minister preached from these words: ' To-day, if ye will hear his voice, harden not your hearts.' (Ps. xcv. 7, 8.) And that sermon proved the voice of Christ to my soul. I was enabled, from what I heard, to believe upon God with all my heart, and for a long time my faith and love were kept in lively exercise. Since then, however, I have been cast down as well as lifted up."

A considerable amount of detail follows this, but without indicating any remarkable change, and, therefore, we shall subjoin only the conclusion.

" To conclude, I think the Lord has given my heart such a touch and turn, that I can through grace say, that there is none either in heaven or on earth whom I desire besides him, or in comparison with him; that I count all things but dross, when compared with the excellency of the knowledge of Christ, and of being found in him, not having my own righteousness, but his; and I have often found so much sweetness in communion with God, through his ordinances, that I esteemed a day in his courts better than a thousand elsewhere, and preferred his favour to every thing else."

We see, from such details as these, much of what was going on in private during the interesting season referred to, much also of how the leaven operates under such visitations; and we repeat the remark before offered, as explanatory also of this case. Persons who have long enjoyed ordinances formally and hypocritically, are likely to have many difficulties special to themselves. It was said by our Lord, " Children, how hard is it for them that trust in riches to enter into the kingdom of God!" (Mark x. 24.) And it may, on similar grounds, be said, How hard is it for formalists and hypocrites to see with their eyes open, so as to receive the truth freely and in the love of it!

3. Elizabeth Jackson, daughter of James Jackson,

elder, a young woman aged nineteen, and occasionally referred to under the last case:—

" When I was a child, my parents often set me to pray, and I usually kept up something like a form of prayer daily. When very young, I also learned psalms. Sometimes, when thinking of the great day, I would say to myself, ' What will become of me?' and for a time I was concerned about myself. I was accustomed to attend church—sometimes hoping to get good, and at other times going only because others went. Sometimes I was for a little impressed with what I heard; but all these favourable appearances soon wore off. At the sacrament in Cambuslang, in 1739, I fell under more than ordinary concern. Mr. Hamilton of Bothwell was preaching from Rev. xxii. 17: ' The Spirit and the Bride say, Come,' &c.; and on the Sabbath following, Mr. M'Culloch preached from Isa. xl. 11: ' He shall feed his flock like a shepherd,' &c. And this concern continued with me about three weeks. But this also wore off, and I became more dead than I had been before. Like Nicodemus, I had no idea of being born again. In September 1741, I went to hear Mr. Whitefield in Glasgow. Some of his first sermons renewed my concern for a time; but those which he delivered on the Tuesday, just before leaving, melted my heart. Some weeks after that, I heard Mr. M'Culloch read some papers concerning the spread of the gospel in foreign parts, which moved me greatly, especially on observing how much good others were getting, while I was let alone. On hearing him afterwards preach from Ps. xxv. 11: ' For thy name's sake, O Lord, pardon mine iniquity, for it is great;' he observed that many asked and received not, because they asked not as the psalmist, earnestly; but as if they did not care whether they received it or not. This came home to me as if I were the very person meant. After that sin had become bitter to me, and also my undervaluing gospel mercies, I was led to see other evils both in my heart and life, and I now saw myself to be a hell-deserving sinner. This impression was confirmed by what the minister said at an examination, namely, that even the wicked would be forced to acknowledge the equity of God at the great day. In December 1741, the minister was preaching from these words, ' Behold, now is the accepted time; behold, now is the day of salvation:' and he remarked, that the city of Nineveh got forty days to repent, but that the sinner has only one, and that, should it be neglected, there is no promise of any other. His soul may that very night be required of him. This caused me to feel the urgency of the gospel; and yet I felt myself unable to move towards God. I was now for a while in great distress. My sleep went from me; and as I awoke, I could not better describe my feelings than in the words of the psalmist, ' As the hart panteth after the water-brooks, so panteth my soul after thee, O God.' On a Sabbath soon after, the minister was preaching from John iii. 3: ' Except a man be born again, he cannot see the kingdom of God:' and he remarked, that the heart might, like a stone, be broken in pieces, and yet not be melted. This seemed to be my case. I was deeply affected, and my legs trembled even on the way home. I now looked more to God for help, feeling my own inability. Various passages of the Word of God came into my mind, bringing relief for a time; but it abode not. In this way I continued till the 10th of February, when, at home, I was enabled to lay hold on a promise, which had before been brought home to me, namely, Isa. xli. 10: ' Fear thou not, for I am with thee; be not dismayed, for I am thy God: I will strengthen thee; yea, I will help thee; yea, I will uphold thee with the right hand of my righteousness. My heart was now drawn out after Christ, so that I was enabled to close with him in all his offices.

"After this, when I heard the gospel preached, it seemed to me as if it were another gospel, and that all it contained was new to me. I now heard with joy, and I read my Bible with like feelings. When I walked in the fields, everything looked as if it also had changed, affording me occasion for pleasant and spiritual meditations. Still my feelings were not so full of joy as many afterwards experienced. On Tuesday the 16th of February, I heard my sister [Catherine] so commend the love of Christ, as to fill me with grief, because I did not feel as she did. I went away to call at a relation's house, and as soon as I reached it, I could not restrain from weeping; and in the presence of all, I began to commend the free grace and love of Christ, in a way I had never done before, and for a considerable time. I was even unable to restrain myself. This frame of mind continued for weeks; yet it was not always so with me. I had afterwards my times of depression as well as of joy; but the Lord often gave me deliverance. On hearing a sermon from Rom. iii. 19, ' Now we know that what things soever the law saith, it saith to them who are under the law, that every mouth may be stopped, and all the world may become guilty before God;' I was melted on account of sin, and made to wonder at the free grace of God. On other occasions, when hearing sermon, as well as in prayer and at our fellowship-meetings, I had similar feelings. One day, in particular, I was hearing the minister preach from Jer. xvii. 9: ' The heart is deceitful above all things, and desperately wicked; who can know it?' and I got a very affecting sense of the evil of my heart, and was greatly humbled before God.

" When the communion arrived, I was in doubt as to what I ought to do, and although I at last ventured, I experienced great deadness. On seeking to ascertain the cause, I was led to see that I had sinned through unbelief and murmuring before God. On hearing Mr. Currie of Kinglassie, on the fast-day before the second sacrament, I was greatly refreshed. His text was John iii. 29: ' He that hath the bride is the bridegroom,' &c. Yet, on Saturday, I felt my heart hard as a stone; and on Sabbath I was in much the same state, so that I was greatly perplexed whether I ought to communicate. At length I did, and obtained some relief. And throughout the whole of the following harvest I was filled with wonder and admiration at the condescension and grace of God to so vile a sinner; yet during the winter it was otherwise with me.

"When I now reflect on the workings of my heart for the last twelvemonth and more, I find that its ordinary and chief bent is after Christ and the things of another world. I cannot pretend to a fixed assurance of my state, but I would not for a thousand worlds be in the state I was in not long ago; and I cherish a humble hope that the Lord will have mercy upon me to eternal life."

The experience of this young woman differs from that of the former in different respects. If all the circumstances were known, perhaps some of these points might be explained. But beyond all that man can reach, there is the sovereignty of God, and purposes under that sovereignty, which will not appear till the end of all things. It may be also well to remind the reader, that although feelings are the expressions of what we experience, they are not always to be regarded as affording proper evidence of our state, and they ought not therefore to be proceeded upon as grounds either of confidence or distrust. It is not because we love our friend that we trust him, but because of the evidence which we have that he loves us; and neither is it because of the coldness of our own affections that we distrust him, but only because of our learning that his affections are cooled towards us. And, in like manner, it is not because of our love to God, but rather of his love to us, that we ought to have confidence before him: and unless we see cause for believing that his love towards us is less, we ought not to distrust him.

4. Catherine Jackson, sister of the former, and introduced from the second volume on account of this connection:—

"It pleased God to preserve me in a great measure outwardly blameless, whether living at home with my father or at service. From infancy, I was taught to observe a form of prayer, and now and then I read my Bible, and I attended divine ordinances. But in none of these did I go beyond mere form. When about seventeen years of age, I fell under deep concern about my state, especially in connection with preparation which I was making before going forward to the Lord's table; but when that occasion was over, I fell back into my usual listless state. In December 1741, I heard Mr. M'Culloch preach from 2 Cor. vi. 1, 2: 'We, then, as workers together with him, beseech you,' &c. This sermon awakened me to a deep sense of my original as well as actual sin, and from that time my convictions went on from day to day. About the beginning of February, a weekly lecture was begun on the Thursdays; and so great was my desire for instruction in the Word, that I sat up a good part of the night at my wheel, that I might go to the meeting next day, without giving cause of offence to my master and mistress. On Sabbath, the 14th of February, the minister preached on John iii. 3. My convictions were greatly increased by what I heard. After sermon, I went with my two sisters to a friend's house near the kirk; and while I sat there weeping, and seeing nothing before me but the blackness of darkness, a preacher [probably Mr. Duncan], and another person, Ingram More, now an elder, came where I was, and spake several things suitable to my case. But for what followed that night, I refer to the following account written out by the minister next morning, from his own recollection, and that of the persons now referred to, and which is also according to what I am able to recall to mind:—

"The preacher asked her what particular sins lay heaviest on her conscience. She bewailed her despising gospel ordinances, her unbelief, that she had received gospel grace in vain, had lost much precious time, that she had been a lover of pleasure more than of God, and that she had murmured at the conduct of Providence in calling, as she believed, her sister, and leaving her. After a little, she was brought by her sisters and the two men to the minister's room, weeping all the way. After she had been seated a little, he asked what ailed her? She could only reply, as she did over and over, ' Oh, what shall I do?' 'Believe,' said he, ' on the Lord Jesus Christ, and thou shalt be saved.' Weeping very bitterly, she cried out, ' But my sins are so great that he will not receive me.' ' Come now,' he repeated, ' and let us reason together, saith the Lord. Though your sins be as scarlet, they shall be as white as snow; though they be red like crimson, they shall be as wool.' ' Oh no,' said she, in great bitterness of spirit, ' he will not accept of me—he will not accept of me.' ' But he will,' said the minister. ' If you be willing to come to him, and to accept of him, I assure you, in his name, that he will accept of you, whatever you have done or been. Where there is a willingness on both sides, what should hinder the concluding of a match between you? Come, then, to him, and be assured that he will in no wise cast you out.' On this she ceased weeping, and seemed calmed for a little. She was now, as she afterwards explained, essaying to believe on Christ. But in a little she burst out anew, weeping and crying, ' Oh, my sins, my sins; he will not receive me—he will not receive me : I am the chief of sinners.' ' Are you a greater sinner,' said the minister, ' than the apostle Paul? He was, as he says, the chief of sinners, and yet he obtained mercy; and he is set forth as an example of the grace of God, that others may be encouraged. Come to him, then, and ye also shall obtain mercy, as the apostle did.' She again repeated the same complaint, when she was told that no evidence of Christ's willingness to save her could be greater than his having shed his very heart's blood, out of love to such as her; that this blood was capable of cleansing her from all her sins—of washing out the deepest stain. After several passages to this effect had been repeated, she again ceased crying, and said, mournfully, ' Oh, but I cannot believe in the Lord Jesus Christ, that I may be saved.' ' Will you not, then,' said he, ' cry out, with that poor man in the gospel, ' Lord, I believe,' or Lord, I *would* believe; ' help thou mine unbelief?'' She now repeated these words, endeavouring to exercise faith, and was in some measure helped to it, as she afterwards said. But although, during this, she refrained from crying, it was but for a little. She again fell a-weeping, and said, 'He will not accept of me.' 'But he will,' said the minister; 'he assures you that he will. Hear his own words: 'Whosoever will, let him take of the water of life freely.'' Still she continued to weep in great bitterness of spirit. 'Come,' said the minister, 'shall we pray for the help of God to draw you to Christ?' 'Oh yes, yes,' said she, and she hastened to rise. We stood, and one present supported her in that attitude. The prayer consisted first of adoring gratitude, because of the love of God in giving his Son, and of the love of Christ in giving himself; after which it turned on the condition of the young woman. It was but a little, when she whispered to the person supporting her, that she felt as if Christ were saying to her, 'I will never leave thee nor forsake thee;' and again, that he had cast all her sins behind his back. After prayer she repeated the promises which had thus been brought home to her, and broke out in a strain of exultation, because of the excellences of Christ's person, and the wonders of his love and free sovereign grace, and lamenting her late unbelief. Then she exclaimed, 'Oh, I would not believe till I felt his power; but now his love hath conquered my heart. He has pardoned even my unbelief; he has drawn me with the cords of love and the bands of a man. I thought that my sins were so great and many that he would not pardon them; but now he hath cast them all behind his back. His thoughts are not as were my thoughts, neither are his ways as my ways.'

"A number of people had by this time gathered into the room, particularly some young women of her acquaintance: and all present being deeply affected, several weeping all the while, the minister said to the young woman, 'You see that there are several daughters of Jerusalem with us, who may be asking in their hearts, 'What is thy beloved more than another beloved?' have you anything to say to them in commendation of Christ?' She immediately turned to them and said, in the most feeling manner, "'My Beloved is white and ruddy, the chiefest among ten thousand; yea, he is altogether lovely.' O come to Christ. Come and trust him. If ye cannot cry to him, long after him. Oh, will ye at least sigh and sob for him? I can now say, ' My beloved is mine, and I am his.''

" This address produced great commotion of feeling. Some were so transported with joy as scarcely to be able to restrain themselves, and there was heard among others such a sound of weeping, as to be audible at a considerable distance. The minister bade them compose themselves and join in praising God; and turning to the young woman, he said, ' Shall we sing part of the 103d psalm?' She readily approved, and they sang the first eight verses, in which she very cheerfully took part. When this exercise was over, the minister said to her, ' I suppose you have been singing with pleasure?' She answered, that she had never up to that time sung as she had just done, nor had she previous to this occasion known Christ.

" She then rose up, with great vigour of body and liveliness of spirit, and turning first to her sister, who had been brought under the power of the truth, as was believed, some weeks before, she embraced her with the greatest tenderness, thanking her for what she had done in counselling her and praying for her. She then shook hands with all present, commending to them Christ, and the sweetness of his love, as well as the riches of his grace. As many as she feared were still strangers to Christ, she invited with great earnestness to come to him without delay; and such as she believed to be in Christ, she asked to join with her in praising him for the wonderful love and favour he had vouchsafed her.

" After this the minister and several others joined in prayer, and so the meeting broke up, after being together for about three hours. Mr. M'Culloch adds, that during the whole of this time, much of the sensible presence and power of God were felt by as many as had previously known the truth, and at least deep concern laid fast hold of others."

In proceeding with her own narrative, she speaks of many varying exercises of mind through which she was brought, but they are very much like those we have already seen. Passing, therefore, over some of these, we find her thus describing her condition the summer following:—

"For some time before the first sacrament, which was in July 1742, I was under great discouragement, having but little of that liveliness and spirituality which I had formerly enjoyed. I went with others to the minister for instruction; and when all was over, he offered me a token, but I did not feel at liberty to accept of it, being under the impression that I had not God's welcome. But on returning home, I was so impressed with that saying, 'My grace is sufficient for thee,' that I resolved on going forward still. During the action-sermon, which was on these words, 'He is altogether lovely,' &c. (Song v. 16), the Lord was pleased to give me great heart-brokenness on account of sin, and to draw out my desires in love towards Christ. He also allowed me much of his presence at the communion-table. On Monday, I heard Mr. Whitefield preach from Phil. ii. 5, and saw much of God in that sermon. I was made greatly to desire that the same mind should be in me which was in Christ; and I was much humbled in thinking how little there was of it in my soul. At the second communion, which was in August, I heard Mr. Currie preach from these words, 'He that hath the bride is the bridegroom,' &c. (John iii. 29); and was greatly refreshed. I was enabled to see that Christ was the bridegroom of my soul. My heart was also drawn out after him above all things, and I had a deep and affecting sense of the dishonour I had done him. At the table, I had a sweet savour of Christ upon my soul. On the Monday, I heard Mr. Hamilton, on these words, 'Pray without ceasing' (1 Thess. v. 17); and my heart was melted under a sense of the love of God, and was drawn out with earnest desires that I might be enabled to comply with the exhortations offered.

"In the course of the harvest, I fell into a state of great darkness and deadness of spirit. One day after coming from secret prayer, and feeling as if I needed not to attempt it any more, seeing the Lord would not hear me because of my sins, that word came to me with commanding power, 'In a little wrath I hid my face from thee for a moment; but with everlasting kindness will I have mercy on thee, saith the Lord thy Redeemer.' (Isa. liv. 8.) From this I was made to see that the Lord had justly hid his face from me on account of my sins; that although it was, as my unbelieving spirit suggested, long, yet was it but for a little moment; whereas his kindness was everlasting, and altogether his own.

"In the course of the winter a story was got up against me, which, though altogether untrue and unjust, I felt most because of the dishonour which might, in this way, be done to God and his cause. One night, while weeping and lamenting this as I lay in bed, I was so distressed as deeply to deplore my having revealed my spiritual condition to any one, as otherwise, say what they might of me, it could not have injured religion. But while in this state these words came to me as if sent by God, 'Be still, and know that I am God.' (Ps. xlvi. 10.) This calmed my fretted feelings and reproved my impatience. I resigned myself and all my ways to God, that he might over-rule my lot as he should see to be best; and I was afterwards confirmed in this temper of mind, by observing that we are required to endure hardness as good soldiers of Jesus Christ.

"In January, the same winter (1743) I heard much of the Lord's gracious dealings in some of the prayer-meetings which were held in the parish; and yet in the meeting with which I was connected there was, as I thought, much deadness. This distressed me greatly, believing, as I did, that we must, in some way, have done dishonour to God.

I was much engaged in prayer on this account, and was led earnestly to plead that God would visit us also at our ensuing meeting, and this although I should not share in the blessing. It seemed as if the Hearer of prayer were intimating his answer by sending home to me that saying, 'Said I not unto thee, that if thou wouldest believe, thou shouldest see the glory of God?' (John xi. 40.) Accordingly at night, when we met for prayer, there were several present so filled and overcome with the love of God, especially during the devotional exercises, that they could not converse for some time after, but were wholly taken up in admiring wonder at the love of God in Christ. I desired much to share with them in this love, but the Lord did not grant me this desire; yet the declarations of his Word were sweet to my soul, and I felt satisfied in waiting his holy will in all that concerned me, sincerely rejoicing in the blessings bestowed upon others. While one of the meeting was engaged in prayer, that word came home to me as appropriate: 'I charge you, O ye daughters of Jerusalem, by the roes, and by the hinds of the field, that ye stir not up, nor wake my love, till he please.' (Song iii. 5.) And when it came to my turn to pray, I got great liberty in blessing and praising the Lord for his goodness to others.

"Some time after this I went to attend on a sacramental occasion in Paisley. There several of us were going together; and I felt as if I ought not to be with them, so much was I borne down with a sense of my sinfulness; yet God dealt very tenderly with me. On Saturday I was broken-hearted, because of sin. During the action-sermon on Sabbath, my heart was filled with a sense of God's love. In the evening I was also filled with holy joy, listening to a sermon from these words, 'And truly our fellowship is with the Father, and with his Son Jesus Christ.' (1 John i. 3.) And on Tuesday morning I was greatly confirmed in my faith, and resolved to serve God.

"To come to a close, I bless the Lord that, down to the present time, the thoughts and desires of my heart are mainly and ordinarily carried out after spiritual and eternal things. Though my heart is sometimes much more dead in reading and hearing from the Word than it is at other times, yet I often long for opportunities of attending gospel ordinances, both on Sabbath and week-days, before the time; and I prize them more than my daily food. I also bless God that he has often made them the means of reviving, strengthening, and comforting my soul. The world, and the things of the world, bulk but little in my eyes; yet I am often humbled because of wandering thoughts when engaged in holy duties. I now find vastly more pleasure in the enjoyment of the light of God's countenance, even for a very short time, than I ever found in all my life before. What I chiefly want and desire is, more communion with Christ, and greater conformity to him in the present state, and to be ever with him in the life which is to come. To him be glory for ever. Amen."

The pious reader can scarcely fail to have been particularly interested with what is said of this young woman; and his interest will not be lessened by our adding, that she was merely a servant girl in a farm-house. So much does grace elevate and enlarge the mind, that even the simple and unlearned think and speak to some extent as if their circumstances had been different. At the same time, there are peculiarities in such cases. In this and similar examples, there is a tendency to count too much on feelings, and also to attach an undue importance to impressions. A more enlarged acquaintance with divine truth, and greater strength of mind, would, with the same measure of spirituality, greatly lessen these. But the prevailing tendency of our age lies in an opposite direction, and may even require such examples as this to show what it is to have the heart fully engaged in the things of God.

5. George Tassie, a married man, aged forty-one years:—

" I was taught to read and write at school, and also to repeat the Shorter Catechism. I was instructed by my parents to engage in prayer when but a child; but as I grew up I became less regular. I usually attended divine ordinances—sometimes heard gladly; and kept up, on ordinary occasions, the worship of God in my family morning and evening. I used also to read the Bible by myself, although I understood nothing of its spirituality. I had likewise pleasure in reading sermon books, but I could never apply what I read to myself; and I cannot say that anything, either read or heard, ever came home to my heart with power, till the end of June 1742. I had still, however, a suspicion that there was something in religion more than I had found, and yet I could not think myself worse than many of my neighbours.

"I continued in this state till the 12th of May 1742, when I heard Mr. Robe of Kilsyth preaching at Cambuslang on these words: 'He heareth the cry of the poor and needy.' He said it was better to cry now than to cry in hell; but adding, that the cry which God heareth is the cry of faith. I fell under great concern, and was made to tremble and shake, although I made no noise. I felt as in the immediate presence of God, and was therefore filled with fear. I put up many petitions for deliverance. The trembling abated, as did also my fear, and I became very much what I was. Reflecting on the probable cause of what had occurred, I thought of that saying, 'The devils believe, and tremble.' This showed me that there was nothing saving in my fear.

"One day, when at home working by myself, I thought much of what was then going on at Cambuslang, and concluded that there must be something very special about it. When thus engaged, these words came into my mind with great power: 'What the law could not do, in that it was weak through the flesh, God sending his own Son in the likeness of sinful flesh, and for sin, condemned sin in the flesh.' (Rom. viii. 3.) This led me to meditate on the law, and I saw it to be just, and good, and so holy that the best man on earth could not keep it, so as to be justified by it before God; and this led me to wonder at the love of God in sending his Son to purchase salvation for law breakers. So much did I wonder at this, that I could not restrain myself from crying out, 'O wonderful, amazing love!' My heart was thus drawn out to accept of Christ in all his offices—as my prophet, my priest, and my king. In doing this, I found the words of Thomas to be as my own: 'My Lord, and my God.' And after this, my desires went out after God, that he would keep and preserve that which concerned me. I had now much sensible love in my heart towards Christ. He was to me, indeed, the chiefest among ten thousand, and altogether lovely. My heart was enlarged to bless and praise God, on account of his many mercies. I had also a deep and humbling sense of my own sinfulness, and especially in having rejected the Saviour so long. When I had settled a little, I began to inquire whether this was to be regarded as really a work of regeneration or otherwise. My own conscience said that it was, but doubts were raised in my mind as to whether such a work could take place in so short a time. I turned up my Bible, and found in it such cases as those of the Philippian jailer and Zaccheus, which showed me that some were converted in a short time. I also observed that several of those described in the New Testament as applying to Christ, addressed him as Lord, and placed themselves under his authority, and that this also I was enabled to do; and thus, instead of stumbling at the Lord's way, I was taught to admire his great goodness in dealing with me as he had done, in carrying me through so mildly and speedily. Their crying and distress, who had been otherwise dealt with, I saw to be because of their being kept so long under a sense of sin, without finding rest in Christ, and I became convinced that, if it had been so with me, I also would have been forced to cry out.

"I continued in this state for some considerable time. All week I was occupied in admiring the love of Christ in obeying and suffering, in yielding satisfaction through the excellency of his divine nature and his sufferings as a man.

I was taught to imitate Christ in all his imitable perfections, to take part with God speaking in the law against the corruptions of my own heart, to watch against every known sin, and to strive after every commanded duty; and I was at the same time made to see in all I did much that was evil; and, renouncing all my deeply-stained performances, to rely wholly on Christ for acceptance and sanctifying grace.

"The Bible was now to me my frequent companion. Many passages appeared in a new light, so as to be quite different from what they had been before. I remember, in particular, how that passage in the 118th psalm, 'The stone which the builders refused, is become the head stone of the corner,' flashed upon me, as condemning many because of unbelief. In conversing with some of my neighbours, whom I had been accustomed to regard as religious, I now found them to be nothing more than I had myself formerly been—mere formalists.

"Next Lord's-day, I went to Cambuslang and heard Mr. Duncan, on that text: 'If any man be in Christ, he is a new creature.' (2 Cor. v. 17.) The marks given I was enabled to find in myself, particularly love towards God and my neighbour. So much did I experience the latter, that I earnestly wished to be reconciled to any with whom I had been at variance. Hearing Mr. M'Culloch preach from these words: 'O Jerusalem, wash thine heart,' &c. (Jer. iv. 14), I did not very well understand what it was to have my heart washed; but afterwards I came to understand and experience it in my own case.

"On the Sabbath preceding the first sacrament at Cambuslang, Mr. M'Culloch preached from these words: 'But let a man examine himself,' &c. (1 Cor. xi. 28), and took occasion to say, that many might get a token from a minister or elder without receiving any token from Christ; adding, that an unconverted soul could not derive any benefit from the Lord's supper. Some of the marks given I had no difficulty in finding, which gave me much peace and joy, believing, as I did, that the Lord made me welcome. Before going to the table I was in a very dead frame of mind; but when there, I could scarcely get another word said than 'My Lord, and my God.' My heart clave to God as its portion for time and eternity, and I was at the same time much humbled because of my own unworthiness. Mr. Whitefield, on preaching from the text, 'Thy Maker is thy husband' (Isa. liv. 5), said, that he was come to woo a bride for his Master, the church's bridegroom; but that before any soul could be admitted into the marriage covenant with Christ, it behoved to become dead to the law and its own righteousness. I had great satisfaction in finding that I had become dead to both, and had betaken myself to Christ for righteousness and strength.

"For several weeks, I was much perplexed how to manage some of my worldly affairs. My thoughts about these became a snare. They haunted me even on the Lord's-day, and I have had to sit till well on in the night reading and praying, lest, on going to bed, they should haunt me there. One Sabbath evening, while so perplexed, these words stole in upon me with a soothing and healing effect:—

> 'Set thou thy trust upon the Lord,
> And be thou doing good;
> And so thou in the land shalt dwell,
> And verily have food.'

I was thus led to ascertain present duty, and to cast myself on the care of Providence for the future.

"And now, reflecting on the time that has passed since June 1742, I find that by grace I have been enabled to go on from day to day in the way of duty, endeavouring to live soberly, righteously, and godly. I find now that my chief end is to live and act for the glory of God, studying in all things conformity to his will. Though obliged to attend to my worldly calling, so as to provide, under God, for myself and family, my thoughts run out more after Christ, and in meditations on his word, than in any other way."

In this case, there is much less feeling, and fewer

changes, than in some of the preceding, and yet is there apparently much evidence of a real change of heart; thus showing us, it may be, how much there is of constitutional dissimilarities, and also of the sovereignty of God in dealing differently with different individuals.

6. Alexander Roger, a youth about fifteen years of age:—

"I obtained the usual education when a boy, and sometimes, but not regularly, I said my prayers, and I usually went to church on Sabbath; but I had no proper understanding of what I addressed to God in prayer, or of what I read in my Bible, or heard from the minister. It was my great loss that, after leaving school, I was for some time in a family where I saw nothing of the fear of God. All this while I restrained prayer before God; I never, while here, so much as bowed my knee in prayer. I forgot my questions [catechism], and seldom turned over a leaf of my Bible. I even lost my reading, and cared for nothing but madness and folly; never reflecting that there was a God, a heaven, and a hell, or that I had a soul to be saved. Having none to reprove me, I went into habits of profane swearing, of Sabbath-breaking, and of lying. On leaving that family, I returned home; and being under restraint, these gross habits were discontinued. I began to recover my reading and questions, and I made a fashion of praying. Soon after this I was sent to learn a trade, but I minded nothing but vanity. I was given to card-playing and other games; and I continued in this hardened state till it pleased the Lord to show me my sin and danger.

"Some time in the month of June 1742, I went to Cambuslang, to hear Mr. Whitefield preach. It was on a Thursday, and his text was, 'The harvest is past, the summer is ended, and we are not saved,' &c. (Jer. lxxx. 20-22.) Among other things, he said, 'Many come out of curiosity to hear a poor child preach; and the same curiosity would induce them to go to the devil.' I thought myself described. I had come from no better motive; and I felt that without repentance I could not be saved. Again, addressing God, he said, 'O Lord, how many trample thy blood under their feet, and despise thee and thy gospel!' This led me to such a view of my sins, that I saw nothing but the wrath of God awaiting me, and hell ready to receive me. I was also deeply pierced with a sense of the evil of those sins which I could remember, as well as of the corruption and depravity of my nature and of my unbelief in not receiving but rejecting Christ, when offered to me in the gospel. My sense of guilt was such, that I would have thought it no injustice, on God's part, had he cast me immediately into hell. I even felt as if I were sinking into the bottomless pit, and that all around were ready to drag me down to it. My feelings of repentance were deep and sincere, and above all, on account of the dishonour which I had done to God.

"Under these awful feelings, I at last fainted away; and on recovering, I was enabled to return with a comrade to my father's house, which was about five miles distant. After reaching home, I attempted to pray, but I could not; my heart was hard as a stone. I had no peace at home, and therefore I returned to Cambuslang, and was in time to hear Mr. M'Culloch's first sermon that day. His text was, 'He hath filled the hungry with good things; and the rich he hath sent empty away.' (Luke i. 53.) When these words were first read, they came home to my mind with power. I thought much upon them; so much as to lose a considerable part of the sermon. My convictions of sin were so strong, that I was at last forced to cry, nevertheless that I did all I could to restrain myself. I continued in this state during all the time of that sermon, during the interval, and also during the second sermon.

"When it was over, I went alone to pray, pleading with God for grace to close with him on his own terms; and while so engaged, that saying of Scripture was powerfully borne in upon my mind, 'Fear thou not; for I am with thee: be not dismayed; for I am thy God: I will strengthen thee; yea, I will help thee; yea, I will uphold thee with the right hand of my righteousness.' (Isa. xli. 10.) I was now filled with joy and wonder at what God had done; and thus I was enabled, with all my heart, to believe on Christ—to receive and embrace him as offered in the gospel. And ever since, the power of sin and of unbelief has been broken. I have not been without doubts of my interest in Christ, and I have in consequence been shy to speak of myself, lest matters should turn out otherwise than I hope; but, on the other hand, I have great pleasure, and even delight, in religious duties, and make conscience of what I owe towards both God and man. I am accustomed to keep a strict watch over my heart, and over my words and actions. One of the greatest crosses I have to do with, is to be found in the vanity and sinfulness of my heart and life. My chief desires are after God and Christ, heaven and holiness; and I am often looking for the coming of the Lord."

The subject of this notice was but young, and the period reviewed was perhaps too short to warrant any very settled opinion concerning him. Still the account which is here given is simple and scriptural, and may be useful, especially to the young. They ought to feel and know that their season of life is, more than any other, an acceptable time and day of salvation.

7. Elizabeth Dykes, a young woman, about sixteen years of age:—

"By the time I was six years of age I could read the Bible, having been taught by my father. I got the catechism by heart, and am still able to repeat it. My parents set before me a good example, and exhorted me to pray to God. Sometimes I did so, and sometimes not; but I had no delight in the duty, and I knew not the God to whom I prayed. The Lord kept me from gross sins, such as appear before men; only I sometimes fell into saying what was untrue, and the profanation of the Lord's-day. I usually attended the house of God; but it was only to see and be seen. I read my Bible when bidden by my parents; but I had far rather read story-books and ballads. On hearing sermons,

I sometimes thought that the gospel condemned me, and that if I died in that state, I must perish; still these things were not laid to heart.

"The first time that I felt the word coming home to me with power, was when hearing Mr. M'Culloch, on the last Sabbath of February 1742. His text was, 'He that believeth not is condemned already, because he hath not believed in the name of the only begotten Son of God.' (John iii. 18.) I heard with much attention, and was made very uneasy. I went to go into the manse with others, but could not get in, there being many about the door. A man whom I knew not said to those standing about, 'Why stand ye idle? ye have need to be looking into the state of your hearts.' I felt this to be true, and particularly applicable to myself. And such was my state of feeling, that I was unable to stand; I was carried into the manse, and remained with others in the hall, in great distress, all night. My sins so pressed upon me, that I could not believe it possible that God would ever pardon my sins, they seemed to me to be so great. I saw nothing before me but hell-fire; and yet my sense of the evil of sin was even greater than my apprehensions of coming wrath. My lying, my Sabbath-breaking, and other sins, were brought fresh to my remembrance, and they lay upon my conscience with a weight which I could not remove. But I had not yet got such a sight of my heart sins, and of the corruption of my nature, as I afterwards got. Towards morning, that word came home to me with power, 'I will heal their backsliding, I will love them freely; for mine anger is turned away from him.' (Hos. xiv. 4.) It seemed as if the Lord had spoken to me in these words; my trouble ceased, and for a time I had peace. But during Monday night, I awoke in great horror, crying out that I was in the gall of bitterness and the bond of iniquity. My former comforts seemed now a delusion. I bethought me that many precious sayings of the word might cast up and be snatched at by those to whom they did not belong, and I concluded that it had been so with me. This brought me into great distress, which continued for about eight days. Next Sabbath I had to remain at home, so as to allow another member of the family to get to the kirk. When engaged in secret prayer, that word came into my heart, ' O thou afflicted, tossed with tempest, and not comforted, behold, I will lay thy stones with fair colours, and lay thy foundations with sapphires,' &c. (Isa. liv. 11–13.) I was made to say, ' Will the Lord, indeed, cleanse so vile and filthy a heart as mine, and make it conformable to his will?' I also found in my heart love to God, and I was made to rejoice in him, and to praise him with my whole heart. My great wish was, if I could get all the world to praise him.

" But this frame did not continue very long. I fell into a state of doubting, and I was unable to take that promise to myself. Many of the threatenings of God's Word came now to my mind, such as that, ' It is a fearful thing to fall into the hands of the living God;' and that, ' Our God is a consuming fire.' I was accordingly brought into great distress. It seemed as if all the threatenings of God's Word were against me. I saw that there was no relief for me, but in Christ; and yet I seemed to be so great a sinner, as that I could scarcely venture to plead for his mercy. While in this distress, and not knowing what to do, that word came home to me with power, ' Great is the Holy One of Israel in the midst of thee.' (Isa. xii. 6.) This made me praise God for his love in Christ Jesus, and so for a time I rested in the promise. But I had not, as yet, seen my need of Christ in all his offices; I was, however, led so to see the corruption of my nature, as to know that there was nothing in me but sin that I could call my own, and that I was otherwise so imperfect, as to be unlike God. I experienced within me as the conflict of two armies—the flesh lusting against the spirit, and the spirit against the flesh. Even when my lusts had been subdued, so as to seem trampled under foot, I found them stealing upon me anew, and drawing away my heart from God and from matters of duty. I saw in this how unwilling I was to come to Christ, how backward I was in duty, and how much inclined to sin; yea, how obstinate I was in sin. I saw my great need of Christ as my prophet, my priest, and my king, and I felt willing to accept of him in all of these offices. But on searching more deeply, I found a secret unwillingness in my heart to submit to him in all things *as my king*. I discovered in me a lusting after things sinful, which I had not power to overcome. I saw in this my own insufficiency, and became persuaded that unless the Lord would undertake for me, and work all my works in me and for me, I would not succeed in doing anything to purpose. My heart seemed deceitful above all things, and desperately wicked, averse to all good, and bent upon all evil. I was, however, enabled to look to the Lord in faith, for grace to conquer these strong lusts and corruptions; and as I thus looked to him, I became stronger, and they became weaker.

"As the Barony communion was approaching, I resolved to attend, to see whether the Lord would be pleased to strengthen my weak faith, and to give me more love to himself. I was sensible of much want of preparation, but I went forward relying on Christ. When at the table, that word came with power: 'And Mary hath chosen that good part which shall not be taken away from her.' (Luke xi. 42.) I did not then know that there was such a passage in the Bible; and it came into my mind as if it had been said, 'Thou hast that good part which shall not be taken away from thee;' and this was accompanied with so much sweetness and power, that I could not enough praise God. After this, I took great pleasure in prayer and other duties, finding all His ways to be pleasantness and peace. On the observance of the first sacrament at Cambuslang, I had a great desire to communicate, but I was overtaken with damps and doubtings, and was left under great deadness.

When the second sacrament came round, I could not find any one to whom I could apply for a token, and so I sat on the brae and heard the tables served. My longings were great to be there, and my love to Christ was so strong that I would have given all I had for a token. I even desired to be dissolved, that I might be with Christ in heaven. I went home with much of this frame upon me, and had for a time great sweetness in reading the Word of God, and in secret prayer.

"Some time after, I again fell into great doubts and fears, concluding that all my experiences were only of the common operations of the Spirit, and that the promises which I had got, as I believed, from God, had been suggested by the wicked one. Many evil thoughts now came into my mind, and I was made to fear that I had committed the unpardonable sin, and was in a state altogether desperate. These thoughts came into my mind so thickly and quickly, as to seem so many fiery darts; and so it continued for about a month. Intending to communicate in Glasgow, in October 1742, I was by myself on the morning of the communion Sabbath, and these words of the prophet came into my mind as of God: 'I will pour water upon him that is thirsty, and floods upon the dry ground.' (Isa. xliv. 3.) I had been thirsting greatly for the righteousness of Christ, and this word encouraged me. I went to the table under a deep sense of my need of Christ, and I got such a view of his fulness as enabled me to go forward resting on his righteousness and strength; and such was my love towards him, that I could have laid down my life for his sake. Yet after a few days, when my feelings of love were somewhat abated, I examined myself, and found that I could not then willingly lay down my life for him. This grieved me, and I earnestly sought after greater perfectness, reckoning myself a wretched creature to be so fickle and so easily led away from the love of Christ. I examined myself as to that faith which worketh by love, and sometimes I was satisfied as to my having such a faith. I found that I could pray from the heart for my friends, my relations, and even my enemies; and I would have been glad of an opportunity to serve them. At other times I was much bowed down, not finding such liberty in prayer. When I had any difference with my neighbours or fellow-servants, I found a rising of corruption in my heart against them; yet, on looking to Christ as meek and lowly, the force of my corruption has been broken, and I have prayed most heartily for them.

"Preparatory to the next communion occasion in Glasgow, I began to read concerning the sufferings of Christ, and was made to see in our sins the procuring cause, and in his sufferings love to poor perishing sinners. I was made greatly to wonder at the love of Christ in that he suffered for his very enemies. When I went to the table, I could not get even a sense of a broken heart, nor one blink of Christ's countenance; but hearing Mr. Bain of Killearn preaching from these words, 'Whatsoever is born of God overcometh the world; and this is the victory that overcometh the world, even our faith' (1 John v. 4), I began to revive, hoping through Christ to overcome the world.

"And now to this day I cannot say that I have an assurance of heaven, but I desire to lay the stress of my salvation on Christ and his righteousness. I find great delight in reading and hearing the Word, and in prayer; and with these, in every other known duty, I am well pleased with the commands of God, and with his disposal of all my ways in providence. But I dare not say much, for fear of presumption, and lest my heart should deceive me. I endeavour, from time to time, to pray for the public interests of real religion. I dare not say that I pray for these on all occasions with that earnestness wherewith I ought; but I wish from the bottom of my heart that Christ's kingdom of grace may be advanced, and that multitudes of souls may be brought to him in a day of his power."

The feeling, probably, produced on the mind of the

reader on finishing with this case, will be, "I had rather that her progress had been more steady." True, and this will often be felt in reading other cases, and even the diaries of persons more highly privileged: and what we should learn from this is, to be humble, to study practically to live near God—to get at God himself as the soul's portion, and not to live by his gifts. It is natural for us, so long as we are but imperfectly sanctified, to live by sense, even in spiritual things, rather than by faith. But in proportion as we are enabled to hear and to feel that we have our portion in God, our peace will be as a river, full and overflowing.

8. James Kirkland, a young man, aged twenty-four:—

"In youth, I got into a way of praying evening and morning, and I attended church every Lord's-day. But many a time I wofully neglected to read my Bible in secret. Sometimes I had of myself a desire to pray, and also to go to church; but usually I went the accustomed round of duty without any sense of the authority of God. When about sixteen years of age, I was admitted to the Lord's table; at which time I thought that I got some views of the folly of my former ways, and that I had somewhat of a concern upon my spirit in the observance both of public and private duties. I had also some resolutions to amend my life. These resolutions I had both before and after the sacrament. When at sermon, I sometimes gave attention to what I heard, but more generally my heart wandered after vanities.

"After this, for four or five years, I in many things followed the multitude to do evil. During this time I went on heedlessly, without concern about a future state, either of happiness or of misery. During all my former attendance on duties, I cannot say that I ever felt the Word of God come home to me with power, so as to make me see and feel my lost condition. I was never led to feel my condition till about the middle of April 1742; and it was thus: —I had gone to Cambuslang, where I heard Mr. M'Culloch preach from these words, 'There are some of you that believe not.' (John vi. 64.) Even then I heard as I had been accustomed to do; but on the Tuesday following, while thinking on that text, I was made to see and judge concerning myself, that I did not yet believe. I continued under this impression for the space of nine days, during which my distress was so great that I was rendered unfit for work, and would scarcely venture to eat, thinking I had no right to the comforts of life, and feeling as if the wrath of God would overtake me when receiving what I did not deserve.

"On the tenth day, acting under the advice of a friend, I tried to give myself to God after the manner of a covenant; but I had little satisfaction. Sometimes that Scripture came into my mind, ' I, even I, am he that blotteth out thy transgressions for mine own sake, and will not remember thy sins.' (Isa. xliii. 25.) But for the time, it had no effect. After a little, however, the latter part of the verse came back upon me with power, namely, that God would pardon for his own name's sake. Under this impression, I was made solidly to trust and believe that he would be as good as his word, and that he would do it for his own name's sake. And from this time, I got a humbling sense of my sins, both in heart and in life, particularly of that great sin, the sin of unbelief, and of distrusting God. I experienced much inward grief on account of inward corruption, the fruit of original sin. I was thus made to own that God would have been just though he had cast me into hell on account of my sins—on account of the dishonour I had done to him by my sins. In this condition I was much engaged in prayer to God; and I found great liberty, so that I was enabled to pour forth tears of sorrow, such as I knew not before. Sometimes I thought that I could not contain myself, or refrain from crying out. But though with difficulty, I was enabled to restrain myself, smothering my grief in my own breast. About this time, I was frequently made to think that all I had found, either from the Word of God or in prayer, was a delusion. At other times, I was led to fear that, after all, I could not obtain mercy, seeing I had been so guilty before God. New convictions shot up in my mind, sometimes when hearing the Word, and sometimes when engaged in other duties. And this is a short account of what befell me till I went back to Cambuslang.

"On returning, I heard Mr. M'Knight of Irvine preach from these words: 'Sir, we would see Jesus.' (John xii. 21.) In opening this subject, he showed what it was to see Jesus, and who were the persons that would see Jesus; and he gave it as a mark of such, that they had a hungering and thirsting after Christ and his righteousness. This enabled me to try myself, and I found that this was the very exercise of my soul; and from this conviction I found relief. That same night, however, when in the hall at the exercise, a cloud returned and settled upon me again. It seemed now as if I had no right to Christ or the promises; and in this condition I returned home much distressed, and continued so for some time.

"On returning, I heard Mr. M'Culloch preach from these words: 'O Jerusalem, wash thine heart from wickedness, that thou mayest be saved; how long shall thy vain thoughts lodge within thee?" (Jer. iv. 14.) In hearing this sermon, I all the while felt as if I were the person pointed at as not cleansed from wickedness. My case seemed now to be blacker and more dismal than ever. All I heard led me so to conclude concerning myself. On Monday morning, I again heard Mr. M'Culloch preaching from that other text, 'Keep back thy servant also from presumptuous sins.' (Ps. xix. 13.) In opening his subject, he showed what presumptuous sins were, under seven or eight heads. In examining myself, I thought that I was guilty of them all, whereupon I fell into such distress that I had to retire to a dyke-side, and there allow myself to burst into tears, for I was no longer able to restrain myself. Afterwards, I was enabled to reason with myself as to the cause of this distress after, as I believed, true comfort, and I came to the conclusion, that it was because I had not received the promises as yea and amen in Christ; and so I was enabled to receive Christ anew, and to see him in the promises.

"And now, as to the ordinary bent of my heart, it is that I may, through grace, be kept at the utmost distance from sin, and in the practice of holiness. I hate every false and wicked way—the sins of my heart as well as those of my life. I now feel, as I think, some delighting in the law of the Lord, after the inner man; and I have pleasure in the duties of religion, particularly in hearing the Word and in prayer. I have, as I trust, though in much weakness, closed with Christ on his own terms; and seeing my need, I have received him in all his offices. And I think that I can say of God in Christ, that he is my chief good and satisfying portion, and that there is none in heaven or in earth that I desire besides him."

This case is short and simple. It is also remarkably free from anything like attaching undue importance to the suggestions of particular passages. But there is in it enough to remind us of that important saying, "Not as though I had already attained, either were already perfect." (Phil. iii. 12.) The mere theorist is ever stumbling at the returning unbelief and distressful condition of persons said to be in Christ. He might as well wonder at the wailing of the infant, and at the tottering steps of the child. "We live by faith, and not by sight;" and yet, earth-born as we all are, we naturally seek rather to walk by sight; and hence our falls. Losing hold of what faith sees, we are again among the pots, and can with difficulty regain our loss.

9. R. Shearer, a young man, aged nineteen:—

"I never used to pray in secret before last year, except when, after committing some sin which smote my conscience, I was for a time driven to it. I went to church, but more from curiosity and custom than anything else. When there, I would sometimes have been glad to be out again, that I might saunter about. Till of late, I was also much given to cursing and swearing, and to the profanation of the Lord's-day. In thinking of death, I fancied that I would then weep and cry to God, and that he would hear me—that I would send for a minister or elder, who would pray for me; and so I concluded that I would in this way get to heaven.

"When the awakening broke out at Cambuslang, I went thither and heard a sermon. It was about the middle of March 1742. Nothing struck me at the time; but about two or three days after, these words came into my mind, 'Blessed are they which do hunger and thirst after righteousness; for they shall be filled.' (Matt. v. 6.) They had merely the effect of leading me to think, and causing me to be more diligent in duty. I now attended at Cambuslang every Sabbath, and usually every Thursday, for about a quarter of a year. Still it was without any sensible effect. I was, however, impressed, in observing so many flock to Christ, and I had some fear that I might be left to perish. On a particular occasion, Mr. M'Culloch preached on these words, 'He that believeth on the Son hath everlasting life: and he that believeth not the Son shall not see life; but the wrath of God abideth on him.' (John iii. 36.) In speaking from this text, he said that the wrath of God rested on as many as believed not, wherever they went or whatever they did. This seemed to me to be very awful, and for a long time I felt as if this were my own case. On the 20th of June, when hearing Mr. Whitefield, the same words struck me as if the sword of divine justice was hanging over me, and even hell seemed less than my iniquities deserved. My feelings were such, that I was forced to cry out among the people on the brae. After sermon, I was assisted into the manse, thinking every moment that I was going to hell. Instructions were given me, but I was unable to attend to them. I was removed to another apartment, that I might engage in secret prayer. I tried to do so, and would fain have sung these lines :—

> ' How long wilt thou forget me, Lord?
>   Shall it for ever be?
>   O how long shall it be that thou
>   Wilt hide thy face from me?' (Ps. xiii. 1.)

But I was unable even to speak, and scarcely to draw breath.

"I was again assisted to go where I might hear sermon; but my distress continued. I remained all night, a good part of which, as well as the morning, I spent in prayer. These words were very terrible to me, 'Because I have called, and ye refused; I have stretched out my hand, and no man regarded; but ye have set at nought all my counsel, and would none of my reproof: I also will laugh at your calamity; I will mock when your fear cometh.' (Prov. i. 24–26.) I felt that it would be just for God so to deal with me. My sins stared me in the face. I saw them as dishonouring to him, especially my profaning the Lord's-day and his holy name, and my going up and down drinking and playing at cards, &c. Still I felt that I could not mourn as it became me. My heart was still hard.

"Soon after I joined a meeting of young lads for prayer. We met twice a-week. I had still a very deep sense of my guilt and unworthiness, wondering that the Lord should have spared me so long, and not cut me down as a cumberer of the ground. And when I observed persons going on in sin, I have been made to tremble; my very hair standing on end. At Calder sacrament, I heard Mr. Warden of Campsie preach from Isa. xlv. 22; and during the sermon these words came forcibly into my mind, 'But unto you that fear my name shall the Sun of Righteousness arise with healing in his wings; and ye shall go forth, and grow up as calves of the stall." (Mal. iv. 2.) This filled me with much joy, only I feared that I was still mixing up my own righteousness with that of Christ's; and I was all the while praying for sanctifying grace. On looking forward to the first sacrament at Cambuslang, where I commonly sat, that other passage proved useful, 'Not unto us, O Lord, not unto us, but unto thy name give glory, for thy mercy, and for thy truth's sake.' (Ps. cxv. 1.) It showed me more of my need to disown all but what is of God. I went to the communion, but profited little. On hearing that there was to be another soon, I was much engaged in preparation, and had joys and sorrows. During the Saturday night, which I spent in a yard near where the tent stood, I had great comfort and confidence in God, and in the unchangeableness of his love. My own heart was so filled with love and joy, that I found it easy to give and devote myself entirely to God, as reconciled to me in Christ; resolving, by his grace, to follow him through good and bad report. On Sabbath morning I was much engaged pleading for his presence that day as a conquering Saviour. When I went to the table, I besought him for a broken heart; and on receiving the elements, I had a lively and affecting sense of the sufferings of Christ brought before me. It seemed as if I had seen him evidently crucified, hanging, and bleeding, and dying on the cross; while my sins seemed saying, with the Jews, 'Crucify him, crucify him.' This sight melted me into tears. They ran down my cheeks. I could have wished they had been tears of blood, so heinous was I in my own sight. Tender expressions of Christ's love now rushed into my soul; and as one of the passages was immediately repeated by the minister serving the table (Mr. Bonar of Torphichen) I was so affected, that I thought I could have died for Christ. On retiring from the table, I went to the place where I had been the night before, and gave God thanks for his great goodness, and devoted myself anew to his service; resolving, with Joshua, that whatever others might do, I would serve the Lord. This frame continued with me a considerable time; and ever since I can say, that though in the former part of my life I could see no beauty in Christ, he is now to me altogether lovely, and I find my heart going out after him above all things. On going out to the fields, that I might engage in secret prayer, I have had lively discoveries made to me of the glory of God as shining forth in all around me—in the heavens, the earth, and the creatures about me; and this caused me the more to wonder at the goodness and love of God to such a sinner as I was. Sometimes I have had great enlargement of heart in prayer and other devotional duties. Sometimes, at my work, I have got such manifestations of the love of God to my soul, that I could have wished, had it been the divine will, to be removed out of this wilderness of sin and vanity, that I might for ever praise God; and yet I was at the same time willing to wait his pleasure and to do his will. And on observing others going on in sin, I wondered at God's patience; and this made me wonder more at his distinguishing love towards me, while others were left.

"After this I had many changes. Returning from Cambuslang, I was grievously tempted of the wicked one. I retired to some distance from those who were with me, and made my appeal to the Searcher of hearts, that God was my only portion, my chief good; and my faith grew stronger. As I arose from prayer, that word came sweetly home to me, 'My grace is sufficient for thee; for my strength is made perfect in weakness.' (2 Cor. xii. 9.) My soul was made again to rejoice. I laid hold anew on the grace and strength of Jesus Christ. I was enabled to renew my acceptance of him, as regarded his cross as well as his crown; and my feelings of love and gratitude were such as I thought eternity alone would suffice to declare. This state of feeling continued also for a considerable time.

"On another occasion, after being led to fear that I was after all a hypocrite, the Lord helped me thus: I had been on Sabbath morning pleading with God that he would enable his servant to speak from the heart to the heart, and that many might be awakened, as in a day of power, and that I might myself find a blessing; and so I went to one of the churches. The minister (Dr. Gillies of the College Church, Glasgow), in his sermon, quoting from Scripture, said, 'And ye will not come to me that ye might have life.' (John vi. 40.) This seemed a call to me, and I was enabled to renew my acceptance of Christ. My whole soul seemed to say, 'Behold, I come to thee; for thou art the Lord my God.' This was a gracious visit from God, for now it was light, whereas before I was in darkness. And this sweet temper of mind remained with me again for another period.

"In February 1743, I again fell into heaviness. Sometimes Satan seemed to restrain me from secret prayer. I persevered, but heavily, till the Lord again delivered me by his word. On the 22d of that month, I heard Mr. M'Culloch lecture on these words, 'I will betroth thee unto me for ever; yea, I will betroth thee in righteousness, and in judgment, and in loving-kindness, and in mercies; I will even betroth thee unto me in faithfulness; and thou shalt know the Lord.' (Hos. ii. 19, 20.) He observed, that the expression 'I will betroth thee,' was said three times. This seemed as if sent the more to confirm me. My faith became strong, my love warm, and mine eyes gushed with the tears of godly sorrow on account of my sins. All things seemed truly but as dross for the excellency of the knowledge of Jesus Christ my Lord. And this frame continues with me to the present day.

"I have often accepted of Christ as my Redeemer in all his offices—as my prophet, my priest, and my king. I now find the Bible to be as a new book. Every word of it is precious. I can scarcely be without it, wherever I go. I long for the Sabbath and other occasions of hearing the gospel, that I may receive another message from God, and love him the more for it. I have much pleasure in meetings for prayer, and am allowed much intercourse with God when so engaged. Besides stated prayer, from day to day, I am often sending up my petitions to God when at my work, and wherever I am."

God alone can truly judge of men's hearts, yet is there much in this case to show how very different the feelings of a man made thoroughly alive to divine things are, from the dreamy observance of religious duties, common among professors. And there is great truth in the remark, that he who would ever live on the borders of Satan's kingdom, ought not to expect the sunshine of Immanuel's land. An apostle speaks of even the righteous being " scarcely saved;" and this, we fear, is a very numerous class. It is our feeling, that much has been forgiven, which will cause us to love much. And this does not so much turn on our having had comparatively much to be forgiven, as on our knowing that our sins, which are in every case great, have been forgiven.

10. R. Barclay, an unmarried man, about twenty years of age:—

" When a child, I was put to secret prayer by my parents, and so long as they lived I kept up the form. Their example and precept urged me, but I had no delight in the exercise. I perhaps fell asleep in the middle of it, and when I awoke I scarcely knew what I had been saying. After the death of my parents, natural conscience urged me for a time to observe prayer, but irregularly and formally. In like manner, I went, though not regularly, to church; but the service seemed wearisome. When the lecture was over, I counted the task as half done, wishing the remaining half to be done also; and sometimes I had scarce patience to wait during the last prayer. One day, I went out at the first prayer, but my conscience checked me, as profaning the Lord's-day; yet was I afraid of returning, lest I should be noticed, and challenged by the elders.

" As regarded my conduct otherwise, I spent much of my time going up and down with my companions, engaging in vain and sinful amusements, such as playing at cards, drinking, and sometimes cursing and swearing. On going to England, I took still greater liberties, having none to reprove me. One time, while there, I heard Mr. Whitefield preach; but I was not benefited. After returning, I went not to any church for some time, making the want of suitable dress my excuse. I came to Cambuslang, that I might not be so much noticed by my acquaintances, and because I heard that many were getting good. The first day I came, Mr. M'Culloch preached from that text: ' He that believeth not God, hath made him a liar; because he believeth not the record that God gave of his Son.' (1 John v. 10.) He spoke much of the heinous nature of unbelief; but I could not at first see how what he said could apply to me, as I reckoned that my belief had all along been sound enough. But he proceeded to show, that if it gives great offence to an equal to be so treated, still more must it to a superior; still more to one who, as a king, is over all; and greatly more to Him who is King of kings, infinitely exalted above all creatures; and that every unbeliever, in every act of unbelief, gave God the lie. These statements did not strike me at the time, but they stuck by me, and had afterwards more effect upon me than all the sermons I had ever heard. That day fortnight, I again heard him from that saying in Luke xi. 21, 22: ' When a strong man armed keepeth his palace, his goods are in peace; but when a stronger than he shall come upon him, and overcome him, he taketh from him all his armour wherein he trusted, and divideth his spoils.' The palace, he said, meant the heart of man; the strong man, the devil; his goods, the lusts of the heart; the armour, those shifts, excuses, and pretences, which sinners, under Satan's teaching, use as covers and fences to their sins. By these, he added, they lull themselves asleep in carnal security. Such are inadequate views of sin, a fancy that they are in the way to heaven; or if awakened to concern, the belief that they are able to repent at pleasure, and that they have yet time enough. All this, and more to the same purpose, seemed to describe my very case. I found myself, my practice, my thoughts, and the workings of my heart, so exactly brought out, that it seemed as if no man could have so laid open my state. It seemed to be God himself convincing me and speaking to my heart. Now I saw that I was indeed an unbeliever, which I could hardly admit on hearing the same minister before. I was now reduced to great confusion and distress.

"Next day, when sitting at my work, the sermon on unbelief, and that on the devil keeping the palace of the heart, came fresh into my mind, and my convictions and distress grew to a great height. I seemed to be a rebel against God, and the most guilty of men; so that I was made to wonder at the patience of God in bearing so long with me, and that the earth did not now open her mouth and swallow me up where I sat. Thinking of myself as in league with Satan, and carrying on a war against God, I was overwhelmed with the thought, that he could at any moment turn the whole world into ashes, and, by his frown merely, send me to hell. I became persuaded that I as really deserved hell-fire as I did the penny which I had earned by my labours. Yet the Lord kept me from sinking into a state of despair. I still thought it possible that God might show me mercy. Satan, indeed, tempted me to conclude, that though there was mercy for others, I had gone beyond it. I was thrown into such a state, that I felt I could not submit my case, as some others had done, to ministers; but I was advised by an acquaintance to read my Shorter Catechism. I did so, and saw things in a new light. On coming to the question, 'What is effectual calling?' I was led to see that the Spirit of God was dealing with me, convincing me of my sin and misery; and I was made to hope that he would, in due time, enlighten my mind in the knowledge of Christ, and also renew my will, and so bring me to embrace and close with Christ in his gospel offer. And reading on till I came to that other question, 'What is repentance unto life?' I found what had till now been a dead letter, become a thing of life. Seeing, from the answer to this question, the mercy of God in Christ to penitent sinners, I wished to feel more of my sins, and to be delivered from them; and resolved, through divine grace, on a course of new obedience.

"From that day till now, nothing could ever satisfy me but a God reconciled in Christ. And this was my experience before hearing that Christ would, as the prophet of the church, reveal to me the will of God savingly, and so direct his ministers as to speak to my case. My thirst after gospel ordinances became now very great; and in returning from these, I usually sought to walk with such as had good memories, and were able to repeat a good deal of what they heard. I joined a prayer-meeting, and was always happy to hear from any what God had done for their souls; and when he was pleased to bless their sayings to me, I was made to rejoice.

"After being satisfied of Christ's ability to save me, I was some time before I got over the difficulty of believing that he was willing; but after a time, I saw that he was more willing than I was, and that, had it not been so, he would never have convinced me of my sin, and drawn my heart to him, so as to make me also willing. I got also a deep sense of my own inability, and became much afraid of mixing up my own righteousness, which I saw to be as filthy rags, with that of Christ's. I now forsook my former companions and sinful practices, and found the very thoughts of them bitter to my soul.

"Hearing that the sacrament was to be dispensed at Cambuslang, I was glad, and attempted some preparation, with the view of communicating. On the fast-day and Saturday I was much taken up with self-examination and prayer. On Sabbath I went to the table with holy fear, earnestly pleading for some token of the divine favour, with a proper sense of my own unworthiness; and the Lord was very gracious. My soul was filled with great joy and thankfulness. In the evening I heard Mr. Whitefield preach from the text, 'Thy Maker is thy husband; the Lord of hosts is his name; and thy Redeemer, the Holy One of Israel; The God of the whole earth shall he be called.' (Isa. liv. 5.) He showed how such as had chosen Christ for their husband should honour and obey him; and he gave some of the marks of such as were in these circumstances. I got liberty to apply these to myself, and was greatly rejoiced in spirit with the satisfying evidence of this my relation to Christ. The views which I now had of the glory of his person, and the sweetness of the relation in which he thus stands to his people, were also satisfying. Doubts were afterwards cast into my mind; yet from day to day I found my love increasing, so that if persecution had arisen, I believed that I could have laid down my life for Christ's sake.

" When I heard of a second communion, I rejoiced at the prospect of again sitting down at the Lord's table. After much prayer and other preparatory exercises, as well as hearing on the fast-day and the Saturday, I concluded that it was my duty to go forward. On sitting down at the table, I was again earnestly pleading; but it was not till the second element had reached, that I experienced as I afterwards did. It seemed as if with the cup it had been said to me by the Master himself, ' This is my blood, shed for the remission of *thy* sins.' This filled me with great joy; and this frame remained with me during the remainder of the day. Again, I was visited with doubt as if all had been a delusion, but through divine grace I was afterwards enabled to believe.

" Since then I have had many down-castings, but also many manifestations of God's love. I have now great delight in reading my Bible; and, blessed be God, he enables me to read it with some knowledge of what was before an unrevealed mystery. I have great pleasure in hearing the gospel, so that I can never hear enough. In every sermon which I hear I find some new and glad tidings. Sin of all sorts I abhor, and that not so much because of the shame and pain which follow, as on account of the dishonour it does to God, its crucifying Christ afresh, and polluting the soul so as to make it loathsome to God. As regards heart sins, I feel as the apostle describes it, from the 20th verse to the end of the 7th chapter of the Epistle of Paul to the Romans. As for my dealings with men, I love plainness and simplicity, and would not, if I could, take advantage of any. Sometimes I have my fears in looking forward to death; at other times I would be glad, were it the Lord's will that I should die instantly; and I often look and long for the blessed hope and glorious appearing of the Lord Jesus Christ, trusting that he will preserve me to his heavenly kingdom."

The general similarity of the change produced on different individuals will lessen the interest felt by many. Their appetite is for excitement, and this requires incident. But as so many specimens of a divine work, it is instructive to observe that, with a diversity of circumstances and dealings, the change is substantially the same in all. Men living in sin, have to be awakened—men already awakened, have to be led to Jesus. In attempting to walk, they cannot; in attempting to look, they cannot: and in these circumstances they cry to God. It is not now a saying of their prayers—they cry to God; and in fulfilment of the promise, the Spirit is given to lead them into truth, through a change of heart; and hence the fruits which now begin to appear.

11. Archibald Bell, a married man, about thirty-eight years of age, and by trade a tailor:—

"I was born in the Highlands; and as my parents lived far from any school, I was about fourteen years of age before I was taught to read, and even then I was at my apprenticeship, and dependent on others for the lessons I got. Still I was enabled to read the Bible, and I got also the Catechism by heart. I was put to secret prayer in my childhood, by my grandfather, and I continued to observe it, but not regularly, nor with good will. I also went to church, thinking it right to hear and read, and my outward conduct was free from gross sins; but I knew nothing of heart holiness, nor had I any liveliness in religious exercises, and I was wholly ignorant of that quickening power which I have since experienced in the gospel. I would have been glad to go to heaven, but I had no idea of what was wanting to prepare me for it. And on observing the miscarriages of some who attended meetings for prayer, I was apt to believe them insincere, or that religion was not what it is said to be.

"During the winter of 1742, I sometimes heard Mr. Hamilton of the Barony, and sometimes Mr. Fisher of the Secession, and found them both excellent gospel ministers. On hearing of the revival at Cambuslang, I thought that it must be of God; but before going there, I went to converse with a young woman of my acquaintance who had been there, and was said to be in great trouble of mind. I found her at the fire-side holding her Bible. I asked her how she came to be so troubled. She told me that it was by hearing Mr. Nasmith, a preacher at Cambuslang, who said, in the course of his sermon, 'He that believeth not, is condemned already.' On hearing these words, she was struck to the heart, and continued in great distress from that time down. This surprised me, as I had never felt in this way; and so I left her, strongly suspecting that there was something in religion of which I was wholly ignorant. And so I fell into a state of great terror. This, however, wore off, and although I went to Cambuslang, I experienced nothing more than ordinary.

"Hearing Mr. Hamilton of the Barony preach one day from these words, 'Blessed are they that mourn; for they shall be comforted' (Matt. v. 4), he remarked concerning the mourners who had this promise of comfort, that persons might be outwardly blameless, and might go the round of duties, might have some concern on account of sin, might go to the Lord's table out of regard to that ordinance, and yet be all the while strangers to true religion. This struck me to the heart, for I saw that I was one of the persons described. I sank down, and covered my face with my napkin, only I did not cry out. This was in the forenoon, and during the remainder of the sermon I continued in great distress. But in the afternoon, I heard a preacher from the words, 'O that men would praise the Lord for his goodness' (Ps. cvii.); showing for how many natural blessings we should praise God; which being unsuitable to *my* case, I allowed my fears again to be forgotten, concluding that they were imaginary.

"Some time after this, I was at Cambuslang, and heard Mr. Willison of Dundee speak, in his first prayer, of Christ coming to draw up poor perishing sinners out of the pit where there was no water, with the cords of salvation. I was made to weep, from mixed feelings of grief because of my condition and joy because of Christ's coming on such an errand of mercy. But this frame did not continue, only it left some concern on my mind about salvation.

" On a Saturday some time after this, I was again at Cambuslang; and after sermon, I went into the manse, where I heard Robert Wright, a good, grave man, pray among the distressed in the hall. At first, he seemed weak and straitened, but towards the end he was exceedingly strengthened. Several others prayed; after which Mr. M‘Culloch gave a short exhortation, dividing those present into several sorts— such as had got convictions, such as had not, or whose convictions had not come to a proper issue. Addressing these, he showed the necessity of convictions in order to conversion; and the others the necessity of conversion, so as to fit for communion with God here and afterwards in heaven. He remarked, that if it were possible for an unconverted man to reach the gate of heaven, and to look in at the employment of the blessed, he would have no wish to enter. He would not be able to witness the glory of Christ; and finding no company like himself, and struck with the fear of what he saw, he would hasten away. These remarks were too much for me. I had to support myself from falling by leaning on the wall, and I turned away my face, that my condition might not be observed. I saw that I was just such a person as had been described. I went home in great distress, praying as I was able by the way. On reaching home, I knew not what to do, but my wife advised me to go to bed. In bed, these words of the psalmist, 'I muse on the work of thy hands,' came into my mind; and so I resolved to meditate on the glorious work of man's redemption, and the great love of Christ in coming into the world to save sinners. I did so for a while, and afterwards fell asleep. In the morning, as I awoke, I blessed God in that I had been spared to see the light of a new day, and then I thought of it as the morning of the Lord's-day, the day of his resurrection, and that, if risen with Christ, I ought now especially to seek those things which are above. After getting up, and putting on my clothes, I went into a barn for secret prayer, and found wonderful enlargement. I became so inflamed and ravished with the love of Christ, that I thought, were it possible, I would fly after him on the wings of the wind. I lamented my having lived so long estranged from him. 'What a wretch,' said I, 'have I been, to live contented with myself so long, and in so woful a condition, not knowing the sweetness which is to be found in Christ and in communion with him!' I went that same Sabbath to Cambuslang, counting on its proving a glorious day of the Son of man, as it proved.

"Multitudes flocked thither, and so much did I feel, that I could, as I thought, have laid down my very life to help any of them to Christ. Mr. M'Culloch preached from these words, 'There are some of you that believe not.' (John vi. 64.) From this he showed, by many marks and characters, who they are that believe not. Every word of that sermon came with power to my heart, as if Jesus had said it, and to me alone. In this way I got a deeper sense of my unbelief, and was enabled to cast myself at his feet for mercy, closing with him on his own terms. My heart became sensibly warmed with love to Christ; and so joyful was I, as to wish that all present had shared my feelings; and I continued in this state all day, and on my way home, resolving to return the day following to join in the giving of thanks for what had been experienced by others as well as by me. And on my way back, I was again so transported with the love and loveliness of Christ, that I wondered how any could refrain from crying out in his praises. I scarcely knew where I was going or what I was doing, so much was I filled with a sense of his condescending grace to one so vile and filthy with sin.

"Again I had comfort in what I had heard, and in the exercises of prayer and praise; but after getting home, unbelief so prevailed, that it seemed as if I had been only deceiving myself. This renewed my distress, which continued for several days, till, in family worship, I was enabled anew to lay hold on Christ, and all my comfort returned.

"On several occasions, the difficulty of living to God had nearly overcome me; but his promises proved my help. When the first communion at Cambuslang came round, I desired much to give myself to God at his table; and after many struggles, as well as preparation, I did communicate, and had much comfort. When I approached the end of the table, the Lord was with me after a very sensible manner, and at the table I had great comfort in giving myself anew to God.

"During the summer of 1742, I went very often to Cambuslang; and although I had not always sensible enjoyment, yet I cannot say that I ever left without being enabled to resolve anew to serve Christ, and in some measure strengthened for his service.

"And now, I am at a point with the world—I care not for its riches or profits. If I have food and raiment, I hope therewith to be content; and these I hope the Lord will not deny me. And as to pleasure, I wish that I may never meet with anything to draw away my heart from things spiritual. I am not without my fears that I may yet fall away, or even have doubts as to my state; but that which usually bears me up under such fears, is some word of promise that the Lord may have before given me, or that he sends me in times of darkness. I hope that he has made with me a well-ordered covenant, sure and everlasting; Christ having in it undertaken for his people, whether as to their debt or their duty. The whole of this is true, and there is more than I can express in words."

In this case, there is more simplicity and fewer changes than in most. It does not, however, spread over so long a period as some, which may be partly the cause. And there is one truth, common to most, but very evident here, namely, that "we live by faith, not by sight." This is a sad stumbling-block to many. They expect that, on obtaining light, it should continue to shine; that on being reconciled to God, his love should ever be their resting-place; whereas these, as to sensible enjoyment, are both dependent on a continued exercise of faith. The condition remains unchanged, but not the feeling of that condition; God's love is unchangeable, but not man's apprehension of it; and so it is that God is still light, though the believer be in darkness. How? Simply because God is what he is of himself, and man is what he is of another, and of that other only through faith, which is an exercise of a changeable and imperfect creature.

12. James Tenant, an unmarried man, about twenty years of age:—

"I was exhorted by my parents to read my Bible, attend public ordinances, and pray in secret; and so long as I was under their care I kept up a form of religion; but on leaving home, I neglected the advices I had received, was led away with light and frothy companions, and had no serious thoughts till within these twelve months past. During my time of neglect, my conscience sometimes smote me; but when the temptation returned, I fell anew into sin. On hearing about the people that had been awakened at Cambuslang, I went to see them. I had no desire to hear on my own account, but wished to see the awakened. On seeing them, I was concerned on their account, but not on my own. Sometimes, on returning home, I wondered what could affect them, seeing I felt nothing. When engaged at my work, it seemed as if their cries were still ringing in my ears, and yet I could not help returning; and as I again heard the mourning of those awakened, I still wondered how it could be so with them and not with me.

Hearing Mr. M'Culloch preach from John v. 42, 'But I know you, that ye have not the love of God in you,' I felt what put me a little to a stand concerning myself and others. But no sooner had I left the place, than my uneasiness left me. Still, I had more and more of a desire to return, and so I was constrained to go out every Lord's-day and every Thursday. I had now some faint resolutions to leave off frequenting bad company, but these always gave way before the temptation, only I could not endure any to speak evil of the work at Cambuslang; and when asked why I left the minister of the place and went there, my answer was, 'Because I had more pleasure in hearing there than at home.'

"But the first thing which really awakened me, was a lecture which I heard there towards the end of June, from Mr. Whitefield, on the conversion of the Philippian jailer. When he was speaking of the jailer's trembling, and falling down, and crying out, 'What shall I do to be saved?' my conscience began to tell me that I was of all others lost and undone, unless the Lord should in pity deliver me. I fell into great terror, and trembled so much, that I had to be supported by those near. Still I had some glimmering of hope, believing Christ to be able and willing to save sinners, and so I began to pray. But not having had *particular* convictions of sin, I saw myself only in the general in a state of condemnation. I was taken to the manse to hear the exhortations usually addressed to the awakened; but as there was no minister present, I went to my quarters, and then to the fields, attempting to pray, and especially pleading for a more thorough sense of my sins and true condition. After being above an hour so engaged, I was much impressed with these words of the Saviour, 'I came not to call the righteous, but sinners to repentance.' (Matt. ix. 13.) From the bottom of my heart, I saw myself to be one of the chief of sinners. Special sins, and particularly such as were gross, as profanation of the Lord's-day, keeping loose company, slighting the admonitions of parents, and doing nothing in church, but looking about me. I went to my quarters, lay in bed for an hour or so, and again went forth to the fields, that I might give vent to my feelings in pleading with God. My chief petition was, that he would enable me to take his yoke upon me, which I felt I was unable of myself to do; and this I was led to hope would be granted.

" On hearing Mr. Whitefield again, I was again seized with great fear and trembling, because of the wickedness of my heart and life, and was therefore unable to follow all he said. After this I followed him to Calder sacrament. Some advised me to go to the Lord's table, but the sense which I had of my own unworthiness prevented me. Still I attended all the days as a hearer, and learned from what I heard much of my own sinful condition. One night, when engaged in prayer with some others in a barn, I got a clear discovery of myself as still in an unconverted state; and so strong and piercing were my convictions that I was forced to cry out before all present. On the meeting being dismissed, I went alone, and besought God not to allow my convictions to abate till I should attain to a thorough change of heart; that he would graciously lift upon me the light of his reconciled countenance, and give me a continued hatred of sin. Now I was enabled to lay hold on the promise, ' Fear thou not; for I am with thee: be not dismayed; for I am thy God: I will strengthen thee; yea, I will help thee; yea, I will uphold thee with the right hand of my righteousness.' (Isa. xli. 10.) My heart was now filled with the love of Christ. I was made to rejoice in him and in all his ordinances, and to praise him because he had dealt so bountifully with my soul. For several days I could do nothing but praise God for what he had done, and pray that he might perfect what I trusted he had begun; and ever since I have felt a strong love to the people of God, whose company before I used to abhor. I love also to be in the house of God, sitting under the droppings of the gospel, whereas before I had a strong aversion to everything of the kind. My

M

Bible also is now my delight, especially as it unfolds to me discoveries of God's love and mercy to poor sinners."

After detailing temptations which were overcome, and how God delivered him from these, he goes on to say:—

" I resumed my visits to Cambuslang on Sabbath and some of the week-days, and on these occasions I have often been quite overcome with a sense of divine love; but sometimes on the way I have been anew tempted with unbelieving thoughts, as if ordinances were vain. After committing my case to God. I saw it to be my duty to persevere in the observance of these and in my course of Christian conversation. This was impressed on me, particularly from these words, ' If any man draw back, my soul shall have no pleasure in him.' (Heb. x. 38.) One good effect of this trial was to awaken in me great fear of backsliding, through the neglect of commanded duty.

" When the first communion was about to be given at Cambuslang, I set about preparation for the due observance of that holy ordinance, especially by pleading for clearer views of my state. On the preparation Sabbath, I experienced, under Mr. M'Culloch's preaching, growing freedom in giving myself to God, a deeper sense of my own unworthiness, and some measure of confidence in looking forward to the ordinance. On the fast-day and Saturday I found no sensible enjoyment, and was in consequence discouraged. On Saturday night and Sabbath morning I was again engaged in prayer. During the action-sermon I was sustained, yet had many fears, till, as Mr. Whitefield addressed the table at which I sat, these all vanished, and the words of the apostle rushed into my mind, ' All are yours, and ye are Christ's and Christ is God's.' On retiring from the table, I engaged in secret prayer, giving God thanks for his great goodness, and beseeching him for grace to walk worthy of the profession I had now made before so many witnesses. These words came then home with power, ' I will have mercy on whom I will have mercy, and I will have compassion on whom I will have compassion.' (Rom. ix. 15.) This was laying open to me a strong foundation, which gave me great comfort; and as I continued pleading, I felt, with Joshua, that as for me I would serve the Lord. Nothing remarkable occurred during the evening or Monday services; but when all was over, I could scarcely settle at my work, I was so taken up with prayers and praises, and with recalling what I had heard. I had even a desire to depart, that I might be free from sin, and that I might not again fall back from my stedfastness; and this frame continued with me very fully for fourteen days, and, although in a less measure, it continued till the time of the second communion.

"On hearing that there was to be a second communion, I greatly rejoiced; and when it came round, I had much peace and comfort, especially on Monday morning, when Mr. Webster read as his text Luke xii. 32: 'Fear not, little flock; for it is your Father's good pleasure to give you the kingdom.' After this, I returned to my work and ordinary place of residence."

From this till the 19th of March 1743, when this account was drawn up, he continued, subject to the changes common to the people of God, to hold on in his Christian course; and the following is the summary which he gives of his condition then:—

"Though now I am not so sensible of the workings of the Spirit of God within me as formerly, yet through grace I can say, with the psalmist,—

'Nevertheless continually,
O Lord, I am with thee;'

And with the apostle, 'My conversation is in heaven, from whence I look for my Saviour;' and that my chief desire is to walk before God, in righteousness and holiness, all the days of my life.' I have been forecasting sufferings for Christ, and sometimes I think that I could lay down my life for him, while at other times I fear that I might draw back; and it is my prayer that the Lord would strengthen me. My feelings are similar concerning death. I have sometimes had a desire to depart and be with Christ, while at other times I shrink from the thought; but my hope is, that He who is to be judge of all, is now my advocate within the veil, and that when he appears, it will be for my salvation. It is my practice to pray for the church of God, that the Lord would revive his own work throughout the land and throughout the earth; that very many, who are now dead in trespasses and sins, may be quickened and brought home to God; yea, I hope that there will be such an ingathering of souls to Christ, as to resemble flocks of doves hastening to their windows. And, in conclusion, I long to be perfect in holiness, and to begin that never-ending song: ' Unto him that loved us, and washed us from our sins in his own blood, and hath made us kings and priests unto God and his Father; to him be glory and dominion for ever and ever. Amen.'"

Let any one now compare the person so speaking of himself with what he was only a twelvemonth before, and then say whether there be not a practical reality in the words of Scripture: " If any man be in Christ, he is a new creature: old things are passed away; behold, all things are become new" (2 Cor. v. 17); and farther, whether if this be the case, very many are not satisfied with a condition which will at last deceive them. " Examine yourselves, whether ye be in the faith; prove your own selves. Know ye not your own selves, how that Jesus Christ is in you, *except ye be reprobates?*" (2 Cor. xiii. 5.)

CHAPTER XI.

A SELECTION OF CASES PREPARED FROM THE SECOND MANUSCRIPT VOLUME.

There are upwards of sixty cases in this volume; and these differ in various particulars from those of the other. They had not been revised, as those of the other volume; most of them have been copied, but not in the same hand, and a few are still in the hand-writing apparently of the parties themselves; they seem to have been drawn up at a later period—some in 1744, and following years; they are also gathered from a wider extent of country. There is an index, from which may be learned concerning them not only the names and ages, but also the circumstances of the parties; not a few stop short in detailing grounds sufficient for any conclusive judgment; but many are full and interesting, containing also fewer repetitions and passages unnecessary for publication, than those of the other volume; and they contain a greater variety of reference to the work of God in different parishes. Still, from the general similarity of circumstances, it would be tedious to rehearse any considerable number, at least fully; and to secure, as far as may be, the advantage of numbers, with the avoidance of repetition, we shall only give a few pretty full, and a greater number more briefly.

1. Bailie Weir of Hamilton, a married man, aged fifty, and who had received in early life a classical education:—

"I was trained to a habit of prayer in early life, but as I

grew up, I very much laid it aside, and never engaged in it with pleasure. I attended church mainly from custom. I was at the same time fond of idle company, and given to card-playing and drinking even to excess, and so it continued till about two years ago. About the end of February 1742, I went to Cambuslang, and hearing Mr. M'Culloch speak of the exceeding sinfulness of sin, as dishonouring to God, and as having pierced the Saviour, I felt *strangely*, and got such a sense of my own sins both of heart and of life, that I could have torn myself to pieces in revenge, and it was with difficulty that I could restrain myself from crying out.

" The distress into which I was now thrown continued for about a month, during which I thought that I should have gone distracted. I went to Cambuslang every Sabbath, and often on week-days, and got clearer and clearer views and convictions of my sinful and lost condition. I was also led more into the exercise, or attempted exercise, of secret prayer. But this I found to be no easy duty. I have been half-an-hour on my knees before I felt that I could pray; and I was often tempted to leave off my fruitless endeavours to turn to God, as if it were now too late. Still I could not but return anew to Cambuslang; and about the end of the month, when turning to a passage cited, that other passage cast up, ' Look unto me, and be ye saved, all the ends of the earth; for I am God, and there is none else.' (Isa. xlv. 22.) O what a greedy grasp did my soul make at Christ on reading these words! My mind became calm. In about an hour, these other words gave me farther help: ' The blood of Jesus Christ, his Son, cleanseth from all sin.' (1 John i. 7.) I came straight home, went to my closet, and found freer access than ever I had before; and as I rose from my knees, I saw in Christ a perfect sufficiency to deliver and cleanse me from all sin, and in the excellences of his person so much of willingness and grace, that I could not but love him and give myself wholly to him in love.

"And ever since that time all things seem new. Hearing God's word preached, praying and praising God in my family, and engaging in my own secret exercises of devotion, give me real delight. In hearing and communicating I see more and more of Christ's beauty and desirableness, more and more of his fulness and suitableness, and my soul is more and more led out into a hearty and rejoicing approval of God's method of saving sinners. My soul now trembles at the very thought of sin; and when I look back and see what I was, the very thought is terrible; and yet I daily feel that I have about me a body of sin and death, which causes me to heave many a heavy groan, and even sigh to be delivered by a removal from the body. My delights are now in converse, not with the men of the world, but the people of God. My love of the world has given way to the preciousness of Christ; so that the things which were formerly matters of ambition and sinful indulgence, are now tasteless. What I now covet is the righteousness of Christ; to whose name be all the glory!"

2. Mrs. Weir, also of Hamilton, apparently the wife of the above, and aged twenty-eight:—

"I had the advantage of being brought up religiously, was taught to pray twice a-day, and this I have continued all along, sometimes enjoying in this and other religious exercises much sweetness. The consciousness of this and the general consistency of my conduct induced the belief that I was in a good way. But in 1740, 1741, and for some years before, I fell off, became worldly-minded, irregular in my attendance on divine ordinances, and listless in their observance. Hearing of the awakening in Cambuslang, I went thither in March, and heard Mr. M'Culloch preach from 2 Cor. v. 17: 'If any man be in Christ, he is a new creature: old things are passed away; behold, all things are become new.' From the mark given, I concluded that I had not undergone this change; and the following words quoted in the sermon went to my heart: 'If any man draw back, my soul shall have no pleasure in him.' (Heb. x. 38.) I continued in deep distress for many days. One morning, on retiring to secret prayer, I found that I could pray none—my heart was hard as a stone; and yet Satan and my own deceitful imaginations would have it that all was nevertheless well. I knew this to be untrue, and taking up my Bible and beseeching God to direct me and give me light, I turned to the 60th chapter of Isaiah, with which I was much affected, particularly the 19th and 20th verses. God so blessed to me the reading of this chapter, that I felt the load taken off, the love of Christ being shed abroad in my heart. I scarcely knew where I was, and my tongue became as the pen of a ready writer. But again darkness settled upon me—all seemed to be but hypocrisy, and I was again in distress.

"I went again to Cambuslang. My soul was lifted up in singing, as we entered, at the beginning of the 34th psalm, and my joy was increased when Mr. M'Culloch read as his text 1 John v. 10: 'He that believeth on the Son hath the witness in himself: he that believeth not God, hath made him a liar; because he believeth not the record that God gave of his Son.' From this sermon I was made to see the great evil of unbelief, which I saw not before. I felt as if I could now cleave to Christ by a living faith; but again after returning home, I was anew thrown back, which sent me anew to prayer and to God's faithful promises, till I was even filled with peace and joy in believing. Since that time I have also experienced many changes—I have been cast down and afterwards lifted up, so as to lay hold on the promises, and thus to essay a life of faith.

"And now I can say—to the glory of His grace be it said—that for upwards of two years, the prevailing and habitual bent of my heart has been on things spiritual, whereas aforetime it was towards the things of this world. Formerly, these were in my thoughts when I went to bed and when I awoke; now God's testimonies take their place. My fellowship is, to some considerable extent, truly with the Father and his Son Christ Jesus. I see a glory in

Christ, and a suitableness to all my wants, and I feel resigned to his will, so that I even sometimes desire to be absent from the body, that I may be for ever with the Lord."

3. John Parker, a wauker and dyer at Busby, in the parish of Carmunnock, unmarried, aged twenty-three:—

"My parents being both religiously disposed, I had the advantage of obtaining a good education and of having a proper example set before me. I was trained to the habit of observing secret prayer, and of waiting on God in family worship and in the services of the sanctuary. These habits I continued all along; and I was in everything external sober, and of becoming conduct. I also recollect that many of my feelings in early life had a religious tendency. I was accustomed to confess my sins before God in prayer; I even bewailed them with many tears. When hearing the word preached, I was sometimes distressed because of my shortcomings, but sought refuge in the saying, that no one does all he should do. I recollect being much affected reading various religious books, such as Willison on the Sacrament, the Life of Elizabeth West, and a work written by Isaac Ambrose. One Sabbath evening, when reading in the Bible concerning Elijah's being carried up to heaven, and Elisha crying out, 'My father, my father! the chariot of Israel and the horsemen thereof' (2 Kings ii. 12), I felt my heart melt wonderfully; but this lasted only for the night. On recovering from a dangerous fever, my father came up to me in the fields, and told me that he had been much exercised on my account during my illness, and that he had vowed to God, should it be his will to spare me, that I should be specially devoted to his service; and proceeding upon this, he exhorted me, with great earnestness, to give myself to God in Christ. I felt much while he addressed me. At another time, I was listening to the exhortation of a communion table in Carmunnock church, and I was so impressed that I almost cried out among the people; and yet, after all, my heart required only temptation to discover its folly. So much was I set on attending fairs and weddings, and enjoying every kind of merriment, that if my money had been equal to my wishes, I would have been ready for every occasion which offered. Although I went the round of all outward duties, I am persuaded that this was little else than the fruit of education and example, and of these acting on a natural conscience. I had flashes of religious feelings, yet they left no *abiding* effects. In this state I was admitted to the Lord's table four times. On the first occasion I was guilty, I fear, of presumption; on the other times I had more searching of heart, striving against corruption, and even meltings because of sin. Many of these things look very like saving grace, yet am I now persuaded that I was all the while in an unchanged state.

"At length, in September 1741, I heard Mr. Whitefield preach on a Sabbath morning, in the High Church-yard of Glasgow, from the text, 'They have healed also the hurt of the daughter of my people slightly, saying, Peace, peace; when there is no peace.' (Jer. vi. 14.) After describing what it is to have a false peace, he said, 'If ye have no other peace but this, it is a peace of the devil's making.' These words came home to me with such power as to throw me into a state of great confusion. I could scarcely attend to what was farther said. I went into the High Church, and during the psalms I felt, as I had often done, a passing glow of emotion. In the evening, I heard Mr. Whitefield again in the church-yard. His text was, 'The kingdom of God is not meat and drink; but righteousness, and peace, and joy in the Holy Ghost.' (Rom. xiv. 17.) As soon as the text was read, my heart began to melt; but as he went on opening up the subject, I felt my whole soul melted, and I became flooded with tears. I felt especially that he was describing my own case, when he said, 'Many of you seem very good and devout during a communion season, but a little after you will be as vain and carnal as ever.' *Now* I felt that I was still in a lost state, and my heart was ever crying,

' What shall I do to be saved? Hearing a minister speak of what it was to look upon Him whom we had pierced, and to mourn for him as one mourneth for his only son (Zech. xii. 10), I felt as if, though all my friends and relations had but recently died, I could not so mourn for them as I then felt and bewailed my sins as dishonouring to God; yet, nevertheless of my deep and very painful sense of the evil of sin, I had no fear of hell or of the wrath to come. When the preacher opened up to us what the kingdom of God is, his words fell on my heart with unwonted power. When exhorting, towards the close of his sermon, he bade such as had obtained a sense of their lost condition, and had not yet found Christ, cast themselves at his feet, there to perish if they were to perish; knowing that *there* no one had ever yet been allowed to perish. I thought this to be good news, and was enabled heartily to comply. During prayer after sermon, I stood up and felt as if my condition had been much altered. I was now calm, and my heart seemed softened. I went home, took my dinner comfortably, and then retired to secret prayer; and when so engaged, I said, among other things, ' Now, O Lord, I renounce all righteousness of my own, and am willing to submit to the righteousness of Christ.' I was thus enabled to close with Christ in all his offices, and, under a deep sense of my own helplessness, to look to him and the fulness which is treasured up in him.

" After this, I continued long in a very desirable frame, enjoying much calmness and satisfaction of mind. Often, when engaged at my worldly calling, my heart was melted because of sin, and much occupied with meditations on things spiritual. I also frequently retired, to be alone with God in prayer. About two weeks after, and on the morning of the Lord's-day, I turned up my Bible, that I might find a suitable passage for meditation while I was on my way to church, and these words occurred: ' That he would grant you, according to the riches of his glory, to be strengthened with might by his Spirit in the inner man.'

(Eph. iii. 16.) They laid deep hold of my mind. I kept meditating on them, and offering them to God as my prayer nearly all the way; and I was so filled with a sense of their power, that my tears scarcely ceased to flow while I walked. Much of this frame continued during worship, especially in the time of singing and prayer, so that I could not forbear saying to myself, 'Lord, I now feel thy blessed Spirit at work in my soul.' On one occasion I had been praying much that the Lord would direct his servant whom I was to hear to what would prove useful to me. He preached on John iii. 3, respecting the new birth; and as he went along explaining it, and fixing the marks of a true change, my heart kept pace, and I was enabled to see them all in my own soul. One night, after having done with my work, I took up 'Vincent on True Love to an Unseen Saviour.' In reading, and praying over what I read, my heart was wonderfully filled with a sense of divine love. When going to bed, and long after, passages expressive of the love which subsists between Christ and his people were ever occurring, as fitly expressing what I felt.

"In these times I began to see many things, which formerly seemed indifferent, now to be sinful; and as I saw them to be so, I left them off. One of these was the practice of associating with others between sermons in the church-yard and elsewhere, and thus spending the interval in carnal conversation. I now saw this to be sinful, and a mean of doing away with impressions which had been made in the forenoon; and from this time forward I have avoided it, seeking rather to be alone for meditation and prayer. Another was the practice of singing foolish and sometimes not over-chaste ballads, to while away the time. I found from experience the evil of this and other kindred amusements, and I committed to memory instead of these, portions of the Psalms, which I chanted over when at my work, and found in them as much delight as I had ever done in the other. Some of the passages which greatly delighted me were, Ps. xxvii. 8, cxix. 60. It was about this time, also, that I found great sweetness in these words: 'For to me to live is Christ, and to die is gain.' (Phil. i. 21.) Repeating these words as my own, it occurred to ask whether I was entitled to speak of myself as an apostle had done. And I was led to see that, though in many things I had no pretension to use his language, yet in this I felt that the language was fitting to me as well as to him.

"Family worship became now very delightful. I can say, to the praise of sovereign grace, that many a time has my soul been delighted when engaged in this exercise. One day in particular, when the master of the family read the 4th chapter of the First Epistle of John, it seemed to me as if it particularly suited my case. These words, 'God is love,' met with such a response in my breast as to convince me that, dwelling in love, I had my dwelling in God, and he in me. (Verse 16.)

"One day when engaged in secret prayer, I found great enlargement in pleading for the revival of God's work throughout the land, and for the spreading abroad of the gospel all over the world; and I was at the same time enabled to plead for my friends, companions, and acquaintances. A minister, preaching on God's answering his people's prayer sometimes by fire, exhorted us to seek that we might obtain answers by the fire of divine love being sent into our hearts. This seemed to be my very experience. On some occasions I had felt so much of the love of God coming into my soul, that I had also fancied my very body to be warmed thereby. At other times, however, I have been straitened in prayer, and have been greatly cast down because of sin and indwelling corruption, even to such an extent as to make me cry out, 'O wretched man that I am! who shall deliver me from the body of this death?' (Rom. vii. 24.) Yet here also the Lord was often very gracious. On one occasion, these words were to me as a healing balsam: 'The Lord will perfect that which concerneth me.' (Ps. cxxxviii. 8.)

"When the awakening broke out in Cambuslang in

February 1742, I was much rejoiced, and went thither to hear sermon; and after coming home, I was so much overjoyed, that I felt it difficult to restrain myself, even during dinner; and hastening to be alone, I had much freedom in believing that God would yet pour forth farther blessings.

" During the spring and summer, my feelings were less lively, yet I had abiding desires after what was good; I continued much in secret duty; I was helped to great earnestness in pleading. I got more and more insight into the hidden springs of my corruption, and I was enabled to abstain from causes of sin. I was often in difficulties, but had many gracious outgates, and often by means of some passage of Scripture, particularly in the Psalms, such as Ps. xxx. 6–12. One time, while meditating on the Redeemer's sufferings, I got my heart melted anew, on account of sin, and because of his great love in dying for poor sinners, and particularly as regarded myself. In March, I heard Mr. M'Culloch at Cambuslang on the text, ' A bruised reed shall he not break, and the smoking flax shall he not quench.' (Isa. xlii. 3.) I was enabled to attend with great earnestness; and on returning home, what I had heard was made useful, as were also various passages, particularly from the 54th chapter of Isaiah. Going again to Cambuslang on a Saturday evening, I heard Mr. M'Culloch preach from that other text, ' The heart is deceitful above all things, and desperately wicked; who can know it?' (Jer. xvii. 9.) This gave me such a view of myself as greatly to humble me. On Sabbath, he preached from these words, ' Thou hast ascended on high, thou hast led captivity captive: thou hast received gifts for men; yea, for the rebellious also, that the Lord God might dwell among them.' (Ps. lxviii. 18.) In speaking from these words, he took occasion to speak of the duty of restitution; and so much was my conscience made to feel alive to whatever appeared duty, that I could not be at peace till I went to my master and offered him some small gratuities I had received in his service, and which, as now appeared, belonged rather to him than to me. He set me right in this matter, and refused to accept of anything. Still I remained in a state of comparative bondage of spirit, till reading a sermon of Mr. Whitefield's on the Evidences of Regeneration, I became again satisfied, and was so far relieved. The 126th psalm came also home to my mind with great sweetness, so that I sung it for very joy, and my bonds seemed loosened.

" Still I was left to know that I was yet in the wilderness, sometimes making way in my journey, and at other times turning back and becoming discouraged because of the way. I was not allowed to be ever singing the song of triumph, as on my escape from Egypt. I went to the communion at Cathcart in May 1742; but both on Saturday and during the forenoon sermon, my heart was very hard and dead, and it was little better at the table, which grieved me much. The minister who addressed the table spoke much concerning the sufferings of Christ, and then offered this as a test, that if any of the communicants failed to be affected with what had been said, they ought not to be there. I was deeply humbled in being so little affected, but felt as if this were going too far. Between sermons, I retired to a secret place, and got some freedom in prayer, particularly in reading and turning into a prayer the last section of the 119th psalm. The evening sermon was on these words, ' O Lord, revive thy work in the midst of the years, in the midst of the years make known; in wrath remember mercy.' (Hab. iii. 2.) In speaking from these words, the preacher said, that such as had never been concerned about the salvation of others had reason to suspect their own state. This was helpful to me, as God had truly given me a heart to be often deeply concerned for others. On Monday, I was still farther refreshed, although my joy fell greatly short of what it had once been.

" I also attended the communion at Kilbride that summer; still seeking Him whom my soul loved; but I had no sensible enjoyment during any of the days. Sitting by myself before the Sabbath evening sermon, I felt myself depressed, and that word, ' No man cared for my soul,' came home as if descriptive of my state; but when in danger of giving way to melancholy feelings, that other word proved a comforter: ' The Lord God hath given me the tongue of the learned, that I should know how to speak a word in season to him that is weary.' (Isa. l. 4.) Matters still remained, however, in a very unsatisfactory state, till the Friday after, when I had become so distressed as, with Jonah, even to desire death rather than life. It was in these circumstances that light as of God broke in upon my mind, conveying to me with great power these precious words: ' But unto you that fear my name, shall the Sun of Righteousness arise with healing in his wings; and ye shall go forth and grow up as calves of the stall.' (Mal. iv. 2.) After praying also that the Lord would satisfy me with his goodness, I was looking for some promise on which I might be enabled to lay hold, when that saying came into my heart with such sweetness and satisfaction, that I could desire no more: ' For the mountains shall depart, and the hills be removed; but my kindness shall not depart from thee, neither shall the covenant of my peace be removed, saith the Lord that hath mercy on thee.' (Isa. liv. 10.) I could wish for nothing more, and therefore I sang to God, with great delight, the whole of the 116th psalm.

"At the first communion which was held at Cambuslang, in July the same summer, I heard a sermon from these words: ' For unto us a child is born, unto us a son is given; and the government shall be upon his shoulder; and his name shall be called Wonderful, Counsellor, The mighty God, The everlasting Father, The Prince of Peace (Isa. ix. 6); which was brought home with great delight to my soul. On Monday, I heard another discourse from the saying, ' Let this mind be in you which was also in Christ Jesus.' (Phil. ii. 5.) On hearing the text, I said to myself, ' Let these words be written in a book;' and the discourse itself was brought home to me with so much sweetness and power, that I besought the Lord to write what I had heard on the pages of my heart.

" After this I was again cast down; and in looking forward to the second communion at Cambuslang, I employed myself in preparatory exercises. I recollected, among other things, that in the observance of the passover, the leaven had to be searched out with lighted candles; and I besought the Lord to give me light in searching my heart, for the leaven of hypocrisy, malice, or wickedness, and to give me help in putting it away. I gave myself also, soul, body, and spirit, to God, accepting in covenant God the Father, Son, and Holy Ghost, as my God, in the capacity of Father, Redeemer, and Sanctifier; and this also I subscribed with my hand unto the Lord. On the fast-day I heard a sermon in the afternoon, from these words, ' He that hath the bride is the bridegroom' (John iii. 29); which proved very refreshing. On Sabbath, after three tables had been served, I went to prayer alone, and had great melting of heart, after which I communicated, but without experiencing anything remarkable. From the table I went to one of the tents, where, hearing from these words, ' He is altogether lovely' (Song v. 16), every word was to me sweeter than honey. Truly, Christ was to my soul altogether lovely.

" And now, to draw to a close. Whereas I had experienced some kind of heart-meltings and feelings of love to God before September 1741, and thought myself sincere and heavenly while these lasted, yet they soon wore away and left me where I was, I cannot otherwise judge of them than that they were not the genuine fruits of a saved state. And whereas ever since that time, the habitual bent of my heart has been after communion with God, and conformity to his will, I cannot otherwise judge than that since that period my state has been different. I admit that my heart often wanders and turns aside from God in duty; but he himself knows *that I am never happy in such a state*—that I can never rest satisfied in such a state; that my poor heart, like the mariner's needle, when *jogged* to either side, is never at rest when turned aside from Christ, till, trembling and disquieted, it returns anew to the point of attraction—a God reconciled in Christ, in whose bosom, and there only, it can find rest. To God, therefore, as reconciled in Christ, be all the glory. Amen."

4. Daniel M'Larty, son to Angus M'Larty, weaver in the parish of Kirkmichael, Knapdale, Argyleshire, unmarried, aged twenty-one, and employed as a servant in Paisley :—

" When twelve years of age I was put to school, where I was taught to read the Bible in English, and the psalm-book in Gaelic, which was my mother-tongue. In early life I was given to many vices, and I was not accustomed to prayer till about five years ago, that I went to reside in a religious family. Observing the others to retire daily to their secret devotion, I seemed to myself singular in the neglect of that duty, and so set about it twice a-day; but my devotion was merely in form. I also read my Bible, and not without some measure of interest; and all along I went to church, and sometimes resolved on following out what I had heard; but my resolutions were not abiding. At length, on hearing of the revival at Cambuslang, in February 1742, I thought that I might get some good by going, and so I went frequently, and was not without concern in hearing, but my desire was to feel greatly more. And so when hearing Mr. Hamilton of Douglas one day preaching from Exod. v. 3, 'The God of the Hebrews hath met with us,' the very words of the text arrested and alarmed me. And when I heard Mr. M'Culloch preach from that other text, 1 John v. 10, and showing the heinous nature of unbelief, in making 'God a liar,' and declare that of this very sin all the unregenerate before him were guilty, I was impressed and astonished. I admitted, concerning myself, that I was guilty of unbelief; but that I was, in this, guilty of a sin similar to that of crucifying Christ, which he said was the case, I could not see, and would not bear to have said; and so I resolved to hear Mr. M'Culloch no more. Next Sabbath I accordingly remained away, but I afterwards returned, and hearing him on that and other subjects, came to feel that I was verily guilty of what he described, and was in consequence very uneasy, but not so distressed as some others, or as I thought necessary to a true sense of my condition. Still I continued to attend at Cambuslang; to pray not only formally, but also in my heart, and my condition was seldom absent from my mind. In these circumstances, I often experienced considerable liberty, and was even haunted with a spirit of self-righteousness. But on hearing Mr. Whitefield, at the sacrament of Kilbride, preach from John ix. 35, 'Dost thou believe on the Son of God?' I found comfort. The marks which he gave of a believing state, and as warranting an approach to the Lord's table, were such as I thought I could claim, and so I resolved to go forward at Cambuslang. But after much thought, examination of my Bible, and prayer, and even after I had got a token from Mr. M'Culloch, I had much fear. On Friday before the sacrament, I spent most of the night in secret prayer on Rutherglen green, where I had some manifestations of the love of Christ, and my soul was filled with joy. This continued on Saturday and on Sabbath during the action sermon; but when at the table, my very body was made to shake, and all was darkness and confusion. In the evening, when hearing Mr. Whitefield from Isa. liv. 5, 'Thy Maker is thine husband,' my joy was such, that I could scarcely refrain from crying out that I was ready to strike hands on the bargain; and on meeting a young man of my acquaintance after sermon, I threw my arms about him, exclaiming, that Mr. Whitefield had married my soul to Christ. I lay down on the brae, and was so filled with the love of Christ and disregard for the world, that I even wished to depart and be with Christ; and ever since, my feelings have been different from what they were before

I never read my Bible, or ask a blessing to my food, or engage in prayer, or hear a sermon, or meditate on spiritual things, which I often do, without experiencing warm and lively feelings; and it is now June 1743. In reading God's threatenings, I am little moved; but his promises melt my soul. In hearing, I am often reminded of the saying of the disciples, by the burning of my heart within me, so that at times I can scarcely restrain myself. Evil and daring thoughts sometimes enter my mind, as fiery darts, and send me to prayer. And, to conclude, I now find my mind running out after spiritual, and not, as before, carnal things—to be spiritually-minded being with me life and peace; I find ordinances to be as living waters, and I long to drink of those rivers of pleasure which are at the right hand of God for evermore."

5. Bessie Lyon, daughter of John Lyon, cooper in Blantyre, unmarried, and aged twenty-three:—

"So far as I recollect, my conduct was always quiet and outwardly irreproachable; but till I was twelve years of age, I had scarcely any form of prayer. About this time, I fell under concern, and for a time I prayed much, often weeping. A friend asked me the cause, which I concealed; and partly from what he said, I became thoughtless, fell in with vain companions, and gradually learned their ways, till, in the end, I was foolish and frothy even as they. My concern occasionally returned, and I thought of becoming serious, but my resolutions were as often broken through, till, when about twenty years of age, a relation being on his death-bed, I was much concerned for his salvation, and also my own. After his death, some very horrid temptations were suggested, which for a time greatly distressed me; but this impression also wore off, and I became vain, fond of companions, and of dress, that I might keep their company. In this way, I continued till the awakening broke out in February 1742. About two or three weeks after it began, I went to Cambuslang, and hearing Mr. M'Laurin from Glasgow preach, I got my mind more staid to hear than it had long been; my sympathies were also drawn out as I observed those in distress; and during the singing of the 126th psalm, I was even melted into tears. Still I had no sense of my own sins. Next Lord's-day, I returned and heard, and I also went into the manse; but my heart remained unmoved. I returned on the Monday, and still my heart remained hard; but after going into the manse, and hearing these words of the 6th psalm given out—

'In thy great indignation,
O Lord, rebuke me not,'

I fell under such a sense of the divine wrath, as to tremble and cry out in agony, and I returned home in a state of very deep distress. I went back almost daily; and walking one day with some others, it was remarked by one, that the persons awakened had been previously very ungodly persons, and, therefore, it was doubtful whether the work could be of God; and this would have caused me to stumble, but recollecting that our Lord himself says, that he 'came not to call the righteous but sinners to repentance,' I was only the more confirmed. It was also suggested to me, that our concern at Cambuslang might be owing to our own endeavours to be stirred up, and therefore I resolved to do nothing but be wholly passive; and yet, in spite of me, I could not *now* but strive and pray continually. On one occasion, Mr. M'Culloch was preaching from these words, 'In whom the god of this world hath blinded the minds of them which believe not, lest the light of the glorious gospel of Christ, who is the image of God, should shine unto them.' (2 Cor. iv. 4.) And under this sermon I got a sense of my sins, and enmity to God and every thing spiritual, which I never had before. Next day, while at home, this apprehension of my state led me to see my danger in a very alarming way. It seemed as if I were like one on the top of a tree, with nothing to hold by above him, and the wind blowing fiercely to cast him down—my place of falling being into hell-fire, which seemed even now ready to receive me. In this state, Mr. Henderson, my parish minister, was sent for, who gave me good advices, but I could not lay hold on any of them. Returning to Cambuslang, I heard Mr. Arrot on the sin of unbelief, which I now saw more clearly than before, and with it many other sins. On my way home, I turned up and read in my Bible the 3d chapter of Zechariah, and wondered at what is there said of the filthy garments being removed and clean raiment bestowed, which I came to understand better on hearing Mr. M'Culloch lecture on the passage, and I was greatly comforted. Some time after, I heard Mr. M'Laurin preach concerning the children of Israel in Egypt having to sprinkle their door-posts with blood, and the necessity of our having our hearts so sprinkled. I was comforted, but I was chiefly moved by what followed in the manse. Robert Wright, a grave old man, was giving out the 91st psalm, and in the reading and singing of these lines,

> ' He that doth in the secret place
> Of the Most High reside,
> Under the shade of him that is
> Th' Almighty shall abide,'

My heart was drawn out towards God, and I sensibly felt something in my heart drawing me back; and as the good old man said in his prayers, 'O for the wings of faith, to fly above the world and all the things of it,' my soul went with his petition, as if mounting up to heaven, while I felt corruption pulling me down. Next day, Mr. Henderson asked if I was wanting to be an open (perhaps ostentatious) professor; to which I replied that I was not, but desired to serve Christ in the hidden man of the heart."

After much detail of her experience, she relates, in particular, her having heard Mr. M'Laurin at Cambuslang, her having retired to the manse, and, at the urgent request of others, having gone into the study to speak with him about her state; and she adds, that while there, and receiving instructions, another minister who was present, turned with his face towards her, *simply repeating* these words of the 89th psalm, " God's mercies I will ever sing." " These words," says she, " filled me with such joy that I could not help crying out, because of his mercy towards me while sinning against him, and because of his preventing me from turning away through unbelief. Now I came to see my great ignorance of God and his ways, to know the value of his unspeakable gift, and to accept of Christ in all his offices, and on his own terms, hoping to sing eternally of the mercies of God in Christ Jesus."

After detailing her farther experience, especially on communion occasions, she thus concludes:—" My former light companions are now unwelcome, and I shun them. I formerly excused myself, though guilty, on being found fault with—now I dare not; formerly I could neglect secret prayer, and think little of my neglect—now my conscience will not allow me; formerly I was ready enough to put in my word, when others spoke of what was good—now I have a sense of fear, lest I should say anything which I feel not. Temptations often assail me, but, through the word, their force is broken; and though I enjoy not always a sense of God's love in Christ, my desires are always towards him."

6. Sarah Gilchrist, daughter of Mr. James Gilchrist, schoolmaster in Cardross, Dumbartonshire, twenty-three years of age, and unmarried:—

" As to my former manner of life, it was, as the world judges, all along blameless. I had the advantage of a religious education, and a proper example set me by my parents. They trained me during childhood to walk in the way I should go, though in many instances I have departed from it. It was my rule to pray to God daily. While very young, and engaged in this exercise, the Lord sometimes brought my mind under conviction, and I also had delight in the exercise. But after some time these impressions wore off, and I became more careless. I also heard many sermons in early life, which impressed me, particularly one by Mr. M'Millan, from Isa. lv. 3: ' Incline your ear, and come unto me: hear, and your soul shall live; and I will make an everlasting covenant with you, even the sure mercies of David.' Many a time during my younger years, when pleading that the Lord would give me a discovery of my condition, has he laid open to me my sin in Adam, the corruption of my whole nature, the defilement of my very best actions, so as to make them appear like filthy rags, and my condemnation even on their account.

"When about seventeen or eighteen years of age, my convictions became, I have often thought, as distressing as any I have seen at Cambuslang during the awakening of 1742, only they were not so observable to others. Though outwardly blameless, I verily thought my heart to be more wicked than any one else, especially in rejecting, through unbelief, the grace and favour of Christ, set forth in the gospel. Under these convictions, I was graciously led to close with Christ as my only Saviour. On one occasion in particular, when engaged in secret prayer, I was in a state of great agony through a sense of sin, original and actual, and through a discovery of the sword of divine justice drawn against me; and was, when in this state, enabled to cast myself at God's feet for mercy, and to place myself under the cover of the Redeemer's blood. In this way I was led to trust God for mercy and pardon, and I found my heart eased of its burden; yet had I no sensible experience of joy. On the 1st of June 1740, which was the Saturday before the sacrament at Cathcart, I was there, and heard Mr. M'Culloch of Cambuslang preach from these words: 'Wherefore he is able also to save them to the uttermost that come unto God by him, seeing he ever liveth to make intercession for them.' (Heb. vii. 25.) On this occasion, I was enabled more distinctly to close with Christ in all his offices, and as an all-sufficient Saviour. After this I was often pleading with God to destroy in me the power of heart-corruption more and more, yet still I found it sometimes to prevail.

"In September 1741, I heard Mr. Whitefield in the

High Church-yard of Glasgow. He insisted much on making *sure* of an interest in Christ, and said, among other things, ' Never call yourselves Christians till he has made you sensible of your lost condition, and has drawn out your soul to close with Christ on his own terms.' I could appeal to God that this had been my experience, but I was still in doubt whether this was enough; and I prayed therefore the more earnestly that he would make me clear in this matter. And I obtained more satisfying views; on account of which I held on in the way of duty, till the awakening broke out at Cambuslang, which brought me into fresh difficulties.

" About ten or twelve days after that awakening began, I went out to Cambuslang, on a Tuesday, and heard Mr. M'Culloch preach from these words: ' A bruised reed shall he not break, and the smoking flax shall he not quench: he shall bring forth judgment unto truth.' (Isa. xlii. 3.) In listening to this sermon, I was led to hope that, though I was as a bruised reed, the Lord would not break, but rather heal me, and that he would blow up the spark of grace which was in my soul into a flame, and also return in mercy to this poor church and land. I went into the manse before sermon, and was engaged on my knees in prayer, when I heard some cry out so as to make me start up, afraid that the work was, after all, as had been said, a delusion; but on observing how the subjects of that work valued and used their Bibles, turning up the places where they had found relief, and bewailing their past unbelief, I altered my opinion of them, and prayed for as many as were still in distress. This led me again to doubt whether my own convictions had been real, seeing that theirs did in some things differ. But after hearing some of the prayers then offered I was greatly refreshed, and went home quite satisfied that the work was of God, and eagerly desiring and hoping that the Lord was about to do great things; and after returning home I was much engaged in prayer for those who had not found deliverance, and for the furtherance of the work.

"I continued to go out to Cambuslang usually thrice a-week, and during the exhortations, prayers, and praises in the manse hall, I have often had great melting of heart and much sweetness of soul, and these while I continued to put up to God secret prayers on behalf of the distressed. I had also much satisfaction in hearing the sermons which were preached. But when I observed the crying and fainting of many of the hearers, I was made to wonder at my own stupidity, in not feeling more sensibly the power of the truth. I recollected well my former convictions, and I saw in those of others the same moral experience; but judging from the bodily effects produced, I concluded that their feelings must have been deeper and more distressing, and this led me to be jealous of myself. The terrors of the law were at this time set forth with great solemnity and power, and perhaps even more, the terrible things contained in the gospel against them that believed not; and these were the views of divine truth which struck terror into the hearts of so many. Yet these very awful addresses had but little effect on me. What affected me most were the sweet and gracious offers of Christ, and the promises of the gospel. These were often made sweetly to cheer, warm, and melt my heart. It was also a source of great delight, when I heard from time to time of many who had been in distress obtaining an outgate, and being filled with great delight on their closing with Christ, as offered to them in the gospel. Knowing all this to be the experience of others, I was often much engaged in prayer, pleading with God for clearer and more satisfying views of my interest in Christ.

"At the first sacrament which was observed during the awakening, namely, in July 1742, I got nothing sensible; but I was much engaged, as I had been pleading with God. On Saturday night Satan was very active, seeking to keep me back from the Lord's table, alleging against me what is said of Esau, that 'when he would have inherited the blessing, he was rejected: for he found no place of repentance, though he sought it carefully with tears.' (Heb. xii. 17.)

By this I was much discomposed, and discouraged. Still I was enabled to persevere in pleading that the Lord would, in his own time, send me some clear and satisfying token of his love and favour, and that I might in the meantime be kept waiting. And while I was thus pleading, these words came home to me as specially sent: ' The vision is yet for an appointed time, but at the end it shall speak, and not lie; though it tarry, wait for it; because it will surely come, it will not tarry.' (Hab. ii. 3.) This enabled me to hope that times of refreshing would yet come, and were drawing near.

" When I heard that the sacrament was to be dispensed a second time at Cambuslang, I was glad, and sought to make some preparation for it; yet this went but wearily on. There was sermon on Friday evening, and before going to church I went alone into the fields, and engaged in the duty of prayer and personal covenanting with God, and I renewed my former pleading for some manifestation of divine grace and favour. On Saturday, I was much affected, hearing especially Mr. Whitefield preaching from that text, ' If I wash thee not, thou hast no part with me.' (John xiii. 8.) That night, after taking some refreshment in my lodging at Cambuslang, I went out to the fields to be alone in prayer. I then pled with God to give me a more affecting sense of my sins, as dishonouring to him, and as the procuring cause of Christ's sufferings. The Lord was pleased to give me the desire of my heart, and more than I could have expected. I then and there got a humbling sight of the exceeding sinfulness of sin, and I was made to see my own sins, especially those of unbelief, as the very nails and the spear which pierced Christ's hands, and feet, and side; and I was made spiritually and by faith, yet in a very lively manner, to see, through the wound in his side, a heart full of love, and that love expressed in the bitterness of his sufferings for me. I saw that, after all the evil I had done, he was willing to forgive, and that he had already forgiven me all my sins, and that now, though my iniquities were to be sought for, they would not be found. Many passages of the 53d chapter of Isaiah were now brought to my mind with greater power than anything I had ever met with, particularly these: 'He was wounded for our transgressions: he was bruised for our iniquities: the chastisement of our peace was upon him, and with his stripes we are healed. He shall see of the travail of his soul, and shall be satisfied.' These sayings were brought home to my heart, with a particular application to myself. I was really persuaded that Christ had after this manner been wounded and bruised for me—that he had purchased for me eternal life, and would see in me of the travail of his soul. When these discoveries were made to me, my very soul rose against sin, and my heart was melted because of God's pardoning love. It seemed as if Christ were now speaking to me in the language of the Song, saying, 'Open to me, my sister, my love, my dove, my undefiled: for my head is filled with dew, and my locks with the drops of the night.' And I was at the same time made to grieve that I had kept him so long knocking at the door of my heart—that I had not more freely and readily opened to him. But now, he was himself pleased to open, enabling me to close with him in all his offices, and to devote myself wholly and unreservedly to him, now, and for ever. This was followed by the entrance of a beam of heavenly light—I know not how else to describe it—shining upon my soul, affording me the most ravishing discoveries of the glory and excellency of Christ in his person as God, more in his offices as our Redeemer, and in his perfect suitableness to all my wants and desires: yea, so as to make me greatly long to be with him. This was followed by the saying of Job sweetly darting into my mind, as the fitting expression of what I now felt: 'I have heard of thee by the hearing of the ear; but now mine eye seeth thee: wherefore I abhor myself, and repent in dust and ashes.' (Job xlii. 5, 6.) And with this I got the most humbling and self-abasing sense of my own vileness through sin. I was made truly to loathe and abhor myself in dust and ashes, and to wonder that he should ever have thought of setting his love on a creature so vile and polluted; and therefore all my confidence was now in his free, sovereign grace.

" While this manifestation of God lasted, I scarcely knew where I was, or how I was, so much was I lifted up with these glorious and ravishing discoveries. But after some time, I began again to reflect on my former treachery and deceitfulness of heart, leading me to break vows and resolutions which I had before made; and therefore I besought God that, if it were consistent with his own purposes and glory, he would take me to himself; but that if his will were otherwise he would undertake for me, and keep my feet from falling. I was led also to forecast and to lay my account with coming trials; and yet such was the courage with which the Lord had inspired me, that I would have been content, if every hair of my head had been a life, to have laid them all down for Christ. This was my feeling of willingness at the time, yet was I afraid that I might faint when the hour came. I was therefore engaged pleading for grace and strength, and these promises came home to me with great sweetness and power: ' When thou passest through the waters, I shall be with thee: and through the rivers, they shall not overflow thee: when thou walkest through the fire, thou shalt not be burned: neither shall the flame kindle upon thee'—' For the mountains shall depart, and the hills be removed; but my kindness shall not depart from thee, neither shall the covenant of my peace be removed, saith the Lord, that hath mercy on thee.' (Isa. xliii. 2, liv. 10.)

" Next day, the Lord was pleased to grant me holy communion with himself during the serving of the tables, and in secret prayer; and so also on Monday, and much of this gracious frame remained with me for weeks after that solemn occasion: and often since I have had much nearness to God in duty.

" And now to conclude: As to the habitual temper of

my mind, I find a principle within me opposing and striving against indwelling corruption and sin of all kinds; and on falling into sin, there is nothing in it so bitter to me, as that it is against so much love, and a God so loving. I look upon all things as enemies, that would separate between me and Christ, or mar and interrupt the communication of his love towards me. His ordinances are very dear to me, yet am I restless and unsatisfied in waiting on them, unless I find Christ's presence in them. I often long to be with him in heaven, and yet I am satisfied to wait his will on earth. The advancement of Christ's kingdom is, among earthly things, my chief desire. 'If I forget thee, O Jerusalem, let my tongue cleave to the roof of my mouth.' Come, O come, Lord Jesus. Come quickly in the manifestation of thy glory, and the advancement of thy kingdom. Amen."

7. Catherine Anderson, daughter of Mr. William Anderson, portioner in Little Govan, near Glasgow, and only thirteen years of age:—

"In reviewing my life before 1742, I have reason to bless God for having preserved me outwardly blameless before the world. But I now see that I was all along a stranger to saving grace. I was indeed taught to pray by myself twice a-day, and I was accustomed to go to the kirk, and for a while to the seceders' meetings. But it was only because I saw others go, and because of my parents' desire. My heart did not lie to these things. I could make no difference between one preaching and another, except as they were long or short, and to me the shortest sermons were always the best, while a long one was, as I thought, a great evil.

"When the awakening broke out at Cambuslang, in February 1742, I heard a woman call it a delusion. A friend of mine, to whom this was said, expressed her regret if it should so turn out, especially under Mr. M'Culloch's ministry. I heard much more on the subject from time to time; and observing that they called the persons who had become serious, *converts*, I wondered what this meant. I went myself to Cambuslang about the end of February, and heard a sermon, but felt nothing. I observed a woman weeping greatly, and pointing to her, I said to the friend that was with me, ' That is perhaps one of the persons they call *converts.*' I was little or scarcely at all affected by any thing I had either seen or heard. I returned next Tuesday, and again saw several weeping on account of their sins. Next time I went, I heard Mr. M'Culloch preach from that text, '.He that believeth not is condemned already.' (John iii. 18.) These words were often repeated in the sermon, and as they were repeated they came home to my heart with power. My sleeping conscience became awakened, and set before me my sins. The first sin of which I became convinced was that of unbelief. I saw myself condemned already, truly in a lost state. But my awakened conscience set before me other sins, and as clearly as if I had seen them in print, and each stood against me as if attested by ever so many witnesses. I was thus brought into great distress, partly on account of my condemned state; for I clearly saw that, if I were to die in that state, there was nothing for me but hell-fire, and that it was perfectly just it should be so; but partly also, and mainly, because through my unbelief I had been doing dishonour to the redeeming love of a God reconciled in Christ. In this there was an amount of evil which I could not bear. God's very love was what in this wounded my spirit. But the Lord had mercy on me. I was made to look upon Him whom I had pierced, and to mourn as one mourns for the loss of the dearest friend. I did not, however, cry out, either at this time or any other, nor did I ever faint. I was made, however, both at this time and often since, to weep abundantly. On some occasions, when sitting in the warm sunshine on Cambuslang brae, I have been so affected while hearing as to tremble with very grief on account of sin, as if I were to be shaken to pieces.

" From this time I continued till August in darkness and

distress, unable to apply any thing to myself in the way of comfort. Yet the Lord was pleased all that time to keep me diligent in the use of means. I went for a long time almost every day to Cambuslang. I often read my Bible alone, and I was much engaged in secret prayer and in mourning for sin; and though I was often at the point of despair, yet the Lord kept me from altogether sinking, granting me from time to time some glimmering of hope.

"At length, when sitting, as I had often done, on the brae, on a Thursday, about the beginning of August, and before sermon, that word came home to me with special power, 'Who is among you that feareth the Lord, that obeyeth the voice of his servant, that walketh in darkness, and hath no light? let him trust in the name of the Lord, and stay upon his God.' (Isa. l. 10.) The Lord showed me that I was such an one as is here described, and I was enabled to take to myself the exhortation, staying myself upon God, and with the hope of his being my God. I was in this way much eased of my burden, and in some measure comforted. Next Lord's-day, which was the preparation Sabbath, my confidence was somewhat shaken. I was afraid lest I had been taking comfort to myself to which I was not entitled; but this also was got over. I had great difficulty in resolving whether I ought to ask admission to the table of the Lord. I was afraid of being rash, and yet I could not allow myself to stay away. A sermon preached by Mr. Robe of Kilsyth, on Saturday, from these words, 'He hath put him to grief: when thou shalt make his soul an offering for sin, he shall see his seed, he shall prolong his days, and the pleasure of the Lord shall prosper in his hand' (Isa. liii. 10), was made useful to me. On Sabbath, when I came to the Lord's table, I may say that the Master took me into his banqueting-house, and his banner over me was love.

"At Cathcart sacrament, in May 1743, that saying was brought powerfully home to me when at the Lord's table: 'I, even I, am he that blotteth out thy transgressions, for mine own sake, and will not remember thy sins.' (Isa.

xliii. 25.) I was made to feel that the Lord had indeed blotted out and freely pardoned all my sins. At the communion of Cambuslang, also, in 1743, I could say, with the spouse, that I was sick of love. I was made greatly to rejoice in this, that Christ was now seated on the throne of my heart. So very lively was my joy, that I had great difficulty in restraining myself from crying out.

"But, that I be not tedious, I shall only further notice my general habit of mind down to the present time, March 8, 1744. It is now about two years since I was awakened out of the sleep of sin, and I trust also out of a state of death. For in looking back over these two years, I cannot but observe a great change. Formerly I was indifferent about ordinances; now I could not think of being away from them, except in cases of necessity; and I have great delight in hearing the gospel, and in taking part in the other services of the sanctuary. I come to hear, expecting Christ to speak through his servant to his people, and in particular to myself. I look for this in the way of conviction, of comfort, and of seasonable instruction as regards duty. And the Lord also has thus graciously dealt with me from time to time. Formerly I had no heart for secret prayer; now I know not how I could live without it, even for one day. I take delight in it as a duty, as profitable also to my soul; and my gracious Lord has given me to experience many answers of prayer, and among these, very precious spiritual blessings. Formerly I did not know what heart-corruptions were; now I feel them very sensibly, and I am often sent to Christ beseeching him to help me to overcome them, that I may be wholly and unrestrainedly his. Formerly I understood not what it was to have recourse to Christ for anything; now he is mine, and I am his, and through him I can do all things. I pretend not to be absolutely assured as to the issue; but I am willing to wait in hope of the mercy of the Lord Jesus unto eternal life. To him, therefore, be all the glory and honour, now and for ever! Amen."

8. Jean Walker, daughter of Archibald Walker, shoemaker in Calder, unmarried, and aged nineteen:—

"As to the earlier part of my life, I was outwardly as other moral and well-doing people. Sometimes I prayed in secret, and sometimes not. Family worship was observed twice a-day during the week, and thrice on Sabbath; but it was a weariness to me. I attended church, and had to bring home some notes of the sermon to my father, and if I succeeded in this, I was satisfied; and religious conversation was very unwelcome to me; and so matters went on till the awakening in Cambuslang, when I attended every Sabbath, and often on week-days.* I now began to have some concern about myself, particularly after hearing a sermon one Sabbath in May. I said to myself, 'O, what is this! what a wretched creature must I be, in going home night after night without having obtained any interest in Christ!' And so I went with others to the manse, but after waiting till about ten o'clock unavailingly, another young woman and myself set out for Glasgow. We had not, however, got far, when she, walking a little way behind, cried out, 'O what shall I do? I am lost and undone!' I ran back and laid hold of her, but as I did so I was myself struck to the heart, and made to repeat the same complaint. My conscience, which was till now asleep, awoke armed with terrors. The young woman returned to the manse; but as another young woman, and a man with her, came up on their way to Glasgow, I was induced to accompany them. The man laid before me, as we walked, many comfortable promises, but I could not lay hold on any. Still my convictions were as yet general, and fearing that they might wear off, I thought of concealing them at home; but I was unable. I was not long home, when my distress so grew upon me as to compel me to cry out, so that some about laid hold on me, to prevent my falling. I returned to Cambuslang next day, when my convictions were renewed and deepened, and they gradually became more par-

* She seems to have been now in Glasgow.

ticular; and for five or six weeks I continued in great distress, and without finding any relief. As I walked along the street it seemed as if I should sink through the ground. I slept little and ate little; and although I tried to work, my mind was so much bent on reading and prayer, that I could do little. One day, when hearing in the Ramshorn Church, I found a secret spring of hope and joy rising in my soul, my heart glowing with love to God; and at night, while my mother was conducting family worship, these words, 'I have loved thee with an everlasting love' (Jer. xxxi. 3), shot up in my mind; and regarding them as applicable to my own case, I was overcome and made to cry out with joy. This was accompanied with a very humbling sense of my unbelief, and of Christ's greater willingness to save me than I was to go to him for salvation; and from that time to this (9th November 1743), which is about a year and a quarter, I never could even once doubt of his love."

Passing over her detailed experience, especially on sacramental occasions at Glasgow and Cambuslang, she says of her usual state: "I was enabled to live much above the world, having my heart in a good measure set upon things which are above. During last winter, I was often so overjoyed, when engaged at work or walking along the street, as scarcely to know what I was about—my soul being in heaven, while there was little more than my body on earth. At other times, I had a sad feeling of the burden of sin, and would even that I should depart to be free from it, and from all imperfections."

9. Andrew Faulds, son of Robert Faulds, at Cambuslang, unmarried, and aged twenty-one :—

" When I was a child, I had some feeling of religion; but as I grew up, all my observances were formal, and I knew not that I was blind and naked, but fancying that all was right with me, I had no concern about myself. But soon after the great hurricane, on the 12th of January 1740, Mr. M'Culloch preached from Ps. cxlviii. 8 : ' Fire, and hail; snow, and vapours; stormy wind fulfilling his word.' And, addressing us, he said: 'Will neither the voice of God in the tempests of the air, nor in the threatenings of devouring fire and everlasting burnings, awaken you?' This question had a reference to two things—to the hurricane, and to the text preached from on the day of the hurricane, namely, Isa. xxxiii. 14: 'Who among us shall dwell with the devouring fire? who among us shall dwell with everlasting burnings?' The question so put, came home to me as a message from God, and I had for a time some impression; but it wore off, till the revival occurred in February 1742; and then these very words came back upon me, and awakened me from my slumber. Hearing Mr. M'Culloch give, as a mark of an unbelieving state, that persons remain secure, I saw that I had been all along in an unregenerate state, and I was thereby thrown into great perplexity. While hearing, these words came into my mind with extraordinary light and power: 'Then shall we know, if we follow on to know the Lord: his going forth is prepared as the morning; and he shall come unto us as the rain, as the latter and former rain unto the earth.' (Hos. vi. 3.) The hope awakened in my mind by these words so grew upon me, that, at a meeting of young people that very evening, I could not forbear telling them that, up till that very day, I could never say I had a right to Christ, but that now I thought I could; that formerly my claim always rested on something of my own, but that now I saw it in Christ, and the words of his promise.

"I thus came to have a reliance on Christ, and therefore to have much love and joy, so that I besought many to join with me in praising God. I continued thus for several days; but afterwards I began to doubt, but was sustained by the promises. On a thanksgiving day in May 1742, the minister preached from Ps. cxxvi. 3: 'The Lord hath done great things for us; whereof we are glad;' and when hearing, I was made clearly to see, from Scripture evidence, that the Lord had done for me the great work of regeneration. On Sabbath evening, after our first communion, I heard Mr. Whitefield preach from Isa. liv. 5 : 'Thy Maker is thy husband,' and was enabled anew to accept and close with Christ, to my great joy and satisfaction.

"And now, on comparing my present state with what it was, I find that whereas before the world was in my heart, and its concerns occupied my thoughts, now God is there, and I mind spiritual things; that whereas formerly I went away, after hearing, giving my opinion of the sermon, I now leave, thinking of myself, as set forth in what I have been hearing; and whereas before I had little feeling of sin, it is now felt to be a burden; so that I earnestly long to be free, even by death."

10. Margaret Borland, daughter of James Borland, tenant in Bothwell, unmarried, and aged twenty-three :—

"When a child, I was put to school, but learned little, from playfulness; but, by following the minister when reading in church, I gradually learned in that way more than in any other. Till I was about fourteen years of age, I prayed not alone; but observing the minister (Mr. Hamilton) in his prayer plead that the worship of God might be set up in every family, that his fear might be in every heart, and that there might not be a prayerless person in the congregation, I thought it sad that I should be prayerless, and resolved on getting home to make the attempt. I went out to a dyke-side twice, but could get nothing to say; and on this I wept. I tried it a third time, and got some expressions to use and some freedom; and on thus succeeding, I usually prayed once a-day; and as my conduct outwardly was regular, I now supposed that all was right. And so, being fast asleep as to my state, when vexed at anything, I sometimes said, 'I wish I were dead,' and this without even thinking where death would send me. And, on reading or hearing of the wickedness of the heart, I would say to myself, 'My heart is not wicked;' but when observing in Scripture that Christ came to call not the righteous, but sinners, I said, 'Well, he is my Saviour; for I sometimes sin;' and thus the strong man kept his house. And thus it continued, till one Sabbath in the spring of 1742, I was at Cambuslang, and heard Mr. M'Culloch preach from John iii. 36 : ' He that believeth on the Son hath everlasting life : and he that believeth not the Son shall not see life; but the wrath of God abideth on him.' From the marks of an unbelieving state given in this sermon, I saw that I was still in that state ; and when he said, addressing himself to such, 'The wrath of God is abiding on you, whatever ye do, wherever ye go ; and even now, as ye sit on that brae, it is hanging over you,' I became deeply concerned. After getting home, I often turned to that text in my Bible ; and as I looked on it I wept, for I saw not how to escape. About three weeks after, I was again at Cambuslang on a Thursday ; and, after sermon, I went into the manse, and heard Mr. M'Laurin exhorting, in the course of which he quoted these words : ' Awake, thou that sleepest, and arise from the dead, and Christ shall give thee light.' (Eph. v. 14.) These words pierced my very heart. I was now more than confirmed in all my fears. I saw myself to be asleep, and my sleep to be the sleep of death. I returned home, and remained in this state for twenty days more, scarcely daring to pray, and scarcely able either to eat or sleep.

" My first relief was found when reading in Isa. i. 19, 20 : ' If ye be willing and obedient,' &c. I thought of the rebellion of my heart, and was perplexed ; and that saying came to my relief : ' It is of the Lord's mercies that we are not consumed, because his compassions fail not.' (Lam. iii. 22.)" Her progress from this time is detailed at considerable length ; but it is so variable, and the account so minute, that we shall only sum it up in this—That her change from darkness to light, though less distinct and assignable to any one period than some others, seems to have been real and abiding. The following is her own conclusion : " Though the world cannot observe any great alteration in my behaviour from what it used to be, as it was all along regular, yet I *find a great change in myself*—a change as great as from darkness to light. Formerly, my mind was ever running out after something worldly; now I am crucified to the world, and the world to me—the Word of God being the man of my counsel. Formerly, I liked to hear the gospel, but the words of the preacher going in at one ear, went out at the other; but now I hear with delight and self-application. Formerly, I loved not Christ, and yet fancied I did; now I love him, and am so grieved at sinning against him, that often I would be with him, to be free from sin."

11. Archibald Smith, mason in Kilbride, married, aged forty:—

" I was taught in childhood to pray, but being for some time in a house wanting in every form of religion, I laid aside the practice; and during my five years' apprenticeship, I thought of it only when in worldly difficulties. On becoming a man, I was carried away with follies, and even worse. On getting married I occasionally prayed, both in secret and with my family, and I was brought into a sense of the divine wrath; which, however, wore off. Generally, I was sober; but sometimes, in passion, I fell into the use of profane language; and in company I used to boast of my being able to make others drunk, while I remained sober; yet I was myself sometimes drunk.

" Hearing of the awakening at Cambuslang, which some said was of God, and others of the wicked one, I one weekday put my Bible in my pocket, remarking, that ere I returned I should know something of it. I soon satisfied myself that the work was of God, especially on observing so much brotherly love on the part of such as had found peace. I heard sermon, and was conscious of a certain awe on my spirit, but nothing more. I came home, but in a day or two after I again went out, taking with me all of my family that could go. This was on Saturday, and I remained, and two of my children with me, till the Thursday following. On Sabbath night I tried to get into the manse, but could not for the crowd, and after standing a while, I went into the garden to pray; and as I returned, I found a son of my own, a boy about thirteen, weeping and crying under deep convictions, and I hastened to carry him away to some house, that something might be done to quiet him. But on the way, a remark which I had heard some days before, on the sin and danger of stifling convictions, sprang up in my mind, so as to overawe me. I came back with my son, and about two in the morning he found some outgate. Another [probably his wife] of my family fell under convictions, at which I was glad; but surprised to think that this person, who had been so much more blameless and attentive to religion than I had been, should be so distressed. This also filled me with indignation at my own stupidity and indifference. I now attended to what I heard more closely, and gave myself to prayer, and the Lord opened my mind to a sense of my condition; sins long forgotten coming fresh into my memory, and imbittered not only as exposing me to wrath, but as dishonouring to God. I went on seeking to know more of myself and of the way of salvation, amidst a mixture of hope and fear. I continued the diligent use of the means of grace, and opened my case to some serious persons of more experience for advice. But after going on for a time in this way, I heard Mr. Whitefield preaching from Gen. xli. 55: 'Go unto Joseph; what he saith to you, do.' From this, he showed us that we ought to go directly to Christ. This was useful to me: I learned to go oftener to him, and less to man. While seeking thus to draw near to him, and while engaged in prayer, these words came home, as if given to me of God: 'Believe on the Lord Jesus Christ, and thou shalt be saved, and thy house.' (Acts xvi. 31.) If my heart deceive me not, I had already 'believed,' fully accepting of Christ in all his offices, especially on hearing Mr. Whitefield, as above; and now my faith went out on behalf of my family, and from this time I was enabled to receive with great sweetness many of the promises. As the first sacrament at Cambuslang approached, I began to think how I should do during so many week-day services. I was at the time making good wages, and counting up what sum the loss of time would cost, I stumbled for a little; but after betaking myself to prayer, I was delivered from all thoughts of the kind, and waiting on the ordinances, my heart was left undisturbed, being filled with peace and joy in believing; and this sweet frame remained with me in a good measure for half a year after. And when my sensible enjoyment abated, I was instructed and taught all the more to wait upon God, living by faith and not by feeling.

"And now, in July 1744, I find a very great difference in my state from what it was before. Formerly I had no relish for the Sabbath and its ordinances; now I weary for both. Sometimes I think that I would even consent to my own ruin, if Christ were to be glorified thereby. Sometimes when walking alone, and meditating on the things of God, I am so carried out of myself, as scarcely to know where I am. And sin seems now to be exceeding sinful, so that I would do anything to be wholly freed from it."

REMARKS.

In narrating these cases, we refrained from offering any remarks; but now that the selection has been completed, it may be well to draw the attention of the reader to some of the more important and obvious reflections suggested by these details:—

And first, every intelligent reader must have been struck with the *texts* preached from during the awakening. It is easy to see, from the choice made, that the preacher had some direct and practical end in view; that he had before him certain conditions of mind and particular classes of hearers. Then the texts themselves were generally free from anything requiring exegetical discussion. They stood forth as so many direct messages from God, or they were such as to hold up to the sinner the very picture of his own state. This characteristic, no doubt, grew out of the circumstances. The preacher was very often engaged in conversation with the awakened; from them he learned much of the actual condition of many, and so he chose his text as the warrior would his weapon or the barrister his plea. Our circumstances are generally different; but in so far as our direct and special end is *conversion*, rather than edification, is there not much to be learned from their example?—much as regards texts, looking forth from the context, and speaking their own meaning, and also as regards the employment of these in plain and direct dealing with souls?

Another reflection suggested, is the very marked difference between an awakened and unawakened state. In the one, there is the most profound unconsciousness of any thing real in practical godliness; and in the other, a living sense of divine things. And in passing out of the one state into the other, the individual is very like one who is being awakened out of deep sleep; thus showing the one state to be as when one dreameth of what is not real, and the other as when the same person, now awake, sees and hears things as they are. The application of this to the existing state of society is very awful. The persons introduced in these cases were not more wicked than others previous to their awakening. They were perhaps, on the whole, no unfair specimens of what we may suppose the classes to which they belonged are among ourselves. They had, in their unawakened state, as little suspicion of anything being wrong as those of the same class have now; and yet, when awakened, they found that the wrath of God had all along been abiding on them, nay, that their very security was itself the effect of strong delusion, and of the power which sin had obtained over them. This is very evident in the cases given; and we may add, that it is equally so in those not given. Here, then, is the concurring testimony of more than *a hundred witnesses*, who once were as many now are, and who declare, that it they had died in that state they must have perished. And what, then, becomes of the hundreds who are dying daily in no other state, so far as appearances go, and of the thousands living it may be soberly, yet altogether unconcerned, at least in the sense meant by the awakened?

There is a similar difference, scarcely less observable, between the times of an awakening and those of general security. Previous to the awakening of 1742, the very persons who were then awakened lived, in many cases, without any suspicion of themselves, and some who had been concerned, were so only as in the occasional awakenings of a sleeping man. Society, as a whole, was buried in thoughtlessness as to everything real in matters spiritual; and had this condition continued, nothing more would have been expected. Everything like the means afterwards employed would have been accounted extravagant—every thing like the earnest seeking and deep concern experienced would have been accounted madness; and yet, when the awakening took place, these were regarded as not more than the comparative importance of the soul required. How do we pronounce upon this?—as during the awakened or unawakened age? and if as the latter, are we right? and can we in this way expect the fruits of an awakened state?

But farther, and closely connected with the above, the proper end of an awakening does not require that it should continue. One of the most common objections to such seasons is that they are temporary. And so ought they. A soul asleep in sin has to be awakened, so as to think of its condition, and be led to Christ; but being awakened, it has only to be kept awake, not to be awakened anew in the same way as before. A church is different in this, that, for the sake of awakening sinners, it has itself to be from time to time awakened; but it would not do, even for a church, to be always in the condition of Cambuslang in 1742 and 1743. Ministers have to study edification as well as conversion, and in this they have to teach the whole counsel of God. The people also have to cultivate holiness in all the duties of life, society itself becoming sanctified through their example and influence. Alternations of activity and rest are almost, if not altogether, universal in nature, and they have a place also in spiritual things. But surely our barren season, as regards the country at large, has already been very long; it has now been winter with us for about a century, and we scarcely venture to expect more than we have. And yet there are many of those very symptoms which preceded the revival of 1742 crowding upon us. God is in effect saying unto us in his providence, "Wherefore criest thou unto me? speak unto the children of Israel that they go forward."

But there is yet one other reflection, more direct than any other. It is the extraordinary clearness and freeness wherewith that saying of Scripture, "If any man be in Christ Jesus, he is a new creature," is brought out. Many apparently of God's people are at a loss to find in themselves anything like full and substantial evidence of a change; but here the difference is, as the saying imparts, all old things having passed away, and all things become new. This was no doubt in part owing to the suddenness of the change and the circumstances in which it occurred. But the evidence so afforded is not the less valuable. Substantially the same change has to take place at one period of life or other in all the redeemed; and therefore are there in these cases two specimens of what ought to be sought in evidence of regeneration. In this respect, it is remarkable how very similar, in everything substantial, the actual experience of so many proved. They answered to one another, even as face answereth to face in a glass; and simply because the lineaments portrayed were all after one likeness—that of Christ; and the workmanship of one Spirit, through whom believers are created anew in Christ Jesus. Let men read what is here brought before them, and then ask themselves, Is it so with me?—not, Has my change been as theirs? but, Is my condition as theirs?

CHAPTER XII.

THE EXTENSION OF THE WORK TO OTHER PARTS OF SCOTLAND.

"From you," says an apostle, addressing the Thessalonians, "sounded out the word of the Lord, not only in Macedonia and Achaia, but also in every place your faith to Godward is spread abroad." (1 Thess. i. 8.) This was not peculiar to the faith of the Thessalonians, neither was it confined to apostolic ages. Wherever the power of the truth is greatly felt, this is the case; and in times of general revival, it is eminently so. The conversation of the day, whether among friends or foes, all turns on it. The correspondence, especially of the pious, hastens to carry into all corners of the land, and into different countries, the gladdening news; and by-and-by, the press sends forth its "flying rolls," proclaiming to all the unusual disturbance of the world's slumber. It has been often noticed, as one of the beautiful provisions in the works of God, that the seeds of some plants are carried by the winds of heaven from field to field, and in some cases from country to country, that thus the world itself may be sown. And the same wisdom, as regards the moral world, may be seen in the curiosity awakened as means of spreading abroad the news, especially of a revival. We see in this how, when God's time comes, whole countries may, without the use of any extraordinary means, be awakened to concern; and how, through the blessing of God, even nations may be born in a day.

It is very much on this account, that we are now to subjoin a few particulars concerning other places in Scotland, which shared in the revival of 1742, 1743. A somewhat extended delineation of these would be interesting, but it would unduly enlarge a single chapter. Moreover, anything professing to give an account of that revival over Scotland, would be necessarily faulty, as our knowledge of what then occurred is mainly dependent on authors connected with particular districts, and whose information, though gathered from distant parts, never proceeded on anything like a general survey. The voluminous correspondence of Mr. Whitefield spreads over a wide extent of country, and would lead one to expect that much of the work of God must have been going on in places of which we otherwise hear little. The Glasgow "Weekly History," which was published during 1742, embraces a very wide extent of intelligence; but as yet the revival was felt only in a few places. The "Monthly History," which followed, obtained information from quarters not noticed in the other; but it also was dependent on the correspondence of the editor, who, though most zealous, could not be expected to reach all. And Dr. Gillies, whose copy of the "Monthly History" we have now before us, marked as it is for the printer, was not only judicious in his selections, but he drew also from other accessible sources, some of them original. Still his work, too, was from the Glasgow press; and his means of information, concerning contemporary events, were much greater as regarded the west country and certain other parts, where correspondence had been kept up, than generally over Scotland.

These remarks seem necessary, to prevent any undue impression concerning the extent of this work in Scotland. It certainly prevailed most in the west of Scotland, and other places to be named, but was, we are persuaded, far more general than many imagine, or than any can well show. There was truly a spring season wherever there was spiritual life, and in many places a shaking among the dry bones.

Looking now at the country, even under the partial lights afforded us, the several sources, more or less independent of each other, may be seen sending forth their healing waters over the land. One of these consisted of separate and hidden springs, that would of themselves have proved blessings, but which flowed much more freely and fully when news arrived of what God was doing in other parts of the world. This was the case, for example, in the remote counties of Ross and Sutherland on the one hand, and various parts of the west on the other. And there was one predisposing cause of these already noticed, namely, that the children of persecuted fathers, who retained among them the piety of an earlier and suffering age, had been driven into their closets before a storm of ungodliness, and were now gathering strength and coming forth as a people dwelling alone and caring for the things of God; and these, God was owning in different parts of the country previous to any general movement.

A second source of reviving power flowed in upon the country from without. The news from America and from England awakened very general expectation among the pious; and when Mr. Whitefield arrived, it seemed as if the waters which had flooded and fertilized other lands had also burst in upon Scotland. According to Mr. Whitefield's own repeated statements, in no country had he so experienced in his own soul the power of divine love, and in no other had he been so enabled to speak as of God; and the effects of his ministrations corresponded. The friends of religion in Scotland ought never to forget how much their country was blessed by the labours of that truly great man. God seems in an eminent manner to have raised him up and sent him forth for the revival of the English-speaking Churches of Christendom; and he may be said, in some sense, to have belonged in some measure to all, and exclusively to none. Born an Englishman, he began his labours in England, but soon after visited also Wales. The colonies were very early his chief care. He visited Ireland in

1751, and several times thereafter. But few, perhaps, are aware that he visited Scotland not fewer than *fourteen times*, generally travelling over large districts of the country, and preaching daily, often several times each day. Moreover, these visits were spread over a period of not less than *twenty-seven years*, namely, in 1741, 1742, 1748, 1750, 1751, 1752, 1753, 1756, 1757, 1758, 1759, 1762, 1763, and 1768. England gave him birth, America retains his bones, and one of Scotland's best ministers had the honour to write his life. Dr. Gillies, his biographer and personal friend, says, of his visits to Scotland:—"Though, after the years 1741, 1742, there were no such extensive new awakenings, Mr. Whitefield's coming was always refreshing to serious persons, and seemed to put new life into them, and also to be the means of increasing their number. His preaching was still eminently useful in various respects. In the first place, it had an excellent tendency to destroy the hurtful spirit of bigotry and excessive zeal for smaller matters, and to turn men's attention to the great and substantial things of religion. Another effect was, that it drew several persons to hear the gospel, who seldom went to hear it from other ministers. Again, young people in general were much benefited by his ministry, and particularly young students, who became afterwards serious, evangelical preachers. Lastly, his morning discourses, which were mostly intended for sincere but disconsolate souls, were peculiarly fitted to direct and encourage such in the Christian life; and his addresses in the evening to the promiscuous multitudes who then attended him, were of a very alarming kind. There was something exceedingly striking in the solemnity of his evening congregations, in the Orphan-house park at Edinburgh and the High Church-yard at Glasgow, especially towards the conclusion of his sermons (which were commonly very long, though they seemed short to the hearers), when the whole multitude stood fixed, and like one man, hung upon his lips with silent attention, and many under deep impressions of the great objects of religion and the concerns of eternity. These things will not soon be forgotten, and it is hoped that the many good effects which, by the divine blessing, attended them, never will.

"His conversation was no less reviving than his sermons. Many in Edinburgh and Glasgow are witnesses of this; especially at Glasgow, when, in company with his good friends, Mr. M'Laurin, Mr. Robert Scott, &c., one might challenge the sons of pleasure, with all their wit, good humour, and gaiety, to furnish entertainments so agreeable. At the same time, every part of it was not more agreeable than it was useful and edifying.

"His friends in Scotland, among whom were many of all ranks from the highest to the lowest, were very constant and steady in their great regard for him, and his opposers grew more and more mild. But, indeed, Mr. Whitefield's whole behaviour was so open to the eyes of the world, and his character, after it had stood many attacks from all quarters, came at last to be so thoroughly established, that several of his opposers in Scotland seemed rather to acquire a certain degree of esteem for him; at least they all thought proper to give over speaking against him. When he was in Glasgow, he always lodged with Mr. James Niven, merchant above the cross, till, towards the end of his life, his asthmatic disorder made the town air disagree with him; and, then, he went out in the evenings, and stayed with his good friend, Mr. M'Culloch, at Cambuslang."

Were we to follow the track of Mr. Whitefield's labours in Scotland, in noticing the extension of the revival, Edinburgh would be our starting-point. This was his usual landing-place, and it was, more than any other locality, the scene of his labours, and, to a large extent, of his triumphs. And then from this, there would be tracks diverging southward, upwards along the Forth, and northward as far as Aberdeen, as well as into the west country.

The third source is less original than either of these, but

it flowed out, if not in a broader, at least in a deeper and more commanding stream; we mean the work of God first and chiefly noticed in the west country, and particularly at Cambuslang and Kilsyth. It was, doubtless, dependent on the influence already noticed, but having about it great breadth and distinctness of character, it drew upon itself the attention of the whole country, and thus the west became at once the centre of intelligence from other quarters, and the place from which the sound that was to awaken the whole land went mainly forth, for several years. And therefore, it is from this that we shall do best to proceed in offering some notices of the extension of the work over Scotland. And bearing in mind, that we have not the means of surveying the whole, and that it forms no part of our plan to attempt it, we shall, for convenience and distinctness, arrange our notices under so many of the ecclesiastical divisions of the church, as bringing before us somewhat of the moral relation, as well as local connection of the parishes referred to.

The Presbytery of Hamilton.—Cambuslang lies in this presbytery. And we have many reasons for believing that the revival extended into other of its parishes, and especially those adjoining, and into several of the Glasgow presbytery lying on the south side of the Clyde, although they are not separately and specially mentioned. The ministers of East Kilbride, Blantyre, Bothwell, and Cathcart, took all part in the work; and one of them (Mr. Hamilton of Bothwell) speaks of its having spread into his own parish. "There are a good many of my people," says he, "mostly young, who have been awakened at Cambuslang; and I have much the same account to give of them. All of them are very serious and concerned about their souls, and very solicitous to have others brought to an acquaintance with Christ and the way of salvation through him; which has, I hope, had this blessed effect, that there seems to be a more than ordinary seriousness among a goodly number in several corners of this congregation, more conscience is made of family worship in several families, who made but too little account of it before; as likewise, there are some new societies for prayer and Christian conference set up in this congregation, wherein several persons, besides those awakened at Cambuslang, have joined."

Many of the manuscript cases also refer to these parishes as the residence of the persons described; but, from their nearness to Cambuslang, they are not spoken of as forming separate companies, but are associated with Cambuslang itself.*

The Presbytery of Irvine.—The chief track along which the awakened parishes lie, is from Glasgow northward. But before entering on it, the extension of the work westward must be noticed. The Cunningham of Ayrshire is separated from Clydesdale by a range of hills across which the godly on both sides were long accustomed to hold intercourse. When Mr. William Guthrie was in Fenwick, in Ayrshire, many went from Glasgow and the surrounding district of Clydesdale very frequently to hear him; the distance from Glasgow being eighteen miles. And many from the country sloping down from Fenwick towards

---

* Since finishing what concerned Cambuslang proper, we have been reminded of certain allegations published in the first statistical account, and of a vindication written by the late Dr. Robertson. We have again examined Dr. Robertson's statement, and beg leave to refer to it in the *Christian Instructor* for August, 1831, as containing a full and satisfactory vindication; and this is all the more valuable, that Dr. Robertson was settled at Cambuslang, while many who recollected the revival were still alive. He was elected as assistant to Dr. Meek in 1795, and ordained on the 22d of August 1797. In preaching his funeral sermon, Mr. James Clason of Dalziel, one of his most intimate friends, said, " Of that blessed revival of religion which took place in 1742, he delighted to speak; and his testimony to the reality of that work is invaluable—sufficient to stop the mouths of gainsayers; for he had been a witness to the Christian life and the peaceful death of some who dated their commencement in the divine life from the saving impressions they received at that most interesting period." Dr. Robertson, whose testimony is thus spoken of, was himself distinguished as a scholar, and esteemed by all who knew him.

Irvine were often at Cambuslang, during the revival. At the second communion, two hundred of the communicants were supposed to be from Kilmarnock, a hundred from Stewarton, and a hundred from Irvine.

About fifty connected with Kilmarnock are said to have been awakened at Cambuslang, and there was to some extent a revival in Kilmarnock itself, which was promoted by the visits of Mr. Whitefield. Other places in the neighbourhood, such as Stewarton and Dreghorn, seem to have shared in it; but the town of Irvine is chiefly spoken of. The godly Mr. M'Knight, as already noticed, was minister here. Writing to Mr. Whitefield on the 21st June, 1742, he says: " Blessed be our glorious God, there are some awakenings among us at Irvine; not only of those who have been at Cambuslang, but several others are lately brought into great concern about their eternal state, and among them several children; the news of which I know will rejoice you, and I hope will encourage you to visit us, to help forward this great and glorious work." Mr. Whitefield did visit that district in the month of August. He preached in Irvine, and, as in other places, held many private meetings.* Speaking of this visit to Irvine and some of the neighbouring parishes, in August 1742, he says: " On Friday I preached three times at Kilbride, and again on Saturday once, and twice at Stevenson; on Sabbath four times at Irvine. On Monday, once at Irvine, and three times at Kilmarnock; on Tuesday, once at Kilmarnock, and four times at Stewarton. I never preached with so much apparent success before. At Irvine, Kilbride, Kilmarnock, and Stewarton, the concern was great; at the three last, very extraordinary." And it is said,

---

* The minister's house was then on the south side of the street, opposite the church, and is now occupied by Mrs. Hunter, a worthy descendant of Mr. Walker, then minister of Dundonald. Here Mr. Whitefield held his private meetings; but he preached to crowds in the golf-fields, an open space not far distant, and on the street at the Tolbooth.

that in October 1743, when the sacrament was dispensed at Irvine, the number of communicants then, and on the preceding occasion, was from *two to three hundred* more than in former years; and this was reckoned from a fourth to a fifth part of the whole.

The Presbytery of Paisley, which then comprehended the whole county of Renfrew, and stretched across from the presbytery of Irvine to the Clyde, shared in the labours of Mr. Whitefield, and the revival at Cambuslang; but no one parish is so marked out as to warrant any separate notice. And therefore, we may now return to those parishes which stretch away through Glasgow northward, as before noticed.

Glasgow.—The ministers of Glasgow whose names occur as most deeply interested in the revival, were Mr. John M'Laurin of the Ramshorn parish, Dr. John Gillies of the College parish, and Dr. John Hamilton of the Barony parish. The names of Mr. John Anderson of the Tron parish, and Mr. Michael Potter, professor of divinity in the university, also occur, though less prominently.*

Speaking of the first three, the first place is due to Mr. John M'Laurin. His father was minister of Glendarual, in Argyleshire, and was distinguished, in his day, as one of the translators of the Psalms into Gaelic. He had three sons, all of more than ordinary talent. One died young, but full of promise; another was the celebrated Colin M'Laurin, the great Scottish mathematician; and John, his eldest, of whom Sir Henry Moncrieff says, that he was " not less distinguished as a divine, than his brother Colin was as a mathematician." He was born in 1693, and studied first at Glasgow, and afterwards at Leyden, in Holland. He was licensed by the presbytery of Dumbarton, and, in 1719, ordained minister of Luss, a parish within that presbytery, and on the banks of Loch Lomond. Here

---

* Mr. Potter's father suffered persecution, and died minister of Dunblane. His son was first minister of Kippen, succeeded professor Simpson in 1740, and died in November 1743.

he remained till 1723, when he was called and inducted to the Ramshorn parish of Glasgow. And now properly his life of labour began. Deeply studious, and thoroughly alive to everything practical, whether in religion or matters of philanthropy, his noiseless steps and active mind were soon in almost perpetual motion. He is said to have been eminently a pastor, as well as an able expounder of the will of God; and he seems, as he advanced in years, to have taken a lead in every scheme, whether of general philanthropy or of religious improvement. One of these was his own. At this time there was no Gaelic church in Glasgow, and Mr. M'Laurin set up, for the benefit of his countrymen, a monthly sermon in Gaelic, which he regularly preached.

In Glasgow, as well as other large towns in which revivals occurred, the zeal of the godly first appeared in attempting the suppression of immorality, and advancing the moral improvement of society. The first opening of the public mind was to apprehend only gross evils; and hence the first efforts of those who afterwards beheld the glory of redeeming grace, and sought chiefly the conversion of the soul, were put forth on behalf of outward reformation. And in these efforts Mr. M'Laurin took an active part. But before these had been long continued, whether in the colonies, in England, or in the cities of Edinburgh and Glasgow, the power of Jehovah, going forth with a preached gospel, was announced over all these countries; and Mr. M'Laurin was one of the first, if not the very first minister in Scotland, who opened an active correspondence, especially with New England and other of the colonies, that had been early visited. When he began, neither Dr. Gillies nor Dr. Erskine had yet entered the field; and it was most probably by him that they were first introduced to their correspondents. At this time the American States were colonies of Great Britain, and Glasgow was the seat of an extensive and active trade with them; and this, no doubt, gave Mr. M'Laurin and others great advantages.

But it is important to observe the fact, as from it we see how Glasgow became, at an early period, an emporium of religious intelligence from the colonies, and then became to the country at large, but especially in the west, a source of influence altogether peculiar. And hence one of the causes that the periodicals of 1742 and 1743, on the state of religion all over the world, were published in Glasgow. But Mr. M'Laurin's correspondence was not merely foreign. When the revival commenced in the west of Scotland, he maintained intercourse very largely with his brethren all around, and, it is said, met weekly in Glasgow, with Christian friends, whether of the city or neighbourhood, for receiving and communicating intelligence. His standing, his talents, and his Christian wisdom, as well as zeal, gave him a chief place among his brethren, as a leader and adviser in whatever concerned the spiritual interests of Zion and Zion's King; and therefore references to his opinions and co-operation are very frequent in the correspondence of the day. It is only necessary to add, that he died in 1754, leaving a memory embalmed in the affectionate regards of an awakened and praying people.

Dr. John Gillies, as already noticed, * was son-in-law to Mr. M'Laurin. He was himself of a like spirit. He co-operated with his more aged relative, as a son with his father; and although different in the cast and character of his gifts, yet he also grew up, so as to occupy the place of a spiritual father, especially in Glasgow. One after another of his early coadjutors departed within the veil, and he was himself so long spared as to be recollected by many of the present generation, who all speak of him as associated with whatever was truly pious, evangelical, and philanthropic in his day. And those who know his works, will regard the light which they shed on the times with which he was connected as that of an evening in summer, leaving behind it the saddening thought, that

---

* See chapter vii.

for a season, at least, the sun which then set has not as yet been restored to the spiritual horizon of our country.

Dr. John Hamilton was inducted minister of the Barony parish in 1737, and was translated to the High Church parish in 1749, where he seems to have remained till his death, which was probably in 1779 or 1780. Sir Henry Moncrieff says, that he was " as eminent for the soundness and vigour of his understanding, as for the steadiness and respectability of his pastoral character." The interest which he took in the work at Cambuslang, and the extension of that work into his own parish, have been already noticed in his attestation. It may be added, that many references occur in the manuscript cases, to the religious services of the Barony Church, showing how much these tended to promote the work of God. But he was also, like Mr. M'Laurin, in the habit of corresponding with friends in the colonies, concerning the progress of the revival there, and communicating, in turn, its progress, especially in the west of Scotland.

The Barony Parish.—This parish still surrounds Glasgow on the north side of the river, so far as it permits, and stretches within a short distance of Cambuslang. At that time, instead of having within it a large portion of the city of Glasgow, it was chiefly rural, being merely studded with villages, and encroached upon by one or two outskirts of the city; and there was connected with it, so far as appears, only the one church, that of which Dr. Hamilton was minister.

One of Dr. Hamilton's colonial correspondents was Mr. Prince of Boston, the Dr. Gillies of that city; and in writing him on the 13th September 1742, he describes the state of matters generally around Glasgow, and especially in the Barony parish. And the account which he gives is perhaps the best introduction that can be had to a review of the district. The extract on this subject is as follows:—

" We in the south and west of Scotland, have great reason to join you in thanksgiving to God, for the days we have been enjoying of the Redeemer's power. Mr. Whitefield came to Scotland, for the first time, in 1741; and in many places where he preached, his ministrations were remarkably blessed, particularly in the cities of Edinburgh and Glasgow. In these places, a considerable number were brought under serious impressions, and they are still following on to know the Lord. This, however, was only the beginning of things yet greater than these. In February last, a great concern appeared among the people of Cambuslang, a small parish lying about four miles south-east of Glasgow, and under the pastoral care of the Rev. William M'Culloch, a man of considerable parts and great piety. This concern was connected with some circumstances very unusual among us, namely, severe bodily agonies, outcries, and faintings, in the congregation. The report spread like fire; vast multitudes were attracted thither. I believe that, in less than two months from its commencement, *there were few parishes within twelve miles* that had not more or less of their people awakened by resorting thither; and many who were awakened there came from places greatly more distant. I am verily persuaded, with your worthy brother Mr. Cooper, in his preface to Edwards' Sermon, that God has made use of these uncommon occurrences to make his work spread the faster.

"But, blessed be God, Cambuslang is not the only place in which the work of God has appeared. The same work is spreading in other parishes. and under the ministrations of their ordinary pastors. This has been the case, particularly at Calder, Kilsyth, and Cumbernauld, all to the north and north-east of Glasgow. And I have no doubt, that since the middle of February, when the work began at Cambuslang, there have been *upwards of two thousand persons awakened;* and almost all of them are, according to the best accounts, in a promising condition. There is greatly more seriousness and concern about religion in most of our congregations than formerly. There is also a great desire after the word, and more prayer—more meetings for prayer and spiritual conference. From these evidences, we have the cheering prospect of seeing the Redeemer's kingdom considerably enlarged. In my own parish, there have been *more than a hundred new communicants* this summer—a number more than five times as many as I ever admitted during any former year. Most of them had been awakened at Cambuslang, some of them in our own church, and some had been the subjects of a gradual and protracted change; and these have had nothing uncommon in their circumstances."

The City of Glasgow.—In noticing what was properly the revival in this city, we must refer to the account contained in chapter iv., of Mr. Whitfield's first visit to Glasgow in 1741. From that time forward, he generally spent some time in it, as often as he came to Scotland; even when unable any longer to travel largely over the country, Glasgow was usually visited by him, as well as Edinburgh. These two cities being comparatively near each other, and both large, they were easily reached, and had a commanding influence over large districts of country. And it is interesting to observe, that so late as 1751, the interest usually excited on his arrival, had by no means ceased. Writing in July 1751, and when about to leave for America, he says: "The parting at Glasgow was very sorrowful indeed. Numbers set out from the country to hear the word *by three or four in the morning*. Congregations increase greatly. I *now* preach daily to many thousands. Many of the best rank attend."

But, besides the influence of such visits as these, much good must have been done by other special means. In October 1744, a general concert for weekly and quarterly prayer-meetings began to be observed, and in the year following to become general among the more pious on both sides of the Atlantic. Many prayer-meetings and other special means of instruction came thus into operation, and were continued long after, preserving, in the midst of a rapidly growing population, a large measure of practical godliness among professors.

Were we to go farther into detail, and to speak of the

ordinary means of grace, particular congregations would require to be distinguished, as blessed with evangelical and devoted ministers, and as cherishing among them a more than ordinary share of the piety of their age. But this, besides its invidiousness, would lead away from our object—the extension of the revival into various parts of Scotland.

It is even necessary, in speaking of so large a city as Glasgow, to avoid going into those desultory illustrations which might in other circumstances be suitable, and very much to confine our farther notices to what was statistically ascertained. And the first evidence which we have of this kind consists of a document apparently drawn up by the general session, or some one speaking with its authority, in the "Monthly History" for December, 1743:—

"The increase of the number of tables, when the Lord's supper was given in October, is computed, by persons fit to give a just account of that matter, to amount to about *eighteen* beyond what was usual for a course of years before the late revival. And it is computed that in almost all the churches, three tables may contain about two hundred communicants (making the amount twelve hundred). This increase is, indeed, supposed to be owing, in some measure, to numbers from the adjacent country, and so to be a confirmation of the revival there; but also owing, in a good measure, to a more than ordinary addition of late years to the number of new communicants in the town itself. And this is the more remarkable, seeing that from the number who have seceded, the ordinary amount would otherwise have been less. There was also a more than ordinary concern manifest both in hearing and communicating, and some are said to have experienced much of divine power."

In 1751, attestations were drawn up and published concerning the fruits of the revival, intimating whether these had continued, or whether they had fallen away. A statement of this kind concerning the city of Glasgow, signed by twenty-five members of the general session, and dated 25th March 1751, was published by Mr. Robe. We quote only an extract. After referring to the above statement, published in 1743, they add: "We reckon *that* computation to be very moderate, and think it requisite to observe that preceding the time of revival, for a course of years, ordinarily there was at most only about fifty-four tables of communicants at giving of the Lord's supper in this place, containing about three thousand six hundred communicants; and that since the revival to this time, there has been little or no decrease of the numbers then given, and which amounted to four thousand eight hundred persons; and that the number of backsliders since that time, so far as we know, or have been able to learn, is comparatively small; that several of those persons, who were the subjects of the late revival, and have since died, gave comfortable evidence of their perseverance to the end. Had it been needful and expedient, we could have been more particular, both as to the number and names of those we write of. That preceding this reviving period, religion seemed to be at a low ebb, and like to degenerate, in its life and power, to mere form. The benefits of this revival and spring-tide of divine influences, were not confined simply to those above-noticed, said to be the subjects of that blessed work, who indeed shared deeply in the convincing and regenerating, yea, and comforting, operations of the ever-blessed and Holy Spirit, but also great numbers who, in the judgment of charity, might be termed God's people, many of them of long standing, and who attended at these places where that blessed work was, did share deeply in these uncommon and extraordinary blessings, and showers of divine influence, to their great joy, confirmation, and upbuilding. And, we may add, that a very uncommon liberty, life, and strength, were bestowed upon numbers of the ministers who were employed at these places, and that they were enabled to speak in evidence and demonstration of the Spirit and of power."

The following letter from Mr. M'Laurin, after he had

seen the above attestation, not only confirms but also farther illustrates the facts attested:—

"Glasgow, May 8, 1751.

"Rev. and Dear Brother,—When you are publishing attestations of the perseverance of goodly numbers of the subjects of the revivals in 1742 and about that time, however much we here came short at that period of other places near us, yet, as that period did, and still does, appear to me the most extraordinary I ever saw as to evidences of the success of the gospel, and as I am almost the only minister of this town that was in that station here during the whole of that period, and have had all along the evidence which things of this kind admit of, and which is sustained in other cases, of the perseverance of goodly numbers of these people, I judge it incumbent on me on these accounts to join with others in attesting what is so fit to be remembered and recorded.

"If facts, that have the important character of public notoriety, are on that account attended with distinguished moral evidence, that character appears plainly applicable to the facts relating to the increase of persevering communicants, so well attested by twenty-five members of sessions of this city, in a letter signed by them and directed to you. It is proper to observe, that though it were only supposed that *one-fourth part* of the increase mentioned in that estimate were inhabitants, it must far surpass anything of that kind known here *these twenty-eight years* that I have been a minister in this place, or, so far as I can learn, in the memory of any now living in it—though it is still to be much regretted that there are not many more communicants (I mean worthy ones) in so populous a place;* that after so uncommon an increase of communicants as in the estimate

* The population of Glasgow in 1740 was seventeen thousand and thirty-four; and as the communicants of the Establishment alone were four thousand eight hundred, and as there were, besides, those of the Secession and the Episcopal congregations, there could scarcely be fewer than one communicant for every three of the population, including persons of all ages.

referred to, had there been so many backslidings as some aspersions imply, a proportional number of suspensions from the sacrament must be presumed to have ensued, which is not the case; that continued admissions are really continued attestations of the perseverance now inquired into; that the attestations implied in such admissions, and those contained in the above-mentioned paper, have the concurring characters which, in other cases, render testimony valid, namely, that the witnesses are sufficient as to their character, their number, and their means of knowing what they testify; that among real backsliders there are, through divine mercy, instances of return; that some, who at first were much suspected to be deceivers, have, for a tract of time, given to those who know them best, strong proofs of their uprightness; that persons whose conduct has occasioned reproach to the revivals, are not always found, upon inquiry, to be persons whose profession of religion began at that period; that the unfavourable things above-mentioned are far from being said in the way of mere charitable conjecture; that, instead of that, they are the consequences of such evidence as arises partly from extensive personal acquaintance with these persons, partly from occasional inquiries about them from time to time, partly from more laborious scrutinies set on foot privately, both formerly and of late, among persons attentive to such things; and, lastly, that if any who possibly know only backsliders, can be supposed to claim a right of judging harshly of those whom they own they do not know by those whom they do know, merely because the religious profession of both began about the same time or place, it must be easy for the unprejudiced to observe what principles such reasoning must be built on, what consequences it must infer, and what affinity it has to some people's way of judging of all professors of religion in general, at whatever time their profession began.—I am yours, &c.

"JOHN M'LAURIN."

The Parish of Calder.—This parish stretches along the north side of the Barony parish. At this time, the minister was Mr. Warden, a relation [probably a cousin] of the minister of Campsie, concerning whom some account will be given. The minister of Calder, of whom we now speak, was pains-taking and devoted. There is a tradition, reported by the editor of the last edition of Mr. Robe's Narrative, concerning the commencement of the work in this parish: "Mr. Warden had been in the habit of preaching occasionally to the people of Auchenloch, a distant part of Calder parish, and had to complain that few comparatively availed themselves of the opportunity. Mr. Warden, on the occasion referred to, had said, on intimating his purpose of preaching at Auchenloch, that it was scarcely worth while to give such notice, as the people seemed to be unconcerned about the meeting, but that he would, God willing, give them another opportunity. He went with very low expectations; but, finding a large meeting, he felt as if he would that he had been more fully prepared, and had misgivings about the work. He took for his text: 'Unto you, O men, I call; and my voice is to the sons of men.' (Prov. viii. 4.) The audience was melted under the word, and a goodly number dated their conversion from that sermon." This appears to have been the meeting on the 11th of May 1742, concerning which Mr. Robe says, that there was much outcrying, and that about fourteen were brought under great concern about their state. And writing somewhat later, he adds that, according to information which he had from Mr. Warden, above a hundred had then been awakened.

The Parish of Baldernock.—This parish lies north and west from Calder, and somewhat out of the track of the other parishes to be mentioned. Moreover, it belongs to the presbytery of Dumbarton, and is in the county of Stirling; but it is sufficiently near the other parishes to be noticed, and it held communion with them chiefly, as regarded the revival—its circumstances also were special. Mr. Robert Wallace had been minister of that parish for upwards of fifty years. He is said to have been pious, faithful, and much beloved by his people. But at the time when the revival commenced, he was gone, and the church was vacant. He had left, however, behind him, a valuable substitute, in the person of Mr. James Forsyth, parish schoolmaster, from whose account of what occurred in this parish, as communicated to Mr. Robe in various letters, we shall give an abstract: "From the beginning of February 1742, he had anxiously sought to instruct the young under his charge in the principles of religion, urging on them personally a practical use of what they had been taught, and the necessity of abstaining from all known sin. These instructions and exhortations laid hold on the minds of the young, and some of the more aged were apparently moved by what they observed among the children. One of the school-boys, who had gone to Cambuslang in March, returned awakened, and asked his teacher whether he would allow two or three of the scholars to meet for prayer and the singing of psalms. This was readily allowed, and in the course of two weeks, ten or twelve more were awakened and under deep convictions. Some of these were not more than eight or nine years of age, and others twelve or thirteen. And so much were they engrossed with the 'one thing needful,' as to meet thrice a-day—in the morning, at mid-day, and at night.

"The account which they gave of themselves was also very rational. They spoke of their sinfulness by nature, their actual sins, and their sins of unbelief; and on being reminded of Christ's ability and willingness to save, they replied, We know it, but our hearts are so hard, that unless God work in them, we cannot believe."

Several of the grown people were first awakened at Cambuslang, Calder, and Kirkintilloch, but the greater part were brought into a state of concern while attending the prayer-meetings, which were set up in the parish. These were held among the awakened, twice a-week, and almost daily meetings of this kind were held in some place or other. At the second of the general meetings, there were nine awakened; at the third, four; and at another, five or six. Among these were some who had been known chiefly for rudeness and profanity; and the impression produced among the parishioners was such as to engross general attention, and to bring some from other parishes to attend their meetings. Among these, two young women, who had been at Cambuslang, and brought back an evil report, expressing wonder that any should so give way as to cry out, came into one of their meetings. But before they had been an hour present, they were so convinced of their lost condition, as to be thrown into the deepest distress. Many also found relief, and were brought into a believing state. In this way the work went on, till the number of the awakened was reckoned to be about a hundred.

The case of this parish is interesting on various accounts, but especially as showing, what many seem unwilling to understand, that all who know God as reconciled in Christ, may and ought to bring others to him; and that now as well as aforetime, God perfects his own praise out of the mouths even of babes and sucklings.

The Parish of Kirkintilloch.—This parish lies north of Calder, and was, when the revival commenced, under the pastoral charge of Mr. James Burnside, who was esteemed an able and judicious, as well as pious minister. There was in this parish, also, a not uninteresting incident connected with the commencement of the revival. In the month of April 1742, about sixteen children in the town were observed to meet together in a barn for prayer. Mr. Burnside heard of it, had frequent meetings with them, and they continued to improve. And this being reported, many were the more impressed. But apparently before this, the ministrations of that good man had begun to take effect, and this was probably but the first remarkable manifestation of what was to follow; for on the 20th of May, Mr. M'Laurin and Mr. Robe were there; and the latter says, " There we saw Zion's mighty King appearing in his glory and majesty, and his arrows sharp in the heart of his enemies; many were awakened and brought under great spiritual distress." And soon after, he learned from the minister, that about a hundred and twenty were under a more than ordinary concern, and praying societies were, as usual, formed. Mr. Burnside died in September 1743. In December (that is, two months after Mr. Burnside's death), the elders drew up and published a statement, in which they declare that a goodly number persevered in seeking God, and generally met once a-week in praying societies. And Dr. Erskine, afterwards of Edinburgh, who was inducted minister of Kirkintilloch in May 1744, confirms their statement, and enlarges on the same subject.

The Parish of Campsie.—This parish lies on the north side of Kirkintilloch, and was at this time under the pastoral charge of Mr. John Warden, a son of Mr. Warden of Gargunnock; in connection with whom a notice will be found concerning the date of his son's induction, and other changes.

Mr. Robe says, that he "had always a singular dexterity in instructing and dealing with the consciences of the people under his charge." As this parish is adjacent to Kilsyth, some of the first awakened there belonged to Campsie, and the work went on to a greater or less extent in both parishes simultaneously. In the course of the summer of 1742, about a hundred were said to have been awakened in Campsie. But as a description of what is seen and heard is usually preferred to mere statistics, we shall here introduce a letter, written by a gentleman in Glasgow to his friend in Edinburgh, concerning the first communion occasion at Campsie, after the commencement of the revival:—

"Dear Sir,—The Lord, in his kind providence, carried me to Campsie on Saturday last, where I stayed during the communion solemnity. But truly, I will not pretend to give you a suitable account of the blessed and visible effects of our glorious Immanuel taking to himself his great power, and there, to a demonstration, going on conquering and to conquer. The first sermon I heard was from 1 Tim. i. 15 : ' This is a faithful saying, and worthy of all acceptation, that Christ Jesus came into the world to save sinners; of whom I am chief'—when there appeared a desirable and attentive congregation. The second discourse was by Mr. R——, K—— [probably Mr. Robe, Kilsyth], from Heb. vi. 18 : ' That by two immutable things, in which it was impossible for God to lie, we might have a strong consolation, who have fled for refuge to lay hold upon the hope set before us.' During this sermon there was great melting and mourning among the people, with some outcrying, but not much. In the evening, there was an exercise or lecture in the church, upon the first three verses of the 40th psalm, by Mr. Burnside of Kirkintilloch, on five minutes' warning or so. In his first prayer, which was not usual with him, the tears were running down his cheeks. A little after he began, the Spirit of the Lord, like a mighty rushing wind, filled the house in such a manner that almost the whole congregation was melted into a flood of tears, accompanied with bitter outcries, on the part of some newly awakened. The minister was obliged to stop; and, after a few exhortations, ended the lecture, and left behind him a multitude of distressed souls, thirsting after a soul-satisfying discovery of the dear Redeemer. Near where I had my quarters, there were five or six of these—two of them gentlemen's servants, known to have been wicked.

" On the Sabbath, Mr. Warden had an excellent sermon on these words : ' For when we were yet without strength, in due time Christ died for the ungodly.' (Rom. v. 6.) The congregation was moved, mourning sweetly and devoutly ; and such a set of communicants as were at the *first* table you never saw. There used to be *nine or ten* tables, some years one or two more, but this year there were *eighteen*. Our sermon within was by Mr. S—— of Fintry, from these words : ' Faith worketh by love' (Gal. v. 6); and he had a most desirable auditory.

"On Monday morning, we again assembled in a very becoming manner. One of my acquaintance told me that, in his quarters, a young woman, who had been mocking the distressed, and who refused to come near family worship that morning, placed herself behind the door to listen, and was pricked to the heart, and constrained to cry out. She was with us to-day hearing sermon, and in great distress. Mr. Warden of Calder preached a desirable sermon from Ps. cxix. 30 : 'I have chosen the way of truth : thy judgments have I laid before me.' There was a pleasant motion among the hearers. Mr. M'Laurin of Glasgow succeeded him, from Isa. xliv. 3 : 'I will pour water on him that is thirsty, and floods upon the dry ground.' But of all the days of power, I never saw the like, considering the size of the meeting. The dear Redeemer, by the influences of his Spirit, went from corner to corner; which appeared not so much in outcries, as in a sweet mourning and low motion. The last was truly the great day of the feast. When the bulk of the meeting was dismissed, they came out of the church-yard like a company or two of soldiers, in three and four abreast, supporting the distressed men and women. The state of the parish before, was eighty under soul distress, who had by this time found relief; but now it is far advanced, besides many from the parishes northward, which were, I know, awakened there that day.—In haste, yours," &c.

A very full statement was published by Mr. Warden, which was written in December 1743; but it is much too long for insertion. In 1748, when now in Perth, he was asked by Mr. Robe to state how far the fruits of the preceding revival had continued. And he then wrote anew, declaring that, up till the time of his leaving Campsie, in 1747, he did not know of more than four who had fallen from their profession; adding : " With great pleasure I yet think on many of them, of whom I could not but entertain the highest opinion, and the greatest hopes. A solid and lively sense of divine things seems to fill them with love to God, humility, self-deniedness, meekness, and charity; and a jealousy of themselves, and their own attainments, seems to animate them with a peculiar earnestness in every religious exercise."

The Parish of Kilsyth.—This parish lies east from Campsie, in the great Scottish vale, through which the Roman wall once passed, and where is now the Forth and Clyde canal. Mr. James Robe, the minister, has already been noticed as one of the earliest promoters of the revival, and as having shared in the triumphs of Cambuslang. But, speaking now of him as the minister of Kilsyth, it is due to observe, that as this parish became very much a second source of influence to the surrounding district, so he became eminently the herald of the day, corresponding with all quarters, collecting intelligence, and publishing it in a variety of forms, but especially in his "Monthly History," and in his "Narrative," which, as before noticed, has been recently reprinted. In consequence of this last publication, it is not necessary to give so full an account of this parish as otherwise its importance would demand. Still, as regards the commencement of the revival in Kilsyth, it is so interesting, that we can scarcely think of doing otherwise than glancing at it as we proceed. The good man had long been on the mount, as the prophet was on Carmel, pleading with God; and many a weary look he cast towards the sea, without observing any sign even of clouds. He preached also much and long on the work of the Spirit, as if to bring the people under its power; and yet, so far as for the time appeared, his preaching was only *of* the work—it wanted evidence of the Worker being himself there. At last the news were brought him of what had occurred at Cambuslang. It appeared very much as the prophet's little cloud; but the good man ventured not, like the prophet, to declare that the heavens would soon be black with clouds, full of rain, and pouring down their treasures on many a parish and district. Still, like a true child of faith, he betook himself anew to prayer, crying continually to God that his fleece should not be left dry, when others were thus wetted; and God heard and answered him—yet not perhaps as he expected. In Cumbernauld, Kirkintilloch, Calder, and Campsie—all neighbouring parishes—there were some who had been awakened at Cambuslang. And the ministers of these parishes, because of this, were full of expectation; but the minister of Kilsyth knew of none belonging to his parish. The godly Mr. Willison had come all the way from Dundee to witness what he had heard was going on at Cambuslang, and was on his way homeward, when, on the 15th of April, he arrived at the manse of Kilsyth. This was Thursday evening. His news awakened the despondent feelings of the tried minister. "You must address my people," said he, "to-morrow morning." Mr. Willison consented. Intimations were sent to all quarters, and short as the warning was, the meeting was large. "Mr. Willison preached," says Mr. Robe, "a distinct, plain, and moving sermon, from Ps. xl. 2, 3 : 'He brought me up also out of an horrible pit, out of the miry clay, and set my feet upon a rock, and established my goings. And he hath put a new song in my mouth, even praise unto our God: many shall see it, and fear, and shall trust in the Lord.'" Still the doings of God were yet in secret. On the Sabbath, Mr. Robe himself preached from Gal. iv. 19 : "My little children, of whom I travail in birth again, until Christ be formed in you." The tide of feeling at last began to rise. The preacher so felt as scarcely to be able to go on; and deep seriousness marked the countenances of the hearers. The Sabbath following, one woman was sensibly awakened, but she belonged to the parish of Campsie; and so the fear recurred, that, after all, Kilsyth was to be as the dry fleece, though all around should be as the wet. On the Sabbath following, nothing remarkable occurred; but by this time several prayer-meetings had begun to be formed, and several girls, between ten and fourteen years of age, had been observed to meet in an out-house for prayer. On Sabbath the 9th of May, four or five were awakened; and, on the Wednesday following, Mr. Robe proceeded to Cambuslang, where he saw evidence of the mighty power of God. Returning on Friday, he called at the house of a friend who had a bleachfield, and employed a number of young women; and, to his surprise, he found six of them who had been awakened at Cambuslang a few days before, in deep distress, and crying out for help. As he was hastening home, he spent but a short time with them, and was about to mount his horse, when the cries of another reached him, then another, and another, till he had other six in the same state with the former. On Sabbath the 16th, he again preached from Gal. iv. 29, and extraordinary power now appeared. There was great mourning now over the congregation, and many crying out—some of them strong young men. The number awakened was believed to be between forty and fifty. But, instead of following out the progress of the work in this parish, we must again refer to Mr. Robe's Narrative, merely adding, that upwards of three hundred were said to be awakened in this place—two hundred of them more or less connected with the parish, and the others strangers; and that, in 1751, upwards of a hundred of those in the parish had either died hopefully, or continued to walk worthy of their profession; and farther, that this reaping with joy turned out to be closely connected with his long sowing in tears, and with Mr. Willison's sermon.

Parishes lying east and north of Kilsyth.—These were connected with the presbyteries of *Glasgow*, *Linlithgow*, *Stirling* in particular, and also *Dumbarton*. To all of them the revival extended, yet not in such a way as to require for each a separate section. Cumbernauld, which lies east and partly south of Kilsyth, had about eighty awakened in it; but as the two parishes are contiguous, the influence of the one mingled with that of the other. In the parish of Torphichen, which is in the presbytery of Linlithgow, seven were awakened at one communion, and the work went noiselessly on. And it was also experienced in Falkirk, and other parishes of the Linlithgow presbytery. And, on entering the presbytery of Stirling, there were awakenings in the parishes of Denny, Larbert, Dunipace, and St. Ninians—in the last of these to a considerable extent. There was a district on the river Carron, called Dundaff, partly in the parish of Kilsyth, and partly in the parish of St. Ninians, but separated from the former by a range of hills, and from the latter by a distance of five miles. Hither the work was also carried in 1742, and there are attestations of its continuance in 1743. And at St. Ninians itself, which stretches all the way from Kilsyth to Stirling, and a great way east, there seems to have been a very considerable awakening. It first appeared at the observance of the communion in August 1742. Several were awakened on the Saturday, many more on the Lord's-day, and a still greater number on the Monday, which was reckoned a great day of the Mediator's power. And the work seems to have been going on months after. West from St. Ninians, also, the work extended into the parishes of *Fintry* and *Killearn*, both in the presbytery of Dumbarton, but in the county of Stirling. Mr. James Bain, the minister of the latter parish, had taken part in the work at Cambuslang and elsewhere, from an early period. In July 1742, when the communion was observed, there was a considerable awakening; especially on the Monday, when professor Potter from Glasgow, and the minister of St. Ninians, preached. In 1751, Mr. Bain wrote, regretting that it had been so limited in his parish beyond many others; but giving God thanks that, even then, some of the most eminent Christians he had ever met were among the fruits of that revival. They were poor in spirit, they attained to high measures of communion with God, and cherished fervent love for the whole human race, even their enemies.

The Parish of Gargunnock.—This parish is in the presbytery of Stirling, and lies immediately west of Stirling itself. The minister was Mr. John Warden, a native of

Falkirk. His father was a merchant in that town, and had taken part in the troublous times of the persecution *against* the covenanters; but his son, deeply lamenting this, gave himself wholly to the work of God as a follower of the faithful; and soon after the revolution, he became minister of Gargunnock. Here he was known as a faithful gospel minister, " well seen," as Boston says of him, " in the doctrines of free grace." Mr. Alexander Archibald, a very eminent Christian of those days, says of him, " Mr. Warden, in an action sermon from Isa. lv. 2, ' Eat ye that which is good, and let your soul delight itself in fatness,' with great clearness and earnestness, held forth Jesus Christ and his fulness, and our warrant as sinners to take him as our own. Trickling tears and eager looks marked the inward frame of almost every hearer. My heart was almost melted with the views of redeeming grace, and filled with joy unspeakable and full of glory." In church courts he was among those who stood on the side of gospel truth in the "Marrow" controversy, and although averse to extreme measures, he remained the friend of such men as the Erskines, regularly assisting Mr. Ebenezer after his removal to Stirling. As an author, he wrote a treatise on baptism, and another on the Lord's supper, which was re-published not very long ago, with a recommendation by Dr. Colquhoun and Dr. Ireland, both of Leith. By the time of the revival in 1742, Mr. Warden was far advanced in life; yet did he rejoice in it, as one would in the bursting forth of a late and long expected spring. Some of his people, who were at Kilsyth, attending the sacrament on the second Sabbath of July, came home in an awakened state; others, who were at Campsie on a like occasion on the last of the same month, were also awakened; and others still, who were at St. Ninians the Sabbath following, also a sacramental Sabbath, returned similarly impressed: and on the Thursday thereafter, Mr. Warden himself preached, and eighteen more were awakened that day. The week following, his son from Campsie arrived; and under his preaching, as well as his father's, the awakening became general, deep, and powerful, the gross number of those affected being reckoned at nearly a hundred, which was then a considerable proportion of the parishioners.*

The Presbytery of Auchterarder. The Parish of Muthil.—The presbytery of Auchterarder, and particularly the parish of Muthil, occupies a central position in the southern division of Perthshire. At this time the minister of Muthil was Mr. William Halley. During the prevalence of episcopacy in the seventeenth century, the parishioners seem to have become substantially episcopalian. When the revolution settlement took place, it was laid upon the presbytery to look out for a proper person to be inducted as presby-

* Mr. Warden, the minister of Gargunnock, died probably in 1756. His son, Mr. John Warden, was ordained minister of Campsie on the 3d of April 1732; was translated to Perth on the 16th of March 1747, and to the Canongate of Edinburgh in 1755, where he died probably in 1765. He was the intimate friend of Dr. Erskine, who, when in Kirkintilloch, and the other in Campsie, was his nearest neighbour, and who in Edinburgh knew him as a fellow-labourer, and always spoke of him with much affection; and he is still known as the able and judicious author of a work called "The System of Revealed Religion." His son, Mr. John Warden, succeeded him in the Canongate. But as his mother was a daughter of the laird of Kirkton, in Campsie, and as that property was entailed on her son and heirs male, he took her name on succeeding to the property about 1775, and is therefore best known by the adopted name of M'Farlan, which his descendants bear. His name occurs in the life of Dr. Erskine, as the author of a pamphlet on the subject of Catholic emancipation, "in which," says sir H. Moncrieff, "there is a display of good sense, moderation, and well-conducted argument, worthy of the high character of its estimable author." He wrote also a work on the poor-laws, similar in its principles to those of Dr. Chalmers; but he died at the early age of forty-nine. This was on the 24th December 1788. Speaking of his death, sir H. Moncrieff says, " Dr. M'Farlan died deeply regretted by the whole community of Edinburgh, who lost in him one of its most useful and valuable members. He will always be remembered by his personal friends, and by every individual who had access to know his worth, with the most perfect respect and affection." Dr. Patrick M'Farlan, now at Greenock, and one of the fathers of the Free church, is his only remaining son; and Mr. John M'Farlan, minister at Monkton, also of the Free church, is *his* son, and the fifth in this ministerial line of descent. Mr. James M'Farlan of Muiravonside is also a grandson of Dr. M'Farlan of the Canongate.

terian minister. They named Mr. Halley. But so much were the people set against both him and the presbytery, and, as would appear, presbyterianism itself, that, armed with swords and staves, they occupied the church-yard, guarded the church doors, and refused to admit either the presbytery or Mr. Halley. He was, accordingly, ordained in the church-yard, where he had for a time to preach, and was sometimes even here pelted with stones. At last this opposition gave way, and he entered, as is said, the church on the 20th of March 1705. It is at least questionable whether, even in the circumstances, such an induction as this was justifiable, or not rather to be condemned; but it ought to be observed, that the opposition was virtually against the revolution settlement, and for the continuance of a system which had proved unrighteous, oppressive, and persecuting. But be this as it may, what we have to do with is the work of God under Mr. Halley's ministry, and which extended to a period of nearly fifty years. He proved alike faithful and painstaking; and the writer of the last statistical account adds, that, in 1837, when that document was written, the name of Halley was still embalmed in the traditional recollections of the people.

As regards the revival in that parish, the earliest notice of it is contained in a letter addressed to a friend in Edinburgh, and published in the colonies. The following is an extract: "About a year before this work came to be openly observed, there was a secret stirring and concern among the people. This I was informed of by some religious elders from different corners of the parish. Something of it appeared on the first Sabbath of January 1742, which happened to be a stormy day. I had prepared a sermon which I wished the whole congregation to hear; and, counting on a small meeting, I changed my text; and finding more than ordinary freedom in preaching, I continued to preach from the same text the Sabbath following. Both days I observed an unusual tenderness among the hearers, and I heard more of it afterwards. I was also told of a spirit of prayer appearing among the people; and so it continued, till the third Sabbath of July, when we had the Lord's supper." Writing to Mr. Robe on the 28th of September, he says, in continuation: "At this time, I think our conquering Redeemer made some visible inroads upon the kingdom of Satan. I hope that there are not a few, both in this and other congregations, that can say that God was in this place, and that they felt his power and saw his glory. But, whatever the Lord was pleased to shed down of the influences of his Spirit upon that solemn occasion, it may, comparatively speaking, be accounted a day of small things, in respect of what a gracious God has been pleased to do amongst us since. I must acknowledge, to the praise of our gracious God, that an unusual power hath attended the word preached *every Sabbath-day since;* few, if any, having passed but some have been awakened, and particularly last Lord's-day, which I hope I may say was a day of the Son of man in this place. For, besides the general concern which was seen in the congregation, about eighteen of whom, I got information that night, were pricked to the heart, and deeply wounded with the arrows of the Almighty, the work of the law has been severe and outwardly noticeable upon all that I have conversed with. Their convictions have been deep, cutting, and abiding; and yet I have not observed in any a tendency to despair. The law has been to many as a schoolmaster leading to Christ, and many seem to have attained to peace and joy in believing. Some have been so filled with heavenly joys, as to be almost too much for their frail bodies. Some old people have been awakened, but they are chiefly such as are younger; some not more than twelve years of age are manifesting very delightful fruits, as in the exercise of prayer. They are said to astonish many. Our Sabbath evening meetings are also greatly blessed. As soon as worship is over, crowds come to the manse, filling both it and the court before the doors. Their thirst for the word is great, and their concern so deep, that their mourning frequently drowns my voice, so that I am obliged to stop till they compose themselves. And, when this meeting is over, I am occupied with the awakened, it may be, for hours longer. Many afford such evidence of real conversion, that, to call it in doubt, would be to call in question the experience of the saints spoken of in Scripture."

Writing again on the 29th, he refers particularly to a little company of his people, who had just returned home, after being all the way to Kilsyth, attending the communion there—a distance of nearly thirty miles : " It gave me much pleasure to hear Mr. Porteous (the minister of Monivaird, a neighbouring parish) and some of my people giving such an account of the work of God with you, at your last sacrament. Such of my flock as attended on that solemn occasion, have not, I hope, lost their travel. About seven-and-twenty of them, all in one company, were overtaken on their way homeward by Mr. Porteous, Mr. Erskine, and Mr. David Erskine, who proved eminently useful to them. Such was the distress of many, that, had they not found relief, they would probably have had to lodge in the desert place, where night would have overtaken them; for they were scarcely able to travel farther. The work here is still advancing. Every Sabbath, since I wrote you last, has been a day of the Son of man. Many are so deeply affected in hearing, as to cause a general sound of weeping throughout the congregation, which sometimes rises till I have to stop. Their conversation, coming and going from the church, is spiritual, and their whole course of life devotional. My Sabbath evening meeting had to be removed to the church, where almost the whole congregation attend, and this after a lecture and two sermons; some having a long dark moor to travel after all. There is also a meeting of themselves in the school-house, after the evening exercise, where some hours are spent in prayer to their own edification, and, in some cases, to the conviction of persons standing and listening at the doors and windows. Our praying societies prosper; they are still growing in numbers. They are frequent in their meetings, and the Lord is observably present with them. The meetings formed of boys and girls, give me great satisfaction. One of them, which began after the late communion, has now increased to about twenty members. They first met in the town; but as several of them fell under deep concern, and I was in consequence sent for, I gave them a room here in the manse, where they meet every night. And O how pleasant it is to hear the poor young lambs addressing themselves to God in prayer! Sometimes, standing outside the room, I am myself often melted into tears, listening. There is another meeting of young ones in a different corner of the parish, where Mr. Robertson teaches a charity school. Some of the children desired his permission to meet in the school-house. This was readily granted, and about twenty of them meet twice a-week, some of them having a considerable way to travel homeward in the dark. Both among old and young, the devotional spirit is quite unprecedented in this quarter."

Writing in January 1743, he speaks of the work as still going on, and notices particularly the progress of the young. "We have now," says he, "three praying societies. One of them, at a place about two miles distant, made me a very agreeable visit on the first Monday of the year—a day that young people especially used to be otherwise employed. We had, I think, upwards of forty of them, and they continued in prayer and other exercises till about ten o'clock at night." Writing again in March, he says: "Though the public awakenings be not so discernible as they were some time ago, yet few Sabbaths pass but we have some pricked in their hearts, and, with great anguish of spirit, crying out, 'What shall we do?' A law-work is long continued with many, and some who had their wounds apparently bound up, have them opened afresh; and when the Lord hides his face, they are exceedingly troubled. Ignorant of God's ways with others, they think that there can be no sorrow like their own. But they will gather experience as the Lord teaches."

Two more of Mr. Halley's letters were published in the "Monthly History," the one dated 28th August, 1744, and the other in November of the same year; from both of which the work of God seems then to have been going silently on; the subjects of earlier awakenings growing more and more into the condition of persons bringing forth the peaceable fruits of righteousness. In the last of these, he mentions that some of his people had been again at Kilsyth, attending the sacrament, and that they had returned greatly refreshed, many more regretting that the lateness of their harvest had prevented them from being there also. But we shall now conclude this article, by giving an extract of his attestation in 1751, ten years after the first observable change. "About six of those persons who were the subjects of that glorious work in 1742, 1743, I have every reason to believe, have gone to partake of the rest which remaineth for the people of God. As they had a gospel walk, and were exercised unto godliness, so at their death they gave a notable testimony to the truth and reality of religion and experimental godliness. With some of them, who had been long in the dark about their state, at evening tide it was light. Their doubts and fears were dispelled, and an abundant entrance was ministered unto them to the heavenly kingdom of our Lord. There are a great many, in this and some neighbouring parishes, yet in the land of the living, who were the subjects of that work, to whom, as far as man can judge, it proved saving; their walk being such as becometh the gospel."

Other Parishes in the Presbytery of Auchterarder.—The *Parish of Monivaird* lies directly north of Muthil, and was, as would be observed, under the pastoral care of Mr. James Porteous, who was ordained in 1730, and died in 1780. He took part with Mr. Robe at Kilsyth. And it was reported concerning his parish, during the revival season, that an unusual attention in hearing was observed; that many families, formerly neglectful, set up the worship of God; that four praying societies were formed; that much concern appeared among the young, who had two meetings of their own.

Crieff lies also to the north, but eastward, and was at this time under the pastoral care of Mr. John Drummond. He was inducted in 1699, and continued till 1755. And during the revival, there were discernible awakenings among his people, and some brought into distress. Not fewer than eight prayer-meetings were also set up.

It is mentioned that in the parish of Madderty, which lies farther east and southward, a few boys were found in the fields engaged in prayer. They were allowed the use of a house. Many joined them, both old and young; and they continued, when the information was communicated, to make progress. And in the parish of Auchterarder, which lies farther south, manifestations of the same spirit appeared in the formation of six prayer-meetings.

It is also important to observe, that the presbytery of Auchterarder resolved, collectively, to divide themselves into meetings for prayer and conference, towards the forwarding of this work. Few things are more hopeful than this at present, in the Free church; some at least of the presbyteries spending more of their time in prayer and brotherly conference, than in ecclesiastical proceedings. And when this shall have become general, and shall be followed out in a proper spirit, a spiritual harvest may at last be expected.

Other parts of Perthshire, and also of Fife which lies south-east, were more or less visited with the revival of 1742, 1743. But we must again look northward, crossing the Tay into Forfarshire. Here, and northwards towards Aberdeen, there is scarcely any place of which it can be said, so far as our information goes, that there was anything like a decided awakening, at least in the sense then understood. We shall, however, collect what is said of Dundee, and one or two other places, and so pass on to the far north.

The Town of Dundee.—Mr. Willison, of whom some account was given in chapter ix., was at this time in Dundee, and likely, above most men, to share in the blessings which were so largely dispensed, and the following is the substance of what we have observed concerning it. On Mr. Whitefield's first visit to Scotland, he was very early solicited by Mr. Willison to visit Dundee, and he probably reached that town on the 4th of September, 1741. And in a letter addressed to Mr. Whitefield, soon after this visit, Mr. Willison says: "As for Dundee, I desire always to bless God for the many tears I saw shed, while you were here preaching, and also since your departure, particularly when your labours are spoken of. A good many of the young people in this place have joined meetings for prayer and repeating sermons. I have myself heard some of these young persons pray, and have been delighted with their fervour, and with the expressions employed, confessing, as they do, that they knew nothing of their state till you came among us." In October, on his way back from Aberdeen, Mr. Whitefield preached at a number of places, both in Kincardineshire and Forfarshire, and lastly at Dundee. Concerning the former, he says: "Wherever I have preached, I hear of the good fruits of it, both in convicting sinners and reviving saints." And, as a specimen of the fruits referred to, we shall take the case of Lundie, as described in a letter by his fellow-traveller, Mr. Thomas Davidson: "In several places, the Lord, I thought, countenanced him in a very convincing manner, particularly at a place called Lundie, five miles north from Dundee, where there is a considerable number of serious Christians, who, hearing that he was to come that way, spent most part of the preceding night in prayer. It was betwixt three and four o'clock ere he reached, and he had still to go on to Dundee. Yet scarcely had he begun, when the presence of divine power was very discernible. Never did I see such melting in any congregation." And his own remark concerning Dundee was, "At Dundee, the concern among the hearers is very remarkable." Again, on the 22d of March, 1742,

Mr. Willison says: "Although here in Dundee, we have not such an effusion as at Cambuslang, or other places, yet we have cause to be thankful for the present hopeful beginnings and promising appearances among the young. We see now *great numbers* of them awakened to seek the Lord and cry after Jesus. And still their numbers are increasing, and prayer-meetings setting up so fast in all places of the town, that our difficulty is to get houses to accommodate them. I get very little rest, as they are constantly coming for instruction. I cannot say that many of them have deep convictions, but they have thirsting desires after Christ, after prayer, after hearing the word, and after Christian fellowship. Many very young persons were admitted to the Lord's table here on the first Sabbath of this month." And writing on the 5th April, 1743, he says, "Blessed be God, we have also a great increase of praying societies in this place. I think there will be above twenty of such societies here, and in several of them between twenty and thirty persons; and much time is spent in them—sometimes whole nights. Yet, alas! we have not the awakenings nor deep humiliation of your people." And when writing in 1745, he says with much feeling: "Surely the glorious marchings of Zion's King for many months along the braes of Cambuslang, and the awful steps of majesty there, should never be forgotten. Oh, to see or hear tell of the like *in the parched braes of Angus and Mearns!*" *

* In one of his letters dated March, 1746, there are some curious notices concerning the rebellion: "We had a good number of fierce lion-like men quartered in this town, who threatened us very much with plundering and killing, if we complied not with their measures, travelling still up and down our streets with guns, swords, and pistols in their hands and bosoms. Hundreds of them came sometimes into our churches, having their pistols loaded with ball, and threatening in private to let them fly at us if we prayed for king George; yet they were restrained when they heard us do so, and were sometimes overheard, on going out, blaming themselves for not executing their intention. One day five of their officers, of the name of Farquarson, M'Intosh, and M'Gilvray, &c., advanced towards the pulpit, and three of them coming up close to me, discharged me from praying for king George. I began

The Synod of Ross.—The district comprehended within this synod forms but a limited portion of the county of Ross, including Cromarty, and lies along the Moray Frith on the south and east, the Dornoch Frith on the north, and is so intersected by the Cromarty Frith, as to have many of its parishes connected therewith, and so to have frequent intercourse, though belonging to different presbyteries. On this account, the parishes to be noticed may be reviewed together, though connected with three separate presbyteries.

The Parish of Rosskeen.—The minister of this parish was Mr. David Bethune. He was ordained in the parish of Ardersier, then also of the synod of Ross, in 1713, and translated to Rosskeen in 1717. " Up till this time," says Mr. Bethune, " the parish had been supplied with an episcopal incumbent, and everything like effective instruction and discipline had to be begun." In 1721, he ventured for the first time to celebrate among his parishioners the Lord's supper, *six or seven only* being admitted. For nine or ten years thereafter, the work of God seemed to go on gradually and hopefully. From 1732 to 1742, this progress appeared to be very much at a stand. But from the harvest of 1742, to Martinmas 1743, there was a remarkable revival. About thirty-six men and women fell under deep concern, and were some weeks thereafter received into a fellowship-meeting. The discourses most owned of God in the commencement of this work were from Hos. xiii. 13 : " He is an unwise son; for he should not stay long in the place of the breaking forth of children "— Gal. iv. 19 : " My little children of whom I travail in birth again, till Christ be formed in you;" and John iii. 3 : " Except a man be born again, he cannot see the kingdom

to reason with them, but the women cried so much that after attempting in vain to calm them, and after singing a psalm with that view, I had to pronounce the blessing and dismiss the congregation. They afterwards sent to my house forbidding me to preach, unless I complied with their terms. It was thought best to leave the churches, and we betook ourselves to private houses in different parts of the town. I was, however, only three Sabbaths out of the church."

of God"—especially the first. Those awakened were thrown into a state of great fear, bordering on despondency, and but slowly attained to the confidence of faith; their walk and conversation, however, and their earnest seeking going along with their fears, and seriousness spreading among others. About twelve children, from nine to fifteen, began to meet in a widow's house for prayer and conference. On Sabbath and Monday nights they met, sang psalms, prayed in turn, and conferred on what they had been hearing in church. Some who overheard them were astonished as they listened; and young as they were, they cared for each other, and watched over each other's conduct with faithfulness and affection.

The Parish of Nigg.—The minister of this parish was Mr. John Balfour. Writing in February, 1744, he describes religion as slowly on the advance from 1730 down, and especially in 1739. He speaks of a great increase in meetings for prayer and religious conference. Of this kind there were two general meetings, in which the minister presided, and ten special meetings, in different parts of the parish, and to which members were admitted only on their giving satisfactory evidence of their seriousness. "Worship," he says, "was observed in every family of the parish, except three or four. After public worship on the Lord's day, the families of each neighbourhood met and joined in reading, prayer, and repeating the discourses. They were also greatly rejoiced to hear of the Lord's work in the south."

Writing in June 1744, he speaks of a farther and increased awakening, the feelings of those affected being deeper and more frequent. They generally resolved their first awakening into some passage of Scripture or searching subject, of which the following is given as an instance: A poor illiterate servant lad had called the day before he wrote, and his account was, that on hearing these words, "Awake, O sword, against the man that is my fellow," he gathered that as the Father had given commission to the sword against Christ, for the sins of his people, it would be commissioned also against him for his own sins, unless he attained to an interest in Christ's sufferings on his behalf. He had often, he said, purposed to turn to God before, and afterwards fallen back into sin, and therefore he now came for advice. The awakening had by this time reached persons of all classes, and as the greater part were uneducated, and understood only the Gaelic, it is interesting to observe how their difficulties were met and overcome. The psalms were then in Gaelic, and these many set about learning to read, not by spelling the words, but by taking them as so many separate characters or signs of sounds, already familiar to them. And as all who could read became teachers, the work went rapidly on. Then such as were able to read English were set up as translators, reading their authors fluently, whether accurately or not, *in Gaelic*, each to a little company of attentive and inquisitive hearers. This was practised in the weekly meetings, and also in families.

And writing again in January, 1745, he speaks of the work still going on. At the communion in July, about twenty were admitted for the first time, ten were on that occasion awakened, and soon after ten more, and altogether, between July and January, there were about forty in addition to those admitted in July.

The Parish of Rosemarkie.—Mr. John Wood was minister of this parish, and writing on the 1st of May, 1744, he speaks of the state of religion being low and discouraging previous to 1743. From the time of their communion, which was in July, there was a growing attention to ordinances and a desire after instruction, and by the month of May, about thirty had waited on him in an awakened state. From the account which they gave, their convictions seemed to have been long gathering strength—in some cases for two years. Others, who had not waited on him, were reported to the number of fourteen or sixteen. And he was then waiting, in the expectation of still greater things. "I am the more earnest in this longing expectation," says he, "when I observe the stedfast eyes, the piercing looks, the seemingly serious and greedy desires of many, who have, as yet, discovered their concern in no other way."

Other Parishes in the same district.—Mr. Wood speaks of a similar awakening, to a greater or less extent, in the parishes of Logie, Alness, Killearn, Cromarty, and Kirkmichael; and Kilmuir-Easter is mentioned both by him and Mr. Balfour.

The Parish of Golspie in Sutherland.—We have now got to one of the two most northerly counties on the mainland of Scotland. Golspie, however, lies in a southern portion of Sutherland, and not very far north from the Dornoch Frith. The minister of this parish was Mr. John Sutherland, and the following is the substance of the account given by himself in August, 1745: "The parish of Golspie was, for some time previous to the revolution of 1688, a sanctuary to several eminent Christians, who had been driven out of a neighbouring county by persecution. Here they were protected by the Sutherland family, who steadily adhered to the interests of religion. And although, at the revolution, they might have returned to their own county, yet, out of attachment to the family by whom they had been protected, they remained, and proved a blessing to others. And under the forty years' ministration of my predecessor, Mr. Walter Denoon, religion flourished. At my admission in 1731, there were many of the people godly, and conversions continued occasionally to take place; but down to 1744, religion was by no means in a thriving state. On receiving the intelligence of the revival elsewhere, I read to my people concerning the American revivals, and those at Cambuslang and Kilsyth, and told them what I had myself witnessed at the two last places, and at Muthil, when I was on my way to the assembly; *yet no effect seemed to follow.* When assisting Mr. Balfour of Nigg, at the communion in August 1743, I lamented to him our sad state. He told me what he had himself done, and with what effect; and on returning, I proposed to some of the serious people that there should be three separate meetings on the Saturday evenings, to plead with God concerning his work on the Lord's-day. These met with the other communicants, to consider the proposal, and it was adopted and acted upon for a whole year, *apparently without fruit*. But when our hopes had well-nigh failed us, a merciful God breathed on the dry bones, and since November last, upwards of seventy persons have waited on me under soul-exercise. Some had been months in this state before they ventured to make it known. I have had sundry conferences with nearly all of them, and they seem to have a proper sense of sin, as directed against the authority of God and his love in Christ Jesus, and to be filled with holy wonder at the mercy of God, and at their own infatuation in past years." He then details their experience, as very much what has been seen in other places, and also their reformation of conduct, as thorough and universal, adding: "The work was advanced in some by quicker, and in others by slower degrees; yet in both, a decent, grave, and solemn deportment, or shedding abundance of tears, which they concealed all they were able, were all the visible signs we had, in time of hearing, of their inward concern. About forty of them have, with weeping eyes and trembling hands, received tokens for the Lord's table, at the late solemn ordinance; and it is hoped that the rest will be encouraged to follow their example. As regards bodily effects, some have spoken of their wanting rest for many nights, and some for many hours every night, through the deep exercises of their minds; some have, for a time, lost nearly all appetite for food; some have felt their health and strength impaired; and a few have owned their being overtaken with trembling; but no other bodily effect has been observed. The far greater number of those awakened are between twenty and fifty years of age, few are under twenty, and only four from sixty to seventy. They are, some of them, farmers; some of them tradesmen, with their wives and servants; and seven of them are poor widows. The doctrines taught and specially owned, were the terrors of the Lord against wilful transgressors and unbelieving despisers of gospel grace; the impossibility of being saved on the score of self-righteousness; the necessity of divine power in effecting a vital union with Christ—that it is through this the blessings of the covenant are enjoyed; and the discourses most blessed, were in a course of lectures on the sufferings, death, and resurrection of Christ, with sermons from Deut. xxxi. 21, 22; Eph. iv. 3; 1 Pet. iv. 17, 18; 2 Pet. ii. 9; Eph. v. 14; and Matt. xxii. 4. "

Other Parishes in the district.—Several seem to be referred to; but Mr. Sutherland, who had made inquiry concerning *Rogart*, says, that in 1740, fifteen were awakened; that these, and other serious persons, finding in 1741, 1742, a sad decay in practical godliness, gave themselves much to special prayer; and that in 1743, 1744, but especially the former, about fifty more were awakened, and that they were in 1745 in a hopeful way.

But we must again look southward, and notice what is said especially of Edinburgh, before concluding this general review—and so end at last, as regards Mr. Whitefield, where we began.

The City of Edinburgh.—Mr. Alexander Webster had, it may be with others, written to Mr. Whitefield, inviting him to Edinburgh, some time before he visited Scotland. In reply to two of his letters, Mr. Whitefield says, on the 16th of May, 1741, "God only knows when I come." His actual arrival at Leith, however, was on the 30th of July 1741, and after meeting with the associate presbytery in Dunfermline, he preached his first sermon in the Orphan-house park, Edinburgh, from these characteristic words: "The kingdom of God is not meat and drink, but righteousness, and, peace and joy in the Holy Ghost." (Rom. xiv. 17.) * This was on the 1st of August, and the day

---

* See on this, his first visit, chapter iv. This sermon, as preached in Glasgow soon after, is in the Appendix.

following he preached in the West Church, where he also heard Mr. Gusthart, and Mr. M'Vicar with much satisfaction. And next day he preached in the Canongate. Writing on the 8th, he says: "I preach to many thousands daily, and several have applied to me already, under convictions." On the 13th, he says: "On Sunday morning, I visited and preached to the orphans here, and in the evening to as many people as the Sunday before. People are daily coming under deep convictions." And again on the 21st, "It would make your heart leap for joy, to be now in Edinburgh. I question if there be not upwards of three hundred in this city seeking after Jesus. Every morning I have a levee of wounded souls, many of whom are quite slain by the law. At seven in the morning, we have a lecture in the fields, attended not only by the common people, but also by persons of great rank. I have reason to think that several of the latter sort are coming to Jesus. Little children are also much wrought upon. Never did I see so many Bibles, nor people look into them, when I am expounding, with such attention. I preach twice daily, and expound at private houses at night, and am employed in speaking to souls great part of the day." And again on the 27th October, he says: "It would delight your soul to see the effects of the power of God. Both in the church and park the Lord was with us. The girls in the hospital were exceedingly affected, and so were the standers by. One of the mistresses told me, that she is now awakened in the morning with the voice of prayer and praise. The master of the boys says, that they meet every night to sing and pray, and that when he goes into their rooms, to see if all be right, he generally finds some at their devotion. The presence of God at the old people's hospital was really wonderful. The weeping of the people was like that in the valley of Hadad-rimmon. They appear more and more hungry. Every day I hear of some fresh good, wrought by the power of God. I scarcely know how to leave Scotland."

In turning to the effects produced, we shall understand them better, if we observe that there are different classes spoken of: and first, the boys of Heriot's hospital. The boys in this hospital had the character of being very unruly, and some of them vicious; but through the blessing of God on Mr. Whitefield's ministry, a remarkable change took place, which is described by one of the masters in a letter dated 8th December: "An external reformation prevails among them, and I hope that God hath wrought effectually on the hearts of many. One night, a number of them came to my room, and on being encouraged, they explained to me their circumstances. One said, 'I am troubled with bad thoughts when I pray;' another, 'I think it exceedingly difficult to believe in Jesus Christ. I can believe him to be the Son of God, and Saviour of lost sinners, but I find it very hard to believe that he is my Saviour.' And so said others. On leaving, they went into the school-room, and spent much of the night in reading and prayer. Before many days, they told me that they had, to a great extent, got over their fears; and they now continue fervent in prayer for themselves and all men. Indeed, nearly all our boys are now in love with their Bibles, and delight in prayer. I have often entered their rooms at ten and eleven o'clock at night, to see that all was right, and stumbled on them in prayer, some in little companies and others alone; and this is their daily practice—the elder teaching the younger. No fault is now concealed, as before; they abhor every vice, love one another, and talk of the things of God with the boys of the other hospitals, with whom they often used to fall out. Heriot's hospital is no longer a den of vicious boys, but a Bethel." A gentleman in Edinburgh, writing about the same time, says of the Trades' hospital, that the change there was equally remarkable; that about sixteen of the girls met for devotional purposes every week, and that two young ladies had joined; and he adds, that their teachers reported concerning their conduct as was said of Heriot's boys. After giving a similar account of the girls in the Merchants' hospital, he adds, "About nine of them meet thrice a-week for prayer, eleven or twelve more meet in smaller companies; and some of those so wrought upon were among the most ignorant and thoughtless in the house." And passing from the hospitals, there was a general awakening among persons of different ages, and instances are given to illustrate the power of the Spirit on those. But as effects are best judged of some time after the immediate season of excitement, we shall pass over the more immediate reports, and copy merely part of the following letter, addressed to Mr. Whitefield by Dr. Webster of Edinburgh, and which was written half-a-year after Mr. Whitefield had left for England:—

"April 20, 1742.

"Rev. and Dear Sir,—Knowing that many are careful to inform you, from time to time, what passes here, I have hitherto delayed answering your most acceptable letter, until I should be able to tell you, *with the greatest certainty*, what were the blessed effects of your ministrations amongst us; and now I can assure you, that they were not more surprising than they are lasting. I do not know or hear of any wrought upon by your ministry who are not holding on in the paths of truth and righteousness. They seem possessed of a truly Christian spirit. Jesus is precious to their souls, and, like the morning light, they are advancing with increasing brightness to the perfect day. The state of religion in this sinful city revives and flourishes. Ordinances are more punctually attended. People hear the word with gladness, and receive it in faith and love. New meetings for prayer and spiritual conference are erecting everywhere. Religious conversation has banished slander and calumny from several tea tables; and Christians are not ashamed to own their dear Lord and Master. Praise is perfected out of the mouths of babes and sucklings, and some stout-hearted sinners are made captive to the obedience of Christ. Amidst all these approaches of

Immanuel's kingdom, the enemy does not, however, cease to rage; and some, of whom better things might be expected, join with infidels in blaspheming the operations of the Holy Ghost; but the work is the Lord's, and the gates of hell shall not prevail against it."

We must now conceive of matters going on thus till, after a few months, Mr. Whitefield again arrived at Leith. He had been earnestly solicited to return by many in different parts of the country, and by none more than by Mr. Webster, in the very letter of which the above is an extract. On the 3d of June, he accordingly landed at Leith, and the following is his own account of his reception: "As soon as I came on shore at Leith, many came blessing me, and, weeping, took hold of me. About four in the afternoon, we came to Edinburgh. Great numbers followed our coach, and almost caught me in their arms, as soon as I came out of it. How did they weep for joy! It would have melted you down to have seen them. When I reached my lodging, many dear friends came to salute us in the name of the Lord. About seven o'clock, I went to see some persons of distinction, whose hearts the Lord had touched when I was here last. Some were ready to faint with joy; and with these I prayed and gave thanks. We were all filled with peace and joy in believing. At eight, I went to a nobleman's house, whose lady and other friends received us with great gladness. The cushions and Bible were immediately brought. I gave a word of exhortation. We sang and prayed, and spent the remainder of the evening most delightfully, in talking of the things of God. When we came home, we joined in blessing God's holy name. Though late, I scarce knew how to go to rest. This morning I received glorious accounts of the carrying on of the Mediator's kingdom. The work of God is beyond expression. Three of the little boys that were converted when I was last here, came to me and wept and begged me to pray for and with them."

The hospital park was again fitted up for his meetings.

He was not generally admitted to the city pulpits, or indeed to those of the presbytery; but the magistrates allowed him the use of a church as often as he came, and the park was fitted up with seats and shades in the form of an amphitheatre, and *there* he preached twice a-day to many thousands. It was now the very middle of summer, the month of June; and especially in the evenings, when the slanting rays of the departing sun fell on the vast assembly, and gradually disappeared in the west, as if to demonstrate the sayings of the preacher concerning the passing moment being alone the acceptable time, the effect is said to have been on some occasions quite overpowering. But to copy reports of what was seen and felt, would be only to repeat what has already been often said. We shall therefore again have recourse to what is recorded of the fruits of this second visit; and, first, from a communication dated 8th August, 1743, by Mr. George Muir, afterwards minister of the Low Church of Paisley: "The prayer-meetings are from twenty-four to thirty in number, and so large that some of them will have to be divided. Among them are several of boys and girls, who, in general, seem to be growing in grace and in sound views of divine truth. There are several meetings of young women, who, as I am informed, hold on well. Many young men meet for mutual instruction and otherwise serving God. Many aged men of high standing in the Christian life meet also for edification. And, generally, all of these make it evident to the world that they have been with Jesus."

On the 23d of October, the communion was dispensed in Edinburgh; and it is said that then the number of communicants was greatly beyond what it had been only two years before, that week-day sermons were much better attended, and that a more than ordinary concern was manifest both in hearing and communicating.

Were it our object to follow out the history of Mr. Whitefield's labours in Edinburgh, it would be necessary to repeat similar accounts very often, as he came to Edinburgh not fewer than fourteen times, and over a period of twenty-seven years. Even as regards the revival in Edinburgh, more than ordinary attention to these visits *is due*, as it was to a greater extent than in most other places dependent on these. But as this is not our object, we shall only farther refer to his *last visit*, when now worn out with labour, and suffering from bodily sickness. He arrived in June 1768, and writing on the 15th of that month, he says: " You would be delighted to see our Orphan-house park assemblies—as large, attentive, and affectionate as ever. *Twenty-seven-year-old friends and spiritual children* remember the days of old; they are seeking after their first love, and there seems to be a stirring among the dry bones." Again, writing on the 2d July, he adds: " Could I preach ten times a-day, thousands and thousands would attend. I have been confined for a few days; but on Monday or Tuesday next, hope to mount my throne again. O, to die there!—too great, too great an honour to be expected." Again, on the 9th of July: " Everything goes on better and better here; but I am *so worn down* by preaching abroad and talking at home almost all the day long, that I have determined, God willing, to set off for London next Tuesday."*

In various parts of the south, indications of more than ordinary attention to divine things were noticed; but these were not so remarkable as to require any separate article. And, therefore, we now take leave with Mr. Whitefield where we began; but, in concluding this general though brief review, there are several questions which suggest themselves, and which are at least worthy of consideration.

And *first*, Is it not true that we also live under the ministration of the Spirit, and as regards everything essential

---

* On the 9th of August, his wife died; on the 4th of September 1769, he embarked for America, this being his seventh visit to that country; and, on the 30th of September 1770, he breathed his last at Newbury, near Boston.

to conversion, as really as did the apostles? See Matt. xxviii. 20; John xiv. 16, 17, xvi. 8-11; and 2 Cor. iii. 11.

Secondly, Is it not equally true that, as a generation, we come sadly short of the power which accompanied the Word during the age of the apostles, and also during the times which we have been reviewing? See concerning the one, 2 Cor. ii. 14-17; and concerning the other, the review just concluded.

Thirdly, Is it not equally true, that an awakening such as that now reviewed is much wanted, because of the prevalence of an ungodly and worldly spirit among professors, and on account of the multitude who make not even a profession of religion? Evidence of both is within the reach of all.

Fourthly, Is it not farther true, as formerly noticed, that there is an important end to be served by awakenings, however temporary, namely, in disturbing the deep slumber of an ungodly and worldly age? The ministry of John the Baptist was awakening, and meant to prepare the way for a fuller gospel; and the day of Pentecost itself was but a day, a day of grace; moreover the apostle Peter seems to refer to something of this kind in Acts iii. 19.

And *lastly*, Might it not, then, be well to consider whether we are not sinning in this *through unbelief?* whether, like the Israelitish lord, we are not sinning against the faithfulness of God to his own promise? " O thou that art named the house of Jacob, is the Spirit of the Lord straitened? are these his doings? do not my words do good to him that walketh uprightly." (Micah ii. 7.)

SERMONS

PREACHED BY

THE REV. GEORGE WHITEFIELD

IN THE

HIGH CHURCH-YARD, GLASGOW.

THE three following sermons were preached in the High Church-Yard of Glasgow; that from Luke iv. 18, 19, on Saturday morning, the 12th of September 1741; that from Jer. vi. 14, on the morning of the Lord's-day, 13th September; and that from Rom. xiv. 17, on the evening of the same day. It had also been preached on the 1st of August, in the Orphan-house park, Edinburgh, on Mr. Whitefield's first arrival in Scotland.

SERMONS.

THE DUTY OF A GOSPEL MINISTER.

"The Spirit of the Lord is upon me, because he hath anointed me to preach the gospel to the poor; he hath sent me to heal the broken-hearted, to preach deliverance to the captives, and recovering of sight to the blind, to set at liberty them that are bruised, to preach the acceptable year of the Lord."—LUKE iv. 18. 19.

THOUGH you are all here, I hope, sitting seriously in the presence of God, with desire to hear his Word to your profit, yet I cannot but think it will engage your attention still the more if I inform you that the words now read seem to be one of the first texts on which our Lord Jesus Christ himself preached, when he came to publish the glad tidings of salvation to a benighted world. The occasion of our Lord's preaching upon these words, we find at the 16th verse of this chapter: "And he came to Nazareth, where he had been brought up; and, as his custom was, he went into the synagogue on the Sabbath-day, and stood up for to read. And there was delivered unto him the book of the prophet Esaias; and when he had opened the book, he found the place where it was written, The Spirit of the Lord is upon me, because he hath anointed me to preach the gospel to the poor; he hath sent me to heal the broken-hearted, to preach deliverance to the captives, and recovering of sight to the blind, to set at liberty them that are bruised," &c.

The words, then, plainly contain a prophecy of the Lord Jesus

Christ. He it is who was here spoken of by the prophet Isaiah; he it is who was anointed and qualified by the Holy Ghost, having received the Spirit of God without measure, in order to enable him to perform the mediatorial office betwixt God and man. But the words may be plainly referred to gospel ministers as well as ⁕ Jesus Christ, and the very words of the text plainly give ministers a direction how they are to preach the gospel. And, therefore, from the words,

I shall *first* endeavour to prove that every minister, before he pretends to have orders to preach the gospel of Jesus Christ, from a full evidence of a work of conversion passing upon his soul, ought to be enabled in some degree to say, "The Spirit of the Lord is upon me, and he hath anointed me to preach the gospel."

Secondly, I shall show you what that gospel is, which ministers thus qualified are to preach.

Thirdly, I shall show you the persons whom this gospel is to be preached unto, namely, "The poor, the broken-hearted, the captives, the blind, the bruised."

Lastly, I shall make application of the whole, hoping that while I am preaching, the people of God will lift up their hearts to Jesus Christ; and who knows but we may have an acceptable morning of the Lord?

1. I would endeavour to show you that every minister, before he undertakes to preach the gospel of the Lord Jesus Christ, from a full evidence of a work of conversion, ought to be enabled to say, "The Spirit of the Lord is upon me, because he hath anointed me to preach the gospel."—It is certain there is now a great degeneracy through all the Christian world, and though there may be many reasons assigned for that deadness, that lukewarmness, both in their principle, discipline, and practice, yet I am verily persuaded one great reason is this, That many pretend to preach the Lord Jesus Christ that are strangers to the power of Jesus Christ upon their own hearts. There are many who do run before they are called of God, and therefore it is no wonder they do not profit the people at all. A dead clergy will make a dead people. It is absolutely necessary, before a minister undertakes to preach the gospel, that he should have an experimental acquaintance with the Lord Jesus Christ. A man when he comes out to preach, should preach so feelingly that all who hear him might take notice of him, as the scribes

and pharisees did, that he has been with Jesus. It is a shocking question which Jesus Christ put to Nicodemus—says he, "Art thou a master in Israel?"—Dost thou pretend to be a teacher of others, a guide to those that are blind, to instruct others in the nature of true religion—" and knowest not these things," art not acquainted with the new birth thyself? If Christ were to come to preach the gospel, how many ministers must he be obliged to put this question to! When there were only deacons to be chosen, the apostles said, "Look ye out among you men of faith, and full of the Holy Ghost." And if it was necessary for the office of a deacon that he was to be thus qualified, who was only to take care of the poor's box, how much more necessary is it that those should be full of faith and of the Holy Ghost who are to deal out bread to the spiritually hungry, starving soul? When there was only a material tabernacle to be built, the Spirit of God came upon two special men to qualify them for that; and if the Spirit of God was necessary to qualify them, how much more is the Spirit of God absolutely necessary to enable men to build up the living temple of the Holy Ghost!

Besides, my dear friends, it is not the business of the ministers of the gospel merely to entertain people with harangues of dry morality, and leave out Jesus Christ. It is not our business to entertain our people, as Cicero, Seneca, and other heathen moralists did; but we are to preach Christ, not ourselves; we are to preach the hidden mysteries of the kingdom of God. Now, if a man is a natural man, he can have no notion of the hidden things of Christ's kingdom. "The natural man discerneth not the things of the Spirit of God, for they are spiritually discerned." And how can a man that does not know them, preach them? It is true a man may study a scheme of divinity, and in order to get into a place, to please a patron or some great man, he may get Calvin's scheme, or any other scheme of religion. What is all this, if it doth not come from the heart? the poor people cannot expect to be profited at all. It is poor preaching to preach an unknown Christ; for my own part, I would not preach an unknown Christ for ten thousand worlds. Such offer God strange fire, and their sermons will but increase their own damnation. It is absolutely necessary, therefore, for all ministers before they undertake to preach the gospel to others, that they are taught of God.

Human learning is an admirable thing, when made use of to

divinity. The apostle Paul was a learned man. Every man that reads his writings, must own he was accurate in his style, and a great orator; yet what was all this unless the Spirit of God was in his heart? Great accomplishments in an unsanctified heart only make a man a more accomplished devil; and the more a clergyman knows, if he is not sanctified, he will only be the more fit for propagating the devil's kingdom. It is indeed impossible, in the very nature of things, that a man should preach Christ that doth not know him. I have often thought the minister that does not know Christ, and preaches him for a maintenance, has the greatest drudgery in the world. He is always preaching the thing he doth not love in his heart—and what a drudgery must it be for a man to do so! It is therefore necessary for all ministers, before they undertake to preach the gospel, to examine themselves, and see whether they have got the Spirit of the Lord in their hearts. It is not the laying on of the hands of the presbytery, and having a call of a particular people, that makes a man a minister. These outward calls are certainly good, and I would have every man called as was Aaron; but if you are not called of God as well as of the people, you are no minister in the eye of Jesus Christ, you are carrying your own condemnation with you in every sermon you preach; you will never preach with power feelingly, while you deal in a false commerce with truths unfelt. Every word a minister preaches should be engraven on his heart. It is, therefore, remarkable (though indeed our clergy as well as the clergy of other kingdoms have sadly fallen from their constitution), that in the church of England, the first question the bishop puts to him is, "Are you inwardly moved by the Holy Ghost?" By which they own that an inward call of the Holy Ghost is absolutely necessary for a gospel minister. Many ordained do not mind that question, or rather they lie, not unto men, but unto God. But it is the opinion of the reformed churches, that the Holy Ghost is absolutely necessary before a man can take on him the office of a minister.

And though I would, with all humility, own myself the chief of sinners, yet if there are any persons here in the ministry, I would exhort you, in the name and by the mercy of the Lord Jesus Christ, to examine your hearts, and see whether you are in Jesus Christ or not, and see whether you feel these truths you are preaching to your congregations or not. It will be but poor, dry, sapless stuff—your people will go away out of the church as cold as they came in—except your ministry be attended with the power of God. I would likewise exhort all people who make up presbyteries, and are intrusted with the laying on of hands on those that are sent out to preach, to examine into their experience before they examine into their learning. Learning is a good thing, I am not for crying down learning; but then, for Christ's sake, when persons come to offer themselves for holy orders, examine into their hearts, see whether they are saints more than scholars; and if they are not renewed and converted, and give a satisfactory account of the work of God on their hearts, let their qualifications be what they will, they ought to be dismissed. There is a great deal of guilt lies on those who lay hands on men suddenly, and I would not for ten thousand worlds lay hands on any without examining into their experiences: you are partakers of other men's sin, and whole parishes together may rise up against you at the great day.

I would likewise, as I am near the university, and perhaps as some young gentlemen are come out this morning to hear me—I would exhort you with all humility, in the name of Christ, to consider the importance of that office you are breeding up for. You are to be ambassadors of the Lord Jesus Christ. Let me therefore exhort you to get acquaintance with Christ in the entry of your studies; study not so much to be great scholars as great saints. Know yourselves and God, and a good experience of Christ in the heart, with a moderate share of learning, will make you noble instruments of doing good to mankind. It is true, God may convert people by the devil if he please; but I believe God neither works by him, neither does he convert others by unconverted men. I would therefore exhort all young men that are now employing their time in studies, to take care, first, that their hearts be renewed; not so much to study the stars as themselves. Study the precious Bible, the book of God. My heart is much drawn out for the sons of the prophets; for it is in vain to hope for a reformation in this kingdom, until it begin in the clergy, and those who are intrusted with the care of youth. O that it might be done here in Scotland as in New England universities! I have at present letters from Boston, giving an account of the glorious progress of the kingdom of Christ there. Not above seven in Cambridge college are left without a witness for their soul! When shall we hear or see such a day of power in Scotland? Until we find a work of God stirring among ministers, we cannot find it among the people. Pour out your prayers for your ministers. Many, perhaps, deserve bad ministers, because perhaps you do not pray for them. Pray, says Christ, pray to the "Lord of the harvest, that he may send labourers into his harvest." Pray for students; pray for those who are tutors to students, that they may be taught of God, that when they come out they may say, "The Spirit of the Lord is upon me." When it is upon them, the whole world will be set on fire of love. I would not speak it out of pertness; I speak as I think, as I hope the Spirit of God gives me freedom, and I wish well to this poor kingdom—but this will never be, until the Spirit of God is poured out on the sons of the prophets.

I think it is plain, from what has been said, that every one, before he undertakes to preach the gospel of Christ, ought to be able to say, "The Spirit of the Lord is upon me."

Before I dismiss this, it may not be improper to relate a story a good man gives an account of. There was a presbytery of ministers met together, and one of their number preached. In his sermon he made a supposition that the last judgment was come, and that Jesus Christ was now upon the throne of his judgment, and calling his ministers to an account. He asked one of them, "What did you preach for?" Says he, "Lord, there was a patronage in the family of £150 a-year; I therefore took orders to get the presentation." "Stand thou by," says he; "verily thou hast thy reward." He asks another, "What did you preach for?" And he said, "I preached that I might be reckoned a fine orator, and to have applause of men." Says he, "Stand thou by; verily thou hast thy reward." A third comes, and he said unto him, "And what did you preach for?" Says he, "Lord, thou knowest my heart—I did not seek to please men; and though many infirmities have passed in my ministry, I did it with an upright design to promote thy glory." Jesus Christ immediately cries out, "Make room, angels, for this my dear servant: thou hast honoured me on earth; sit here by me on my throne." O that this story may have the same effect on ministers now, as it had when preached; for we hear they went away affected, and said they would preach Jesus Christ more than ever.

2. But we shall go to the *second* thing, and point out what ministers are to preach—the gospel: "The Spirit of the Lord is upon me, because he hath anointed me to preach the gospel." Observe, we are to preach the gospel, not to preach up moral

harangues. Morality is a good thing, but we must preach the gospel of Christ. The gospel we are to preach is—that Jesus Christ came into the world to save sinners. God the Father entered into an eternal covenant with God the Son; he made Christ the head, the representative of the elect, as Adam was the head, the representative of all his seed. For these the Lord Jesus Christ undertook to fulfil the covenant of works. For these Jesus Christ died a painful, cursed, ignominious death; and by his obedience, and by his death, wrought out an everlasting righteousness for them. So that now, whosoever believeth on the Lord Jesus Christ, whether Jew or Gentile, he shall be saved; let him be what he will, be who he will, if he believe on Christ, there is no condemnation for him. This is, in a few words, the gospel. It is glad tidings of great joy to all who feel their want of Christ. And this gospel is to be preached to all. We are to make an offer of Jesus Christ to you all. "Whosoever thirsteth, let him come to the water of life, and drink freely."

I take the gospel here, more particularly, as signifying the comforts of the gospel; and, therefore, though we are to preach Christ Jesus to all freely, to all indefinitely, yet people will never accept of him, and we can give them no comfort, until that we find they are made sick of sin, and made willing to embrace an offered Jesus.

3. The persons, therefore, we are to preach this gospel to, are described in the latter part of the text: "He hath appointed me to preach the gospel to the poor." Who are we to understand by the poor? We are not merely to understand those who are poor as to outward circumstances, though indeed they are the poor that generally receive the gospel. There are a great many of you perhaps who wish to be great, whereas you should be thankful to God that you are poor. Christ hath pronounced a woe against the rich, and hath told us, "Not many mighty are called;" but it is the poor who receive the gospel gladly. The poor Christ hath chosen, to make them rich in faith. There are many poor people, clothed in rags, who are as proud as the devil himself. But by the poor, you are to understand the poor in spirit; those who feel their poverty, who bewail their misery; those who feel they are lost and undone on account of their original and actual sin, and on the account of the deficiency of their own righteousness. They find they must accept of salvation, or be damned of God for evermore; they find they have nothing to

buy salvation with—they must be entirely beholden to God for it. Are there any such here? And perhaps we have all more knowledge than practice. Are ye poor now? Do ye feel convictions fastening on you? And are you really poor sinners? Can you say from your heart, God be merciful to me, a poor sinner? Many of you may say you are sinners; but if another say so, you will not believe him. But do you feel yourselves lost, undone, poor, miserable, blind, and naked, without Jesus Christ? Do you say so? Then I hope the Spirit of the Lord will enable me this morning to preach the comforts of the gospel to your souls. Ye poor souls, God hath chosen you to make you rich in faith; to you I bring the gospel, the glad tidings of great joy. For you Christ was born; for you the Son of God was given; for you the Lord Jesus Christ became poor, that he might make you rich—to purchase a crown of glory for you. The Lord Jesus, having shed his own precious heart's blood, hath said, "Blessed are ye, for yours is the kingdom of heaven."

You may be as poor as Lazarus, and not have a bit to put into your mouth; you may be glad to be fed with the crumbs that fall from the rich man's table; but fear not, you are rich—you shall be heirs with God, and joint heirs with Jesus Christ. If you are willing to accept of him, behold, the Lord Jesus Christ is willing to accept of you. Though you are poor, the Lord Jesus Christ will not disdain you; the Lord Jesus Christ will take care of you; the Lord Jesus Christ will make you heirs of God; you shall be joint heirs with Jesus Christ; you shall have crowns on your heads, and sit on God's right hand in the kingdom of God. This is the gospel—this is glad tidings to you who are poor.

The next persons are the broken-hearted: "He hath sent me to heal the broken-hearted." By nature we are whole-hearted; and while we are whole, while we are righteous, we need not the Physician; while we do not feel the want of Christ, Jesus Christ and his gospel are not precious to us. Our hearts, by nature, are harder than the nether millstone: they are so hard, that none but God can break them. We reckon it a great misfortune, if we say that such a person has broken his heart—for that sorrow of the world which worketh death is a pitiful case indeed; but do not be angry at me, when I pray God to break every one of your hearts. But what shall it be broken with? With the sight of a wounded Saviour?—of a bleeding, panting, dying Redeemer? The heart broken is the result of looking to Him—of the soul's looking to him whom it has pierced, and mourning as a woman mourneth for her first-born. Are there any poor broken-hearted creatures in this congregation? And, indeed, how can you look up to Christ hanging on an accursed tree, and yet not have your hearts broken? The rocks rent, the graves opened, when Jesus Christ was giving up the ghost; nay, the sun itself withdrew its light, as ashamed and blushing, as it were, to see the God of nature suffer. And shall we see Christ crucified before us, and yet our hearts remain hard and unbroken still? For such as are unbroken, and not changed, I cannot give them comfort; but if there are any broken-hearted creatures here, there is healing in Christ for them; he hath sent me to heal broken-hearted sinners—first to break them, to wound them, and then to heal them. I know very well, when your hearts are broken with a sense of sin, the devil will strike in with terror, and tell you ye are past recovery; the devil will bid you despair of mercy, and not trust in Jesus Christ. But what says the text? "He hath sent me to heal the broken-hearted." Though this is impossible with men, yet it is possible with God.

Jesus Christ feels every sigh, every pang, every throe of your poor soul; Jesus feels the load with you, and he will take the load off from you. Jesus Christ has got a sovereign remedy to heal you. What is that? It is his precious blood—it is a soul-saving remedy. Here is a healing remedy; and, therefore, if your hearts are broken with a sense of sin, come away to the blood of Christ. There is the remedy the poor creature shall have for the accepting of. No one came to Jesus Christ, and went away uncured. And when the Lord undertakes to cure you, he will do it to purpose. Come to Jesus Christ—look at him—do not look to yourselves too much; look out of yourselves, and look up to Christ. The more you look to yourselves, the more you will fall into unbelief; but look out of yourselves to Christ by a direct act of faith, and one look of faith will heal your hearts. You will feel the power of Christ's blood—it is omnipotent! it is almighty! it can cure all broken hearts! Come to the Lord Jesus Christ, and he will heal you. He can but speak the word, and it is done; and the more you come, the more welcome you are to Jesus Christ.

Well, the next is the captive: "He hath sent me to preach deliverance to the captives." By captives we may here first understand all mankind. We are all captives by nature—led captive by the devil, by the world, by our own corrupt hearts;

we are led captive by the devil at his will; by nature we tempt the devil to tempt us; we love the broad way; we hate God and his laws, and bid God depart from us; we are willing drudges to the devil. We are captives in general; but more particularly those who, though they are in captivity, yet feel the misery of captivity. Those who are desirous to get rid of captivity, these we are in a special manner to preach deliverance unto. It is just like a proclamation from the king to the captives in Babylon: they who were fond of their captivity, stayed in Babylon; but they who were weary of it, they had leave given them to go back to Jerusalem. We issue out a proclamation from the King of kings, to all poor captive souls now taken captive by the devil. Is there any of you weary of your burden?—or do you hug your chains, and look on ministers as troublers of Israel?—or do you say, O that my heart were set at liberty! O that I were delivered from the guilt and power of sin! O that my heart-lusts were mortified! O that old things were passed away, and all things were become new in my soul! Is this the language of your heart? Then, behold, I preach to you deliverance by the blood, by the power and Spirit of Jesus Christ. Jesus Christ has led captivity captive; Jesus Christ has the keys of death and hell in his hand. Jesus Christ can open the prison doors; and though you are prisoners, yet you are prisoners of hope. But yet you may say, I have been such a sinner against God, that there is no ransom can be paid for my sin—I deserve to be kept captive, and damned for ever; and I despair of having a sufficient ransom paid for me. But I say, The blood of Christ is the ransom. Christ has bought thy deliverance with a great price—the inestimable price of his blood; Jesus Christ hath purchased it by his precious blood, and God the Father is as willing to release you, as God the Son is to have you released. The great question is, Whether you are willing to come out of your Sodom, to the new Jerusalem? Are you so? Behold, then, your Jesus, the finisher of your salvation, that triumphed over his enemies on the cross, is willing to deliver you. Fear not deliverance! When Jesus is your deliverer, he will deliver you from the guilt and from the power of sin; he will make you new creatures; you shall have love, and peace, and joy, and sweetness, and meekness, in your hearts; and being delivered from death and hell, you shall be invested with eternal glory. This is the deliverance we preach to all who are led captive—who are weary of their captivity. Behold, we preach deliverance to you from captivity this morning; may the Lord give you a heart to accept of it!

Again, we are to preach recovering of sight to the blind. We are all by nature blind; and this is our great misfortune, we do not know it—we think we see. There are some men think they are mighty seeing men, but they do not see; they say they see, and yet they do not see original sin—they do not see the corruption of their hearts. These poor creatures are blind: we are blind by nature; we know not the way, by nature, of being reconciled to God, more than a man born blind knows how to describe the sun. But the blind here mentioned are those who, like Bartimeus, are sensible of their blindness, and desire to see the Lord Jesus Christ. There are a great many of you here; but who of you is a blind beggar, and cries out: "Jesus, thou Son of David, have mercy on me?" If God were to ask you what you want, can any of you say, with blind Bartimeus, "Lord, I want to receive my sight?" Do you want to receive Christ? If you know him, you will long to see him again; he is the fairest among ten thousand, and altogether lovely. Are any of you really willing to see Christ? Are you like the Greeks that came up to worship at Jerusalem, that came to Andrew, saying: "Sir, we would see Jesus?" Then Jesus you shall see. But you say, I am blind. I know you are. There are scales on the eyes of your mind, and a veil on your heart, which intercepts your sight of Christ. But what says Christ to the church of Laodicea? "I counsel thee to come to me and buy eye-salve, to anoint thine eyes, that thou mayest see!" We are blind; though we did see when we came first out of the hand of our Maker, yet now we are blind. But yet, blessed be God, there is recovering of sight to such blind souls as we are. How are we to recover our sight? It is by our Lord Jesus Christ; it is Jesus who opened the eyes of the man that was born blind; the same Jesus who touched this man's eyes, must touch your eyes, and must cause the scales to fall from your eyes, as they fell from Paul's, otherwise you shall be damned for ever. You shall see Christ, indeed, whether you be born again of God or not; but if you are not born again of Christ, you shall see him only to damn you—you shall see him once, that it may be your judgment to see what you have lost. But never, never, shall you see him any more. Blind soul, look up to Jesus Christ. Now some of you may be drooping, and think you shall never see Christ, because you have been in the dark for some time; but do not despair, Jesus Christ has recovered the sight of thousands of millions; why may not each of you say, Lord, why wilt thou not give sight to me also? Can you not put in a word? If you can mix faith with the promise, and look up to Jesus Christ, you shall see. What shall you see? You shall see wonders; you shall see Christ, and you shall be so ravished with his beauty, that you shall be scarcely able to contain yourself. You shall see fulness and righteousness in the Son of God—something in Christ that will satisfy all your wants; you shall see your interest in him; you shall see that you shall be with him for evermore; you shall see him here by faith, and see him as he is in heaven; you shall see wondrous things. May God recover the sight of all you poor blind sinners!

Once more, Christ says, "The Lord hath sent me to set at liberty them that are bruised." We are described as poor, broken, blind, bruised creatures. What a poor helpless creature is man in his natural state! We are all bruised even unto death, and if you want to know how we come to be thus bruised: by falling out with God, the devil bruised our heel most wretchedly. But, blessed be God, we shall yet bruise his cursed head. Our whole head is sick, our whole heart is faint; from the crown of the head to the sole of the foot, we are full of wounds, bruises, and putrefying sores. In our flesh there dwelleth no good thing. We are like the poor creature that fell among the thieves—quite destitute and forlorn; and there shall for ever lie, unless Jesus Christ come to set us at liberty. Are any here feeling their bruises? What signifies your hearing without feeling? Are any here made sensible of their dreadful fall from God? then do not despair, your case is not desperate, the Lord Jesus Christ will set your hearts at liberty. " He hath sent me to set at liberty them that are bruised." Christ will open the prison-door, and let your bruised souls come forth. God the Father sent Christ, and Jesus Christ never came to do the thing he will not perform; therefore he will take care of poor, bruised souls. Christ shall pour in the wine of his consolation into your souls; Christ will do more for you than what the Samaritan did for the wounded traveller. You are so bruised that you cannot walk and come to God; but take comfort, Christ has borne thy sins in his own body on the tree. The Samaritan carried that man on his own beast; but Jesus Christ has carried thy sins on his own body. You want to be taken care of: Jesus Christ will take care of you; he will put you into the inn of the visible church, he will give his ministers charge to nurse you up, until he come and call you to judgment. You cannot tell how tenderly and lovingly he will deal with you. He has wounded you, but indeed he will heal you thoroughly, and present you at last blameless and spotless before his Father, saying, "Behold me, O Father, and these children thou has given me." Thus shall it be done to all you who are bruised, and are willing to be set at liberty by Jesus Christ. Here, then, I preach the gospel to all such poor creatures that feel the want of a Redeemer, that are blind. poor, broken-hearted, bruised; this will be acceptable doctrine to your souls.

4. But what shall I say to you (and perhaps the greatest part of this congregation consists of such), who, instead of being poor, are rich. You do not want Jesus Christ; you will be saved by your own morality. What shall I say to you who, instead of being broken-hearted, your hearts are hard as the nether millstone?— they are so hard and impenetrable, that they cannot be moved at the thoughts of a crucified Jesus. Instead of being blind, you think you see; you see no want of Christ, no want of the divinity of Christ, no want of free justification through the imputed righteousness of Christ—what shall I say to you? You love the ways of the devil, hate God in your hearts, and are every day tempting the devil to tempt you—what shall I say to you? You think you are mighty fine creatures, and hate those ministers that describe man in such a black colour. Shall I preach the gospel to you? Thus far I will preach it; you are welcome to Christ if you will accept it; but if you continue in this condition, I will preach hell to you. Ye poor miserable creatures, what a damnable condition are your souls in! Ye poor blind souls, ye poor whole-hearted creatures, you think you lack nothing, but, alas! you know not that you are poor, miserable, blind, and naked. What shall I say to you? For Jesus Christ's sake, consider the danger you are in; the next step you may go to hell—you may go to the devil directly. You may scoff at Christ and despise the offer of a blessed Redeemer—the preaching of the gospel may to your hardened hearts be foolishness, and you may bid God depart from you, as you desire not the knowledge of his way; and because all things continue as they were, you may mock and say, "Where is the promise of his coming? for since the fathers fell asleep, all things continue as they were from the beginning." But remember, Jesus Christ will avenge himself of his adversaries by-and-by.

God may bear with you long, but God will not forbear with you always. Now the time is coming when God will vindicate his injured honour, when God shall lay hold on his glittering sword, when God shall sheathe his sword in your heart's blood; and if you will not come to Jesus Christ now, Christ shall say, "Depart from me, ye cursed," when he comes to judgment. Hear, then; I preach the law to you, to you that will not come to Christ; and O that God would give this word a commission as once Moses' rod got. I would strike the rock of your hearts through and through, but out of love, that your poor souls should come to Christ to be saved in the day of the Lord Sinners! sinners! how will you escape, if you neglect the great salvation—salvation wrought out for poor sinners by a bleeding Saviour? Do you think God will take it kind? He hath left fallen angels to perish in their sin, he hath sent fallen man the offer of a Saviour; and if you deny Christ, and will not come to him, you commit a crime the devil never did commit, and justly will you be made to say, I am damned for evermore.

O sinners, I would fain turn to preach the comforts of the gospel, but I must speak a little more of the law to you. You are hanging over the fiery furnace, over hell-fire, by a single thread of this life. God Almighty knows but this may be the last time you shall hear this word, and out of Christ you will find God to be to you a consuming fire. "Kiss the Son, then, lest he be angry, and ye perish from the right way." Indeed, it is out of love and sincere affection to your souls I speak so. Let me prevail upon some one of you, do not at all despise Jesus Christ, but accept of salvation by Christ. There is no entering into the gates of heaven but by Christ; he is the way, he is the truth, he is the life. Are there any of the children of God here? I hope there are many. I have heard that this place was famous for the work of God. Sure there are some few names in Sardis, who have not defiled their garments. Help me by your Christian prayers, and wrestle with God, that the Spirit of the Lord may wound them that are sinners, and convince them of their danger, and make them willing to accept of Jesus Christ. O! what shall I say? How shall I prevail? I know I can do nothing without God; but I hope God will send his Spirit to bring some of you home to himself.

It would be my meat and drink to hear of your coming to Christ, more than to hear that your corn and wine increaseth. Beg of God to wound you, that you may see your want of a Redeemer.

THE DUTY OF A GOSPEL MINISTER.

As for you who do see him, I open all the magazine of God's storehouse to you; I proclaim peace to you, be you what you may; come eat of Christ's bread, and drink of Christ's wine—you are welcome. Come and feed on a crucified Lamb. Jesus Christ is become our passover; he is the Lamb slain from the foundation of the world. Come and feast on fat things full of marrow, you poor, broken-hearted souls; poor sinners that feel your poverty, you are welcome to Jesus Christ. O that God may make this an acceptable morning of the Lord to some of your souls! My dear friends, I would have you feed on Christ by faith with thanksgiving; that is real feeding on Christ. Those who know what it is to be born again, can feed on Jesus Christ. I hope some of you are feeding on Christ, and I am sure you have precious food. I have been but a little while in Christ's service, but I hope I have fed on him, and O! he is mighty, mighty sweet. May God give you to feed on him; as you grow in years, so may you grow in grace. Let ministers preach Jesus, let them venture their souls for preaching Christ; if the Spirit of the Lord is upon them, they will be able to do wonders. May God do wonders on ministers and people; and may we meet together to feed on Christ in the beatific vision hereafter. Amen.

THE METHOD OF GRACE.

"They have healed also the hurt of the daughter of my people slightly, saying, Peace, peace, when there is no peace."—JER. vi. 14.

As God can send a nation or people no greater blessing than to give them faithful, sincere, and upright ministers, so the greatest curse that God can possibly send upon a people in this world, is to give them over to blind, unregenerate, carnal, lukewarm, and unskilful guides. And yet, in all ages, we find that there have been many wolves in sheep's clothing, many that daubed with untempered mortar, that prophesied smoother things than God did allow. As it was formerly, so it is now; there are many that corrupt the Word of God and deal deceitfully with it. It was so in a special manner in the prophet Jeremiah's time; and he, faithful to his Lord, faithful to that God who employed him, did not fail from time to time to open his mouth against them, and to bear a noble testimony to the honour of that God in whose name he from time to time spake. If you will read his prophecy, you will find that none spake more against such ministers than Jeremiah, and here especially in the chapter out of which the text is taken, he speaks very severely against them—he charges them with several crimes; particularly, he charges them with covetousness: "For," says he in the 13th verse, "from the least of them even to the greatest of them, every one is given to covetousness; and from the prophet even unto the priest, every one dealeth falsely." And then, in the words of the text, in a more special manner, he exemplifies how they had dealt falsely, how they had behaved treacherously to poor souls: says he, "They have healed also the hurt of the daughter of my people slightly, saying, Peace, peace, when there is no peace." . The prophet, in the name of God, had been denouncing war against the people, he had been telling them that their house should be left desolate, and that the Lord would certainly visit the land with war. "Therefore," says he, in the 11th verse, "I am full of the fury of the Lord; I am weary with holding in; I will pour it out upon the children abroad, and upon the assembly of young men together; for even the husband with the wife shall be taken, the aged with him that is full of days. And their houses shall be turned unto others, with their fields and wives together; for I will stretch out my hand upon the inhabitants of the land, saith the Lord." The prophet gives a thundering message, that they might be terrified and have some convictions and inclinations to repent; but it seems that the false prophets, the false priests, went about stifling people's convictions, and when they were hurt or a little terrified, they were for daubing over the wound, telling them that Jeremiah was but an enthusiastic preacher, that there could be no such thing as war among them, and saying to people, Peace, peace, be still, when the prophet told them there was no peace. The words, then, refer primarily unto outward things, but I verily believe have also a further reference to the soul, and are to be referred to those false teachers, who, when people were under conviction of sin, when people were beginning to look towards heaven, were for stifling their convictions and telling them they were good enough before. And, indeed, people generally love to have it so; our hearts are exceedingly deceitful, and desperately wicked; none but the eternal God knows how treacherous they are. How many of us cry, Peace, peace, to our souls, when there is no peace! How many are there who are now settled upon their lees, that now think they are Christians, that now flatter themselves that they have an interest in Jesus Christ; whereas if we come to examine their experiences, we shall find that their peace is but a peace of the devil's making—it is not a peace of God's giving—it is not a peace that passeth human understanding. It is matter, therefore, of great importance, my dear hearers, to know whether we may speak peace to our hearts. We are all desirous of peace; peace is an unspeakable blessing; how can we live without peace? And, therefore, people from time to time must be taught how far they must go, and what must be wrought in them, before they can speak peace to their hearts. This is what I design at present, that I may deliver my soul, that I may be free from the blood of all those to whom I preach—that I may not fail to declare the whole counsel of God. I shall, from the words of the text, endeavour to show you what you must undergo, and what must be wrought in you before you can speak peace to your hearts.

But before I come directly to this, give me leave to premise a caution or two. And the first is, that I take it for granted you believe religion to be an inward thing; you believe it to be a work in the heart, a work wrought in the soul by the power of the Spirit of God. If you do not believe this, you do not believe your Bibles. If you do not believe this, though you have got your Bibles in your hand, you hate the Lord Jesus Christ in your heart; for religion is everywhere represented in Scripture as the work of God in the heart. "The kingdom of God is within us," says our Lord; and, "He is not a Christian who is one outwardly; but he is a Christian who is one inwardly." If any of you place religion in outward things, I shall not perhaps please you this morning; you will understand me no more when I speak of the work of God upon a poor sinner's heart, than if I were talking in an unknown tongue. I would further premise a caution, that I would by no means confine God to one way of acting. I would by no means say, that all persons, before they come to have a settled peace in their hearts, are obliged to undergo the same degrees of conviction. No; God has various ways of bringing his children home; his sacred Spirit bloweth when, and where, and how it listeth. But, however, I will venture to affirm this, that before ever you can speak peace to your heart, whether by shorter or longer continuance of your convictions, whether in a more pungent or in a more gentle way, you must undergo what I shall hereafter lay down in the following discourse.

First, then, before you can speak peace to your hearts, you must be made to see, made to feel, made to weep over, made to bewail, your actual transgressions against the law of God. According to the covenant of works, "The soul that sinneth it shall die;" cursed is that man, be he what he may, be he who he may, that continueth not in all things that are written in the book of the law to do them. We are not only to do some things, but we are to do all things, and we are to continue so to do; so that the least deviation from the moral law, according to the covenant of works, whether in thought, word, or deed, deserves eternal death at the hand of God. And if one evil thought, if one evil word, if one evil action, deserves eternal damnation, how many hells, my friends, do every one of us deserve, whose whole lives have been one continued rebellion against God! Before ever, therefore, you can speak peace to your hearts, you must be brought to see, brought to believe, what a dreadful thing it is to depart from the living God. And now, my dear friends, examine your hearts, for I hope you came hither with a design to have your souls made better. Give me leave to ask you, in the presence of God, whether you know the time, and if you do not know exactly the time, do you know there was a time, when God wrote bitter things against you, when the arrows of the Almighty were within you? Was ever the remembrance of your sins grievous to you? Was the burden of your sins intolerable to your thoughts? Did you ever see that God's wrath might justly fall upon you, on account of your actual transgressions against God? Were you ever in all your life sorry for your sins? Could you ever say, My sins are gone over my head as a burden too heavy for me to bear? Did you ever experience any such thing as this? Did ever any such thing as this pass between God and your soul? If not, for Jesus Christ's sake, do not call yourselves Christians; you may speak peace to your hearts, but there is no peace. May the Lord awaken you, may the Lord convert you, may the Lord give you peace, if it be his will, before you go home!

But further: you may be convinced of your actual sins, so as to be made to tremble, and yet you may be strangers to Jesus Christ, you may have no true work of grace upon your hearts. Before ever, therefore, you can speak peace to your hearts, conviction must go deeper; you must not only be convinced of your actual transgressions against the law of God, but likewise of the foundation of all your transgressions. And what is that? I mean original sin, that original corruption each of us brings into the world with us, which renders us liable to God's wrath and damnation. There are many poor souls that think themselves fine reasoners, yet they pretend to say there is no such thing as original sin; they will charge God with injustice in imputing Adam's sin to us; although we have got the mark of the beast and of the devil upon us, yet they tell us we are not born in sin. Let them look abroad into the world and see the disorders in it, and think, if they can, if this is the paradise in which God did put man. No! everything in the world is out of order. I have often thought, when I was abroad, that if there were no other argument to prove original sin, the rising of wolves and tigers against man, nay, the barking of a dog against us, is a proof of original sin. Tigers and lions durst not rise against us, if it were not for Adam's first sin; for when the creatures rise up against us, it is as much as to say, You have sinned against God, and we take up our Master's quarrel. If we look inwardly, we shall see enough of lusts, and man's temper contrary to the temper of God. There is pride, malice, and revenge, in all our hearts; and this temper cannot come from God; it comes from our first parent, Adam, who, after he fell from God, fell out of God into the devil. However, therefore, some people may deny this, yet when conviction comes, all carnal reasonings are battered down immediately, and the poor soul begins to feel and see the fountain from which all the polluted streams do flow. When the sinner is first awakened, he begins to wonder—How came I to be so wicked? The Spirit of God then strikes in, and shows that he has no good thing in him by nature; then he sees that he is altogether gone out of the way, that he is altogether become abominable, and the poor creature is made to lie down at the foot of the throne of God, and to acknowledge that God would be just to damn him, just to cut him off, though he never had committed one actual sin in his life. Did you ever feel and experience this, any of you—to justify God in your damnation—to own that you are by nature children of wrath, and that God may justly cut you off, though you never actually had offended him in all your life? If you were ever truly convicted, if your hearts were ever truly cut, if self were truly taken out of you, you would be made to see and feel this. And if you have never felt the weight of original sin, do not call yourselves Christians. I am verily persuaded original sin is the greatest burden of a true convert; this ever grieves the regenerate soul, the sanctified soul. The indwelling of sin in the heart is the burden of a converted person; it is the burden of a true Christian. He continually cries out, "O! who will deliver me from this body of death," this indwelling corruption in my heart? This is that which disturbs a poor soul most. And, therefore, if you never felt this inward corruption, if you never saw that God might justly curse you for it, indeed, my dear friends, you may speak peace to your hearts, but I fear, nay, I know, there is no true peace.

Further: before you can speak peace to your hearts, you must not only be troubled for the sins of your life, the sin, of your nature, but likewise for the sins of your best duties and performances. When a poor soul is somewhat awakened by the terrors of the Lord, then the poor creature, being born under the covenant of works, flies directly to a covenant of works again. And as Adam and Eve hid themselves among the trees of the garden, and sewed fig leaves together to cover their nakedness, so the poor sinner, when awakened, flies to his duties and to his performances, to hide himself from God, and goes to patch up a righteousness of his own. Says he, I will be mighty good now—I will reform—I will do all I can; and then certainly Jesus Christ will have mercy on me. But before you can speak peace to your heart, you must be brought to see that God may damn you for the best prayer you ever put up; you must be brought to see that all your duties—all your righteousness—as the prophet elegantly expresses it—put them all together, are so far from recommending you to God, are so far from being any motive and inducement to God to have mercy on your poor soul, that he will see them to be filthy rags, a menstruous cloth—that God hates them, and cannot away with them, if you bring them to him in order to recommend you to his favour. My dear friends, what is there in our performances to recommend us unto God? Our persons are in an unjustified state by nature, we deserve to be damned ten thousand times over; and what must our performances be? We can do no good thing by nature: "They that are in the flesh cannot please God." You may do things materially good, but you cannot do a thing formally and rightly good; because nature cannot act above itself. It is impossible that a man who is unconverted can act for the glory of God; he cannot do anything in faith, and "whatsoever is not of faith is sin." After we are renewed, yet we are renewed but in part, indwelling sin continues in us, there is a mixture of corruption in every one of our duties; so that after we are converted, were Jesus Christ only to accept us according to our works, our works would damn us, for we cannot put up a prayer but it is far from that perfection which the moral law requireth. I do not know what you may think, but I can say that I cannot pray but I sin—I cannot preach to you or any others but I sin—I can do nothing without sin; and, as one expresseth it, my repentance wants to be repented of, and my tears to be washed in the precious blood of my dear Redeemer. Our best duties are as so many splendid sins. Before you can speak peace to your heart, you must not only be sick of your original and actual sin, but you must be made sick of your righteousness, of all your duties and performances. There must be a deep conviction before you can be brought out of your self-righteousness; it is the last idol taken out of our heart. The pride of our heart will not let us submit to the righteousness of Jesus Christ. But if you never felt that you had no righteousness of your own, if you never felt the deficiency of your own righteousness, you cannot come to Jesus Christ. There are a great many now who may say, Well, we believe all this; but there is a great difference betwixt talking and feeling. Did you ever feel the want of a dear Redeemer? Did you ever feel the want of Jesus Christ, upon the account of the deficiency of your own righteousness? And can you now say from your heart, Lord, thou mayst justly damn me for the best duties that ever I did perform? If you are not thus brought out of self, you may speak peace to yourselves, but yet there is no peace.

But then, before you can speak peace to your souls, there is one particular sin you must be greatly troubled for, and yet I fear there are few of you think what it is; it is the reigning, the damning sin of the Christian world, and yet the Christian world seldom or never think of it. And pray what is that? It is what most of you think you are not guilty of—and that is, the sin of unbelief. Before you can speak peace to your heart, you must be troubled for the unbelief of your heart. But, can it be supposed that any of you are unbelievers here in this church-yard, that are born in Scotland, in a reformed country, that go to church every Sabbath? Can any of you that receive the sacrament once a-year—O that it were administered oftener!—can it be supposed that you who had tokens for the sacrament, that you who keep up family prayer, that any of you do not believe in the Lord Jesus Christ? I appeal to your own hearts, if you would not think me uncharitable, if I doubted whether any of you believed in Christ; and yet, I fear upon examination, we should find that most of you have not so much faith in the Lord Jesus Christ as the devil himself. I am persuaded the devil believes more of the Bible than most of us do. He believes the divinity of Jesus Christ; that is more than many who call themselves Christians do; nay, he believes and trembles, and that is more than thousands amongst us do. My friends, we mistake a historical faith for a true faith, wrought in the heart by the Spirit of God. You fancy you believe, because you believe there is such a book as we call the Bible—because you go to church; all this you may do, and have no true faith in Christ. Merely to believe there was such a person as Christ, merely to believe there is a book called the Bible, will do you no good, more than to believe there was such a man as Cæsar or Alexander the Great. The Bible is a sacred depository. What thanks have we to give to God for these lively oracles! But yet we may have these, and not believe in the Lord Jesus Christ. My dear friends, there must be a principle wrought in the heart by the Spirit of the living God. Did I ask you how long it is since you believed in Jesus Christ, I suppose most of you would tell me, you believed in Jesus Christ as long as ever you remember—you never did misbelieve. Then, you could not give me a better proof that you never yet believed in Jesus Christ, unless you were sanctified early, as from the womb; for, they that otherwise believe in Christ know there was a time when they did not believe in Jesus Christ. You say you love God with all your heart, soul, and strength. If I were to ask you how long it is since you loved God, you would say, As long as you can remember; you never hated God, you know no time when there was enmity in your heart against God. Then, unless you were sanctified very early, you never loved God in your life. My dear friends, I am more particular in this, because it is a most deceitful delusion, whereby so many people are carried away, that they believe already. Therefore, it is remarked of Mr. Marshall, giving account of his experiences, that he had been working for life, and he had ranged all his sins under the ten commandments, and then coming to a minister, asked him the reason why he could not get peace. The minister looked to his catalogue, Away, says he, I do not find one word of the sin of unbelief in all your catalogue. It is the peculiar work of the Spirit of God to convince us of our unbelief—that we have got no faith. Says Jesus Christ, "I will send the Comforter; and when he is come, he will reprove the world" of the sin of unbelief; "of sin," says Christ, "because they believe not on me." Now, my dear friends, did God ever show you that you had no faith? Were you ever made to bewail a hard heart of unbelief? Was it ever the language of your heart, Lord, give me faith; Lord, enable me to lay hold on thee; Lord, enable me to call thee *my* Lord and *my* God? Did Jesus Christ ever convince you in this manner? Did he ever convince you of your inability to close with Christ, and make you to cry out to God to give you faith? If not, do not speak peace to your heart. May the Lord awaken you, and give you true, solid peace before you go hence and be no more!

Once more, then: before you can speak peace to your heart, you must not only be convinced of your actual and original sin, the sins of your own righteousness, the sin of unbelief, but you must be enabled to lay hold upon the perfect righteousness, the all-sufficient righteousness, of the Lord Jesus Christ; you must lay hold by faith on the righteousness of Jesus Christ, and then you shall have peace. "Come," says Jesus, "unto me, all ye that are weary and heavy laden, and I will give you rest." This speaks encouragement to all that are weary and heavy laden; but the promise of rest is made to them only upon their coming and believing, and taking him to be their God and their all. Before we can ever have peace with God, we must be justified by faith through our Lord Jesus Christ, we must be enabled to apply Christ to our hearts, we must have Christ brought home to our souls, so as his righteousness may be made our righteousness, so as his merits may be imputed to our souls. My dear friends, were you ever married to Jesus Christ? Did Jesus Christ ever give himself to you? Did you ever close with Christ by a lively faith, so as to feel Christ in your hearts, so as to hear him speaking peace to your souls? Did peace ever flow in upon your hearts like a river? Did you ever feel that peace that Christ spoke to his disciples? I pray God he may come and speak peace to you. These things you must experience. I am now talking of the invisible realities of another world, of inward religion, of the work of God upon a poor sinner's heart. I am now talking of a matter of great importance, my dear hearers; you are all concerned in it, your souls are concerned in it, your eternal salvation is concerned in it. You may be all at peace, but perhaps the devil has lulled you asleep into a carnal lethargy and security, and will endeavour to keep you there, till he get you to hell, and there you will be awakened; but it will be dreadful to be awakened and find yourselves so fearfully mistaken, when the great gulf is fixed, when you will be calling to all eternity for a drop of water to cool your tongue, and shall not obtain it.

Give me leave, then, to address myself to several sorts of persons; and O may God, of his infinite mercy, bless the application! There are some of you perhaps can say, Through grace we can go along with you. Blessed be God, we have been convinced of our actual sins, we have been convinced of original sin, we have been convinced of self-righteousness, we have felt the bitterness of unbelief, and through grace we have closed with Jesus Christ;

we can speak peace to our hearts, because God hath spoken peace to us. Can you say so? Then I will salute you, as the angels did the women the first day of the week, All hail! fear not ye, my dear brethren, you are happy souls; you may lie down and be at peace indeed, for God hath given you peace; you may be content under all the dispensations of providence, for nothing can happen to you now, but what shall be the effect of God's love to your soul; you need not fear what fightings may be without, seeing there is peace within. Have you closed with Christ? Is God your friend? Is Christ your friend? Then, look up with comfort; all is yours, and you are Christ's, and Christ is God's. Everything shall work together for your good; the very hairs of your head are numbered; he that toucheth you, toucheth the apple of God's eye. But then, my dear friends, beware of resting on your first conversion. You that are young believers in Christ, you should be looking out for fresh discoveries of the Lord Jesus Christ every moment; you must not build upon your past experiences, you must not build upon a work within you, but always come out of yourselves to the righteousness of Jesus Christ without you; you must be always coming as poor sinners to draw water out of the wells of salvation; you must be forgetting the things that are behind, and be continually pressing forward to the things that are before. My dear friends, you must keep up a tender, close walk with the Lord Jesus Christ. There are many of us who lose our peace by our untender walk; something or other gets in betwixt Christ and us, and we fall into darkness; something or other steals our hearts from God, and this grieves the Holy Ghost, and the Holy Ghost leaves us to ourselves. Let me, therefore, exhort you that have got peace with God, to take care that you do not lose this peace. It is true, if you are once in Christ, you cannot finally fall from God: "There is no condemnation to them that are in Christ Jesus;" but if you cannot fall finally, you may fall foully, and may go with broken bones all your days. Take care of backslidings; for Jesus Christ's sake, do not grieve the Holy Ghost—you may never recover your comfort while you live. O take care of going a gadding and wandering from God, after you have closed with Jesus Christ. My dear friends, I have paid dear for backsliding. Our hearts are so cursedly wicked, that if you take not care, if you do not keep up a constant watch, your wicked hearts will deceive you, and draw you aside. It will be sad to be under the scourge of a correcting

Father; witness the visitations of Job, David, and other saints in Scripture. Let me, therefore, exhort you that have got peace to keep a close walk with Christ. I am grieved with the loose walk of those that are Christians, that have had discoveries of Jesus Christ; there is so little difference betwixt them and other people, that I scarce know which is the true Christian. Christians are afraid to speak for God—they run down with the stream; if they come into worldly company, they will talk of the world as if they were in their element; this you would not do when you had the first discoveries of Christ's love; you could talk then of Christ's love for ever, when the candle of the Lord shined upon your soul. That time has been when you had something to say for your dear Lord; but now you can go into company and hear others speaking about the world bold enough, and you are afraid of being laughed at if you speak for Jesus Christ. A great many people have grown conformists now in the worst sense of the word; they will cry out against the ceremonies of the church, as they may justly do; but then you are mighty fond of ceremonies in your behaviour; you will conform to the world, which is a great deal worse. Many will stay till the devil bring up new fashions. Take care, then, not to be conformed to the world. What have Christians to do with the world? Christians should be singularly good, bold for their Lord, that all who are with you may take notice that you have been with Jesus. I would exhort you to come to a settlement in Jesus Christ, so as to have a continual abiding of God in your heart. We go a-building on our faith of adherence, and lose our comfort; but we should be growing up to a faith of assurance, to know that we are God's, and so walk in the comfort of the Holy Ghost and be edified. Jesus Christ is now much wounded in the house of his friends. Excuse me in being particular; for, my friends, it grieves me more that Jesus Christ should be wounded by his friends than by his enemies. We cannot expect anything else from Deists; but for such as have felt his power, to fall away, for them not to walk agreeably to the vocation wherewith they are called—by these means we bring our Lord's religion into contempt, to be a by-word among the heathen. For Christ's sake, if you know Christ keep close by him; if God have spoken peace, O keep that peace by looking up to Jesus Christ every moment. Such as have got peace with God, if you are under trials, fear not, all things shall work for your good; if you are under temptations, fear not, if he has spoken peace to your hearts, all these things shall be for your good.

But what shall I say to you that have got no peace with God?— and these are, perhaps, the most of this congregation: it makes me weep to think of it. Most of you, if you examine your hearts, must confess that God never yet spoke peace to you; you are children of the devil, if Christ is not in you, if God has not spoken peace to your heart. Poor soul! what a cursed condition are you in. I would not be in your case for ten thousand, thousand worlds. Why? You are just hanging over hell. What peace can you have when God is your enemy, when the wrath of God is abiding upon your poor soul? Awake, then, you that are sleeping in a false peace; awake, ye carnal professors, ye hypocrites that go to church, receive the sacrament, read your Bibles, and never felt the power of God upon your hearts; you that are formal professors, you that are baptized heathens; awake, awake, and do not rest on a false bottom. Blame me not for addressing myself to you; indeed, it is out of love to your souls. I see you are lingering in your Sodom, and wanting to stay there; but I come to you as the angel did to Lot, to take you by the hand. Come away, my dear brethren—fly, fly, fly for your lives to Jesus Christ, fly to a bleeding God, fly to a throne of grace; and beg of God to break your hearts, beg of God to convince you of your actual sins, beg of God to convince you of your original sin, beg of God to convince you of your self-righteousness—beg of God to give you faith, and to enable you to close with Jesus Christ. O you that are secure, I must be a son of thunder to you, and O that God may awaken you, though it be with thunder; it is out of love, indeed, that I speak to you. I know by sad experience what it is to be lulled asleep with a false peace; long was I lulled asleep, long did I think myself a Christian, when I knew nothing of the Lord Jesus Christ. I went perhaps farther than many of you do; I used to fast twice a-week, I used to pray sometimes nine times a-day, I used to receive the sacrament constantly every Lord's-day; and yet I knew nothing of Jesus Christ in my heart, I knew not that I must be a new creature—I knew nothing of inward religion in my soul. And perhaps, many of you may be deceived as I, poor creature, was; and, therefore, it is out of love to you indeed, that I speak to you. O if you do not take care, a form of religion will destroy your soul; you will rest in it, and will not come to

Jesus Christ at all; whereas, these things are only the means, and not the end of religion; Christ is the end of the law for righteousness to all that believe. O, then, awake, you that are settled on your lees; awake you Church professors; awake you that have got a name to live, that are rich and think you want nothing, not considering that you are poor, and blind, and naked; I counsel you to come and buy of Jesus Christ gold, white raiment, and eye-salve. But I hope there are some that are a little wounded; I hope God does not intend to let me preach in vain; I hope God will reach some of your precious souls, and awaken some of you out of your carnal security; I hope there are some who are willing to come to Christ, and beginning to think that they have been building upon a false foundation. Perhaps the devil may strike in, and bid you despair of mercy; but fear not, what I have been speaking to you is only out of love to you—is only to awaken you, and let you see your danger. If any of you are willing to be reconciled to God, God the Father, Son, and Holy Ghost, is willing to be reconciled to you. O then, though you have no peace as yet, come away to Jesus Christ; he is our peace, he is our peace-maker—he has made peace betwixt God and offending man. Would you have peace with God? Away, then, to God through Jesus Christ, who has purchased peace; the Lord Jesus has shed his heart's blood for this. He died for this; he rose again for this; he ascended into the highest heaven, and is now interceding at the right hand of God. Perhaps you think there will be no peace for you. Why so? Because you are sinners? because you have crucified Christ—you have put him to open shame—you have trampled under foot the blood of the Son of God? What of all this? Yet there is peace for you. Pray, what did Jesus Christ say to his disciples, when he came to them the first day of the week? The first word he said was, "Peace be unto you;" he showed them his hands and his side, and said, "Peace be unto you." It is as much as if he had said, Fear not, my disciples; see my hands and my feet how they have been pierced for your sake; therefore, fear not. How did Christ speak to his disciples? "Go tell my brethren, and tell broken-hearted Peter in particular, that Christ is risen, that he is ascended unto his Father and your Father, to his God and your God." And after Christ rose from the dead, he came preaching peace, with an olive branch of peace, like Noah's dove: "My peace I leave with you." Who were they? They were enemies of Christ as well as we, they were deniers of Christ once as well as we. Perhaps some of you have backslidden and lost your peace, and you think you deserve no peace; and no more you do. But, then, God will heal your backslidings, he will love you freely. As for you that are wounded, if you are made willing to come to Christ, come away. Perhaps some of you want to dress yourselves in your duties, that are but rotten rags. No, you had better come naked as you are, for you must throw aside your rags, and come in your blood. Some of you may say, We would come, but we have got a hard heart. But you will never get it made soft till ye come to Christ; he will take away the heart of stone, and give you an heart of flesh; he will speak peace to your souls; though ye have betrayed him, yet he will be your peace. Shall I prevail upon any of you this morning to come to Jesus Christ? There is a great multitude of souls here; how shortly must you all die, and go to judgment! Even before night, or to-morrow's night, some of you may be laid out for this kirk-yard. And how will you do if you be not at peace with God—if the Lord Jesus Christ has not spoken peace to your heart? If God speak not peace to you here, you will be damned for ever. I must not flatter you, my dear friends; I will deal sincerely with your souls. Some of you may think I carry things too far. But, indeed, when you come to judgment, you will find what I say is true, either to your eternal damnation or comfort. May God influence your hearts to come to him! I am not willing to go away without persuading you. I cannot be persuaded but God may make use of me as a mean of persuading some of you to come to the Lord Jesus Christ. O did you but feel the peace which they have that love the Lord Jesus Christ! "Great peace have they," says the psalmist, "that love thy law; nothing shall offend them." But there is no peace to the wicked. I know what it is to live a life of sin; I was obliged to sin in order to stifle conviction. And I am sure this is the way many of you take; if you get into company, you drive off conviction. But you had better go to the bottom at once; it must be done—your wound must be searched, or you must be damned. If it were a matter of indifference, I would not speak one word about it. But you will be damned without Christ. He is the way, he is the truth, and the life. I cannot think you should go to hell without Christ. How can you dwell with everlasting burnings? How can you abide the thought of living with the devil for ever? Is it not better to have some soul-trouble here, than to be sent to hell by Jesus Christ hereafter? What is hell, but to be absent from Christ? If there were no other hell, that would be hell enough. It will be hell to be tormented with the devil for ever. Get acquaintance with God, then, and be at peace. I beseech you, as a poor worthless ambassador of Jesus Christ, that you would be reconciled to God. My business this morning, the first day of the week, is to tell you that Christ is willing to be reconciled to you. Will any of you be reconciled to Jesus Christ? Then, he will forgive you all your sins, he will blot out all your transgressions. But if you will go on and rebel against Christ, and stab him daily—if you will go on and abuse Jesus Christ, the wrath of God you must expect will fall upon you. God will not be mocked; that which a man soweth, that shall he also reap. And if you will not be at peace with God, God will not be at peace with you. Who can stand before God when he is angry? It is a dreadful thing to fall into the hands of an angry God. When the people came to apprehend Christ, they fell to the ground when Jesus said, "I am he." And if they could not bear the sight of Christ when clothed with the rags of mortality, how will they bear the sight of him when he is on his Father's throne? Methinks I see the poor wretches dragged out of their graves by the devil; methinks I see them trembling, crying out to the hills and rocks to cover them. But the devil will say, Come, I will take you away; and then they shall stand trembling before the judgment-seat of Christ. They shall appear before him to see him once, and hear him pronounce that irrevocable sentence, "Depart from me, ye cursed." Methinks I hear the poor creatures saying, Lord, if we must be damned, let some angel pronounce the sentence. No, the God of love, Jesus Christ, will pronounce it. Will ye not believe this? Do not think I am talking at random, but agreeably to the Scriptures of truth. If you do not, then show yourselves men, and this morning go away with full resolution, in the strength of God, to cleave to Christ. And may you have no rest in your souls till you rest in Jesus Christ! I could still go on, for it is sweet to talk of Christ. Do you not long for the time when you shall have new bodies—when they shall be immortal, and made like Christ's glorious body? and then they will talk of Jesus Christ for evermore. But it is time, perhaps, for you to go and prepare for your respective worship, and I would not hinder any of you. My design is, to bring poor sinners to Jesus Christ. O that God may bring some of you to himself! May the Lord Jesus now dismiss you with his blessing, and may the dear Redeemer convince you that are unawakened, and turn the wicked from the evil of their way! And may the love of God, that passeth all understanding, fill your hearts. Grant this, O Father, for Christ's sake; to whom, with thee and the blessed Spirit, be all honour and glory, now and for evermore. Amen.

THE KINGDOM OF GOD.

"For the kingdom of God is not meat and drink; but righteousness, and peace, and joy in the Holy Ghost."—ROM. xiv. 17.

THOUGH we all profess to own one Lord, one faith, one baptism; though Jesus Christ never was, and never will be, divided in himself; yet the followers of Jesus Christ have in all ages been sadly divided among themselves: and what has rendered the case the more to be pitied, is, that they have generally been divided about the circumstantials of religion, they have generally received one another to doubtful disputation, and imbittered one another's hearts, by talking about those things which they might either do or not do, either know or not know, and yet at the same time be the true followers of the meek and lowly Jesus. I am verily persuaded that this is the great artifice and engine of the devil. He knows if he can divide Christians, he will get the better of them; and therefore he endeavours to sow the tares of division among them, in order to make them a common prey to their enemies. And, indeed, this God hath permitted in all ages of the Church. In consequence of this, the early ages of Christianity were not altogether free of it. No, this text gives us a pregnant and sufficient proof of it.

It seems the first converts of Christianity consisted of two sorts of people—either those who were Jews before they became Christians, or those who were heathens, and never had been subject to the law of Moses, but were converted from a state of Gentilism, from a state of heathenish darkness, and brought to the marvellous gospel light. The first of these, knowing that every rite, every ceremony of the law of Moses, had a divine superscription wrought upon it, they thought themselves obliged, notwithstanding they believed in the Lord Jesus Christ, to abstain from such meats and drinks as were forbidden, and to submit to such festivals as were enjoined by the law. Whereas, on the contrary, the heathen, who never were brought under this yoke, nay, even the Jews themselves who were better instructed in their Christian liberty, knowing that every creature of God was now good, if sanctified by the Word of God and prayer; knowing that, "Touch not, taste not, handle not," were no longer precepts for those who believed in the Lord Jesus Christ; they could not submit to them—they could not submit to the new moons and Sabbaths—they ate what was set before them, and made no scruple about meat or drink. But, however, it seems there were two contending parties—many right souls, no doubt, on both sides. What must, then, the great apostle do? Why, like a true follower of the meek and lowly Jesus, he preached up to both sides the golden rule of moderation, and endeavoured to persuade them to dispute no more about these outward things.

If we will, therefore, look to the 1st verse of this chapter, we shall find the apostle giving them a healing advice. "Him," says he, "that is weak in the faith, receive ye"—do not separate from him, do not forbid him to come into your Christian fellowship; "receive him"—look upon him as a disciple, receive him with open arms into your communion; "but not to doubtful disputation"—do not fall into disputing with him as soon as ever he comes into your church. "For," says he, in the 2d verse, "one," that is well instructed in his Christian liberty, "believeth that he may eat all things," without scruple. Why, "another that is weak," and hath not got so much light concerning gospel liberty, thinks himself obliged to abstain from such meats as were forbidden by the law, and therefore, for conscience' sake, "eateth herbs." Why then, says the apostle in the 3d verse, "Let not him that eateth, despise him that eateth not," though he be but a novice in grace: on the other hand, "let not him that eateth not, judge him that eateth," as though he took more liberty than God Almighty or the rules of the gospel allowed him; "for God hath received him." Though he is weak, he is a believer in the Lord Jesus Christ; God hath received him into his favour, and how, then, dare you refuse to receive him into your communion?

In order, therefore, that the apostle might put a stop to this spirit of division and opposition that was among them, he goes on, and tells them that their despising, that their judging and disputing with one another at this rate, was taking Christ's prerogative out of his hand. For, says he in the 10th verse, "Why dost thou judge thy brother?" On the other hand, "Why dost thou set at nought thy brother? we shall all stand before the judgment-seat of Christ." And Jesus Christ, who seeth the springs of our actions, can bear with us, though we cannot bear with one another. For, says he, "One man esteemeth one day above another, another esteemeth every day alike; let every man be fully persuaded in his own mind;" that is, let every man take the utmost care to inform his conscience, according to the rule of God's Word; and after he has done that, let him bear with other people, though they may not follow him in all things. And then, as the most prevailing and most cogent argument the apostle could possibly bring, to put an end to their divisions, he tells them, in the words of the text, that religion doth not consist in these things. "For," says he, "the kingdom of God is not meat and drink, but righteousness, and peace, and joy in the Holy Ghost." As though he had said, My dear friends, beware of disputing, beware of dividing from one another on account of the circumstantials of religion, beware of receiving one another to doubtful disputations about meat or drink, or observing holy days. "For," says he, "the kingdom of God is not meat and drink; but righteousness, and peace, and joy in the Holy Ghost."

This is a short, but when I read it, I think it is one of the most comprehensive verses in the whole book of God. And I am sure if ever it was necessary for a minister to preach upon such subjects as these, it must be in the days wherein we live; for, my friends, the devil is getting advantage over us by our manifold divisions. We have been settled upon our lees. we have had no outward persecution; and now God, in his righteous judgment, has suffered us to divide among ourselves. It is high time, therefore, for ministers to stand in the gap, to preach up a catholic spirit, to preach out bigotry, to preach out prejudice; for we will never be all of one mind, as long as we are in the world, about externals in religion; that is a privilege reserved to heaven, to a future state. But while we have different degrees of light, it is absolutely necessary that we should bear with all who cannot in all things follow with us. I am by no means for bringing the church into a state of anarchy and confusion; but that we should bear with one another: we should not divide from one another, so as not to keep fellowship with one another, because we are not of the same mind in some particular circumstances. I verily believe Jesus Christ suffers us to differ, to teach us that his kingdom is of a spiritual nature—it is not such a legal dispensation as the Jewish was; and therefore we should not divide about externals. Besides, by being left thus to differ with one another in our sentiments about externals, we learn to exercise our passive graces. I am sure there is one good effect which division has on my own and many other people's hearts—it makes us long for heaven, where we shall be all of one mind and one heart. It will be our perfection in heaven, to be all of one heart; and therefore it must be our imperfection on earth to be divided.

There are two things which those who call themselves Christians, want much to be convinced of, namely, *First*, What religion is not; *Second*, What religion positively is. Both these are in the words of the text plainly taught, and therefore, as God shall enable me, I shall endeavour, 1*st*, To explain what you are to understand by "the kingdom of God;" 2*dly*, I shall endeavour to show that "the kingdom of God is not meat and drink;" and 3*dly*, I shall show you what "the kingdom of God" positively is, namely, "righteousness, and peace, and joy in the Holy Ghost."

1*st*, I am to explain to you what you are to understand by "the kingdom of God." By the kingdom of God in some places of Scripture, you are to understand no more than the outward preaching of the gospel, as, when the apostles went out and preached that "the kingdom of God and the kingdom of heaven was at hand." In other places of Scripture, you are to understand it as implying that work of grace, that inward holiness, which is wrought in the heart of every soul that is truly converted and brought home to God. The Lord Jesus Christ is king of his church, and the Lord Jesus Christ has got a kingdom; and this kingdom is erected and set up in the hearts of sinners, when they are brought to be subject to the government of our dear Redeemer's laws. In this sense, therefore, we are to understand the kingdom of God, when Jesus Christ said, "The kingdom of God is within you," in your hearts; and when he tells Nicodemus, that "unless a man be born again, he cannot see the kingdom of God," he can have no notion of the inward life of a Christian. In other places of Scripture, the kingdom of God not only signifies the kingdom of grace, but the kingdom of grace and of glory also; as when Jesus said, "It is easier for a camel to go through the eye of a needle, than for a rich man to enter into the kingdom of God;" that is, either to be a true member of his mystical church here, or a partaker of the glory of the church triumphant hereafter. We are to take the kingdom of God in the text as signifying that inward work of grace, that kingdom which the Lord Jesus Christ sets up in the hearts of all that are truly brought home to God; so that when the apostle tells us, "The kingdom of God is not meat and drink," it is the same as though he had said, "My dear friends, do not quarrel about outward things; for the kingdom of God, or true and undefiled religion, heart and soul religion, is not meat and drink."

2*dly*, By meat and drink, if we compare the text with the context, we are to understand no more than this, that the kingdom of God, or true religion, doth not consist in abstaining from a particular meat or drink. But I shall take the words in a more comprehensive sense, and shall endeavour to show you on this head, that the kingdom of God, or true and undefiled religion, doth not consist in any, no, not in all outward things, put them altogether. And,

First, The kingdom of God, or true and undefiled religion, doth not consist in being of this or that particular sect or communion. Perhaps, my dear friends, were many of you asked what reason you can give of the hope that is in you, what title you have to call yourselves Christians—perhaps you could say no more for yourselves than this, namely, that you belong to such a church, and worship God in the same way in which your fathers and mothers worshipped God before you; and perhaps, at the same time, you are so narrow in your thoughts, that you think none can worship God but those that worship God just in your way. It is certainly, my dear friends, a blessing to be born as you are, in a reformed church; it is certainly a blessing to have the outward government and discipline of the church exercised; but then, if you place religion merely in being of this or that sect—if you contend to monopolize or confine the grace of God to your particular party—if you rest in that, you place the kingdom of God in something in which it doth not consist—you had as good place it in meat and drink. There are certainly Christians among all sects and communions that have learned the truth as it is in Christ Jesus. I do not mean that there are Christians among Arians, Socinians, or those that deny the divinity of Jesus Christ—I am sure the devil is priest of such congregations as these; but I mean there are Christians among other sects that may differ from us in the outward worship of God. Therefore, my dear friends, learn to be more catholic, more unconfined in your notions; for if you place the kingdom of God merely in a sect, you place it in that in which it doth not consist.

Again: as the kingdom of God doth not consist in being of this or that sect, so neither doth it consist in being baptized when you were young. Baptism is certainly an ordinance of the Lord Jesus Christ—it ought certainly to be administered; but then, my dear friends, take care that you do not make a Christ of your baptism, for there have been many baptized with water as you were, who were never savingly baptized with the Holy Ghost. Paul had a great value for circumcision; but when he saw the Jews resting upon their circumcision, he told them circumcision was nothing, and uncircumcision was nothing, but a new creature. And yet most people live as if they thought it will be sufficient to entitle them to heaven, to tell Jesus Christ that their name was in the register-book of such and such a parish. Your name may be in the register-book, and yet at the same time not be in the book of life. Ananias and Sapphira were baptized—Simon Magus was baptized; and, therefore, if you place religion merely in being baptized, in having the outward washing of water, without receiving the baptism of the Holy Ghost, you place the kingdom of God in something in which it doth not consist—in effect, you place it in meat and drink.

But further: as the kingdom of God and true religion doth not consist in being baptized, neither doth it consist in being orthodox in our notions, or being able to talk fluently of the doctrines of the gospel. There are a great many who can talk of free grace, of free justification, of final perseverance, of election, and God's everlasting love. All these are precious truths—they are all connected in a chain; take away one link, and you spoil the whole chain of gospel truths. But then I am persuaded that there are many who talk of these truths, who preach up these truths, and yet at the same time never, never felt the power of these truths upon their hearts. It is a good thing to have a form of sound words; and I think you have got a form of sound words in your Larger and Shorter Catechism. But you may have orthodox heads, and yet you may have the devil in your hearts; you may have clear heads, you may be able to speak, as it were, with the tongues of men and angels, the doctrines of the gospel, but yet, at the same time, you may never have felt them upon your own souls. And if you have never felt the power of them upon your hearts, your talk of Christ and free justification, and having rational convictions of these truths, will but increase your condemnation, and you will only go to hell with so much more solemnity. Take care, therefore, of resting in a form of knowledge—it is dangerous; if you do, you place the kingdom of God in meat and drink.

Again: as the kingdom of God doth not consist in orthodox notions, much less doth it consist in being sincere. I know not what sort of religion we have got among us. I fear many ministers as well as people want to recommend themselves to God by their sincerity; they think, If we do all we can, if we are but sincere, Jesus Christ will have mercy upon us. But pray what is there in our sincerity to recommend us to God? There is no natural man in the world sincere, till God make us new creatures in Jesus Christ; and, therefore, if you depend upon your sincerity for your salvation, your sincerity will damn you.

Further: as the kingdom of God doth not consist merely in sincerity (for nothing will recommend us to God but the righteousness of Jesus Christ), neither doth it consist in being negatively good; and yet I believe, my dear friends, if many of you were to be visited by a minister when you are upon a death-bed, and if he were to ask you how you hope to be saved, why, you would say, Yes, you hoped to be saved; you never did man, woman, or child, any harm in your life; you have done nobody harm. And, indeed, I do not find that the unprofitable servant did any one harm; no, the poor man, he only innocently wrapt up his talent in a napkin; and when his Lord came to call him to account, he thought he should be applauded by his Lord, and therefore introduces himself with the word, lo—"Lo, there thou hast what is thine." But what says Jesus Christ? "Cast ye the unprofitable servant into outer darkness: there shall be weeping and gnashing of teeth." Suppose it to be true that you had done nobody harm, yet it will not avail you to salvation. If you bring forth only the fig-leaves of an outward profession, and bring not forth good fruit, it will not send you to heaven—it will send you to hell.

Again: some of you perhaps may think I have not reached you yet; therefore I go on further to show you that the kingdom of God doth not consist in a dry, lifeless morality. I am not speaking against morality—it is a blessed thing, when Jesus Christ is laid as the foundation of it; and I could heartily wish that you moral gentlemen, who are for talking so much of your morality, I wish we could see a little more of it than we do. I do not cry down morality, but so far as this, that you do not rest in your morality, that you do not think you are Christians because you are not vicious—because you now and then do some good action. Why, self-love will carry a man to perform all moral actions. A man, perhaps, will not get drunk for fear of making his head ache; a man may be honest, because it would spoil his reputation to steal. And so a man who has not the love of God in his heart, may do moral actions. But if you depend on morality, if you make a Christ of it, and go about to establish a righteousness of your own, and think your morality will recommend you to God, my dear friends, you are building upon a rotten foundation; you will find yourselves mistaken, and that the kingdom of God is not in your hearts.

Again: as the kingdom of God doth not consist in doing nobody hurt, nor in doing moral actions, neither doth it consist in attending upon all outward ordinances whatsoever. A great many of you may think that you go to church, and receive the sacrament once or twice a-year (though I do think that is too seldom by a great deal to have it administered), you may read your Bibles, you may have family worship, you may say your prayers in your closets, and yet at the same time, my dear friends, know nothing of the Lord Jesus Christ in your hearts. You may have a token, and receive the sacrament, and perhaps at the same time be eating and drinking your own damnation. I speak this, because it is a most fatal snare that poor professors are exposed to—we stop our consciences by our duties. Many of you, perhaps, lead a lukewarm, loose life—you are Gallio-like; yet you will be very good the sacrament week; you will attend all the sermons, and come to the sacrament; you will be very good for some time after that, and then afterwards go on in your former way till the next sacrament. You are resting on the means of grace all the while, and placing religion in that which is only a mean of religion. I speak from mine own experience. I know how much I was deceived with a form of godliness. I made conscience of fasting twice a-week, I made conscience of praying sometimes nine times a-day, and received the sacrament every Sabbath-day, and yet knew nothing of inward religion in my heart, till God was pleased to dart a ray of light into my soul, and show me I must be a new creature, or be damned for evermore. Being, therefore, so long deceived myself, I speak with the more sympathy to you, who are resting on a round of duties and model of performances. And now, my friends, if your hearts were to be searched, and you were to speak your minds, I appeal to your own hearts whether you are not thinking within yourselves, though you may have so much charity as to think I mean well, yet I verily believe many of you think I have carried matters a little too far; and why is this, but because I come close to some of your cases? The pride of your hearts does not care to admit of conviction; therefore you would fain retort on the preacher, and say he is wrong, whereas it is your hearts that are wrong all the while.

Others, again, perhaps may be saying, Well, if a man may go thus far and not be a Christian, as I am sure he may, and a great deal farther, you will be apt to cry out, Who, then, can be saved? And O that I could hear you asking this question in earnest! for, my friends, I am obliged, wherever I go, to endeavour to plough up people's fallow ground; to bring them off from their duties, and making a Christ of them. There are so many shadows in religion, that if you do not take care, ye will grasp at the shadow and lose the substance. The devil has so ordered the affairs of the church now, and our hearts are so desperately deceitful, that if we do not take a great deal of care, we shall come short of true religion —of the true kingdom of God in the soul. The great question, then, is, Whether any of you are convinced of what has been said? Does power come with the word? When I was reading a book, entitled "The Life of God in the Soul of Man,"* and reading that a man may read, pray, and go to church, and be constant in the duties of the Sabbath, and yet not be a Christian, I wondered what the man would be at; I was ready to throw it from me, till at last he told me, that religion was an union of the soul with God—the image of God wrought upon the heart, or Christ Jesus formed in us. Then God was pleased with these words to cast a ray of light into my soul; with the light there came a power, and from that very moment I knew I must be a new creature. This perhaps may be your case, my dear hearers. Perchance many of you may be loving, good-natured people, and attend the duties of religion; but take care, for Christ's sake, that you do not rest on these things.

I think I cannot sum up what has been said better, than to give

* This must have been Scougal's well known work.

you the character of the apostle Paul. Are you a Christian, do you think, because you are of this or that sect?—Paul was a Jew and a Pharisee. Are you a Christian because you are baptized, and enjoy Christian privileges?—Then Paul was circumcised. Are you a Christian because you do nobody hurt, and are sincere? —Paul was blameless before his conversion; and was not a Gallio in religion, as many of us are: he was so zealous for God, that he persecuted the church of Christ. But yet when God was pleased to reveal his Son in him, when God was pleased to strike him to the ground, and let him see what heart-religion was, then Paul dropt his false confidence immediately; those things which he counted gain, which he depended on before, he now counted loss, that he might win Christ, and be found in him; not having his own righteousness, which is of the law, but that righteousness which is by faith in Christ Jesus. It is time, my dear friends, to proceed to,

3*dly*, The next thing proposed, namely, To show you what the kingdom of God, or true religion, positively is. I have told you what it is not; I shall now proceed to show you what it is. It is "righteousness, and peace, and joy in the Holy Ghost." But before I proceed to this, I must make a little digression. Perhaps curiosity has brought many here who have neither regard to God nor man. A man may be a member of the purest church, a man may be baptized, do nobody harm, do a great deal of good, attend on all the ordinances of Christianity, and yet at the same time may be a child of the devil. If a man may go thus far, and yet at the same time miss salvation, what will become of you who do not keep up a form of religion, who scarcely know the time when you have been at church and attending sermons, unless curiosity brought you to hear a particular stranger? What will become of you who, instead of believing the gospel and reading the Bible, set up your corrupt religion in opposition to divine revelation? What will become of you, who count it your pleasure to riot in the day time, to spend time in rioting and wantonness; who are sitting in the scorner's chair, and joining with your hellish companions, who love to dress the children of God in bear-skins? What will become of you who live in acts of uncleanness, drunkenness, adultery, Sabbath-breaking? Surely, without repentance, you will be lost—your damnation slumbereth not. God may bear with you long, but he will not forbear always. The time will come when he will ease himself of his adversaries, and then you will be undone for evermore, unless you come to him as poor, lost sinners.

But I now go on to show you what true religion positively is; "it is righteousness," it is "peace," it is "joy in the Holy Ghost." And

First, The kingdom of God is "righteousness." By righteousness we are here to understand the complete, perfect, and all-sufficient righteousness of the Lord Jesus Christ, as including both his active and his passive obedience. My dear friends, we have no righteousness of our own; our best righteousnesses, take them altogether, are but as so many filthy rags; we can only be accepted for the sake of the righteousness of our Lord Jesus Christ. This righteousness must be imputed and made over to us, and applied to our hearts; and till we get this righteousness brought home to our souls, we are in a state of death and damnation—the wrath of God abideth on us.

Before I go farther, I would endeavour to apply this. Give me leave to put this question to your hearts. You call yourselves Christians, and would count me uncharitable to call it in question; but I exhort you to let conscience speak out, do not bribe it any longer. Did you ever see yourselves as damned sinners? Did conviction ever fasten upon your hearts? And after you had been made to see your want of Christ, and made to hunger and thirst after righteousness, did you lay hold on Christ by faith? Did you ever close with Christ? Was Christ's righteousness ever put upon your naked souls? Was ever a feeling application of his righteousness made to your hearts? Was it, or was it not? If not, you are in a damnable state—you are out of Christ; for the apostle says here, "The kingdom of God is righteousness;" that is, the righteousness of Christ applied and brought home to the heart.

It follows, "peace." "The kingdom of God is righteousness, and peace." By peace I do not understand that false peace, or rather carnal security, into which so many are fallen. There are thousands who speak peace to themselves, when there is no peace. Thousands have got a peace of the devil's making; the strong man armed has got possession of their hearts, and therefore their goods are all in peace. But the peace here spoken of is a peace that follows after a great deal of soul trouble; it is like that calm which the Lord Jesus Christ spoke to the wind, "Peace, be still; and immediately there was a great calm;" it is like that peace which Christ spoke to his disciples, when he came and said,

"Peace be unto you"—"My peace I leave with you." It is a peace of God's making, it is a peace of God's giving, it is a peace that the world cannot give, it is a peace that can be felt, it is a peace that passeth human understanding—it is a peace that results from a sense of having Christ's righteousness brought home to the soul. For a poor soul before this is full of trouble; Christ makes application of his righteousness to his heart; and then the poor creature, being justified by faith, hath peace with God through our Lord Jesus Christ. My dear friends, I am now talking of heart-religion, of an inward work of God, an inward kingdom in your hearts, which you must have, or you shall never sit with Jesus Christ in his kingdom. The most of you may have peace, but for Christ's sake examine upon what this peace is founded—see if Christ be brought home to your souls, if you have had a feeling application of the merits of Christ brought home to your souls. Is God at peace with you? Did Jesus Christ ever say, "Peace be to you"—"Be of good cheer"—"Go thy way, thy sins are forgiven thee"—"My peace I leave with you, my peace I give unto you?" Did God ever bring a comfortable promise with power to your soul? And after you have been praying, and fearing you would be damned, did you ever feel peace flow in like a river upon your soul? so that you could say, Now I know that God is my friend, now I know that Jesus is my Saviour, now I can call him, "My Lord, and my God;" now I know that Christ hath not only died for others, but I know that Jesus hath died for me in particular. O my dear friends, it is impossible to tell you the comfort of this peace, and I am astonished (only man's heart is desperately wicked) how you can have peace one moment, and yet not know that God is at peace with you. How can you go to bed this night without this peace? It is a blessed thing to know when sin is forgiven; would you not be glad if an angel were to come and tell you so this night?

But there is something more—there is "joy in the Holy Ghost." I have often thought, that if the apostle Paul were to come and preach now, he would be reckoned one of the greatest enthusiasts on earth. He talked of the Holy Ghost, of feeling the Holy Ghost; and so we must all feel it, all experience it, all receive it, or we can never see a holy God with comfort. We are not to receive the Holy Ghost, so as to enable us to work miracles; for, "Many will say in that day, We have cast out devils in thy name, and in thy name done many wonderful works." But we must receive the Holy Ghost to sanctify our nature, to purify our hearts, and make us meet for heaven. Unless we are born again, and have the Holy Ghost in our hearts, if we were in heaven we could take no pleasure there. The apostle not only supposes we must have the Holy Ghost, but he supposes, as a necessary ingredient to make up the kingdom of God in a believer's heart, that he must have "joy in the Holy Ghost." There are a great many, I believe, who think religion is a poor melancholy thing, and they are afraid to be Christians. But, my dear friends, there is no true joy till you can joy in God and Christ. I know wicked men and men of pleasure will have a little laughter; but what is it, but like the crackling of a few thorns under a pot? it makes a blaze, and soon goes out. I know what it is to take pleasure in sin; but I always found the smart that followed was ten thousand times more hurtful than any gratification I could receive. But they who joy in God, have a joy that strangers intermeddle not with—it is a joy that no man can take from them; it amounts to a full assurance of faith that the soul is reconciled to God through Christ, that Jesus dwells in the heart; and when the soul reflects on itself, it magnifies the Lord, and rejoices in God its Saviour. Thus we are told that "Zaccheus received Christ joyfully," that "the eunuch went on his way rejoicing," and that "the jailer rejoiced in God with all his house." O, my friends, what joy have they that know their sins are forgiven them! What a blessed thing is it for a man to look forward, and see an endless eternity of happiness before him, knowing that everything shall work together for his good!—it is joy unspeakable and full of glory. O may God make you all partakers of it!

Here, then, we will put the kingdom of God together. It is "righteousness," it is "peace," it is "joy in the Holy Ghost." When this is placed in the heart, God there reigns, God there dwells and walks—the creature is a son or daughter of the Almighty. But, my friends, how few are there here who have been made partakers of this kingdom! Perhaps the kingdom of the devil, instead of the kingdom of God, is in most of our hearts. This has been a place much favoured of God; may I hope some of you can go alongs with me and say "Blessed be God, we have got righteousness, peace, and joy in the Holy Ghost?" Have you so? Then, you are kings, though beggars; you are happy above all men in the world—you have got heaven in your hearts; and when the crust of your bodies drops, your souls will meet with God, your souls will enter into the world of peace, and you shall be happy with God for evermore. I hope there is none of you who will fear death; fy for shame, if ye do! What! afraid to go to Jesus, to your Lord? You may cry out, "O death, where is thy sting? O grave, where is thy victory?" You may go on your way rejoicing, knowing that God is your friend; die when you will, angels will carry you safe to heaven.

But, O, how many are here in this church-yard, who will be laid in some grave ere long, who are entire strangers to this work of God upon their souls! My dear friends, I think this is an awful sight. Here are many thousands of souls, that must shortly appear with me, a poor creature, in the general assembly of all mankind before God in judgment. God Almighty knows whether some of you may not drop down dead before you go out of the church-yard; and yet, perhaps most are strangers to the Lord Jesus Christ in their hearts. Perhaps curiosity has brought you out to hear a poor babbler preach. But, my friends, I hope I came out of a better principle. If I know anything of my heart, I came to promote God's glory; and if the Lord should make use of such a worthless worm, such a wretched creature, as I am, to do your precious souls good, nothing would rejoice me more than to hear that God makes the foolishness of preaching a means of making many believe. I was long myself deceived with a form of godliness, and I know what it is to be a factor for the devil, to be led captive by the devil at his will, to have the kingdom of the devil in my heart; and I hope I can say, through free grace, I know what it is to have the kingdom of God erected in me. It is God's goodness that such a poor wretch as I am converted; though sometimes when I am speaking of God's goodness, I am afraid he strike me down dead. Let me draw out my soul and heart to you, my dear friends, my dear guilty friends, poor bleeding souls, who must shortly take your last farewell, and fly into endless eternity. Let me entreat you to lay these things seriously to heart this night. Now, when the Sabbath is over, and the evening is drawing near, methinks the very sight is awful (I could almost weep over you, as our Lord did over Jerusalem), to think in how short a time every soul of you must die—some of you to go to heaven, and others to go to the devil for evermore.

O my dear friends, these are matters of eternal moment. I did not come to tickle your ears; if I had a mind to do so, I would play the orator; no, but I came, if God should be pleased, to touch your hearts. What shall I say to you? Open the door of your heart, that the king of glory, the blessed Jesus, may come in and erect his kingdom in your soul. Make room for Christ; the Lord Jesus desires to sup with you to-night; Christ is willing to come into any of your hearts, that will be pleased to open and receive him. Are there any of you made willing Lydias? There are many women here, but how many Lydias are there here? Does power go with the word to open your heart? and find you a sweet melting in your soul? Are you willing? Then Christ Jesus is willing to come to you. But you may say, Will Christ come to my wicked, polluted heart? Yes, though you have many devils in your heart, Christ will come and erect his throne there; though the devils be in your heart, the Lord Jesus will scourge out a legion of devils, and his throne shall be exalted in thy soul. Sinners, be ye what you will, come to Christ, you shall have righteousness and peace. If you have got no peace, come to Christ, and he will give you peace. When you come to Christ, you will feel such joy that it is impossible for you to tell. O may God pity you all! I hope this will be a night of salvation to some of your souls.

My dear friends, I would preach with all my heart till midnight, to do you good, till I could preach no more. O that this body might hold out to speak more for my dear Redeemer! Had I a thousand lives, had I a thousand tongues, they should be employed in inviting sinners to come to Jesus Christ! Come, then, let me prevail with some of you to come along with me. Come poor, lost, undone sinner, come just as you are to Christ, and say, If I be damned, I will perish at the feet of Jesus Christ, where never one perished yet. He will receive you with open arms; the dear Redeemer is willing to receive you all. Fly, then, for your lives. The devil is in you while unconverted; and will you go with the devil in your heart to bed this night? God Almighty knows if ever you and I shall see one another again. In one or two days more I must go, and, perhaps, I may never see you again, till I meet you at the judgment-day. O my dear friends, think of that solemn meeting; think of that important hour, when the heavens shall pass away with a great noise, when the elements shall melt with fervent heat, when the sea and the graves shall be giving up their dead, and all shall be summoned to appear before the great God. What will you do then, if the kingdom of God is not erected in your hearts? You must go to the devil—like must go to like—if you are not converted Christ hath asserted it in the strongest manner: "Verily, verily, I say unto you, Except a man be born again, he cannot enter into the kingdom of God." Who can dwell with devouring fire? Who can dwell with everlasting burnings? O, my heart is melting with love to you. Surely God intends to do good to your poor souls. Will no one be persuaded to accept of Christ? If those who are settled Pharisees will not come, I desire to speak to you who are drunkards, Sabbath-breakers, cursers and swearers—will you come to Christ? I know that many of you come here out of curiosity: though you come only to see the congregation, yet if you come to Jesus Christ, Christ will accept of you. Are there any cursing, swearing soldiers here? Will you come to Jesus Christ, and list yourselves under the banner of the dear Redeemer? You are all welcome to Christ. Are there any little boys or little girls here? Come to Christ, and he will erect his kingdom in you. There are many little children whom God is working on, both at home and abroad. O, if some of the little lambs would come to Christ, they shall have peace and joy in the day that the Redeemer shall set up his kingdom in their hearts. Parents, tell them that Jesus Christ will take them in his arms, that he will dandle them on his knees. All of you, old and young, you that are old and grey-headed, come to Jesus Christ, and you shall be kings and priests to your God. The Lord will abundantly pardon you at the eleventh hour. "Ho, every one of you that thirsteth." If there be any of you ambitious of honour, do you want a crown, a sceptre? Come to Christ, and the Lord Jesus Christ will give you a kingdom that no man shall take from you.

THE END.